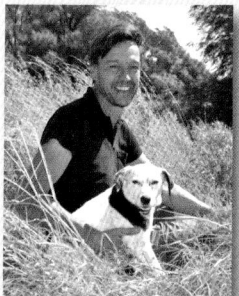

HE
guic
the
Kili
Had
co-a
West
with
DAIS
expe
has already completed all the trails above with Henry and her ambition is to walk all 15 National Trails.

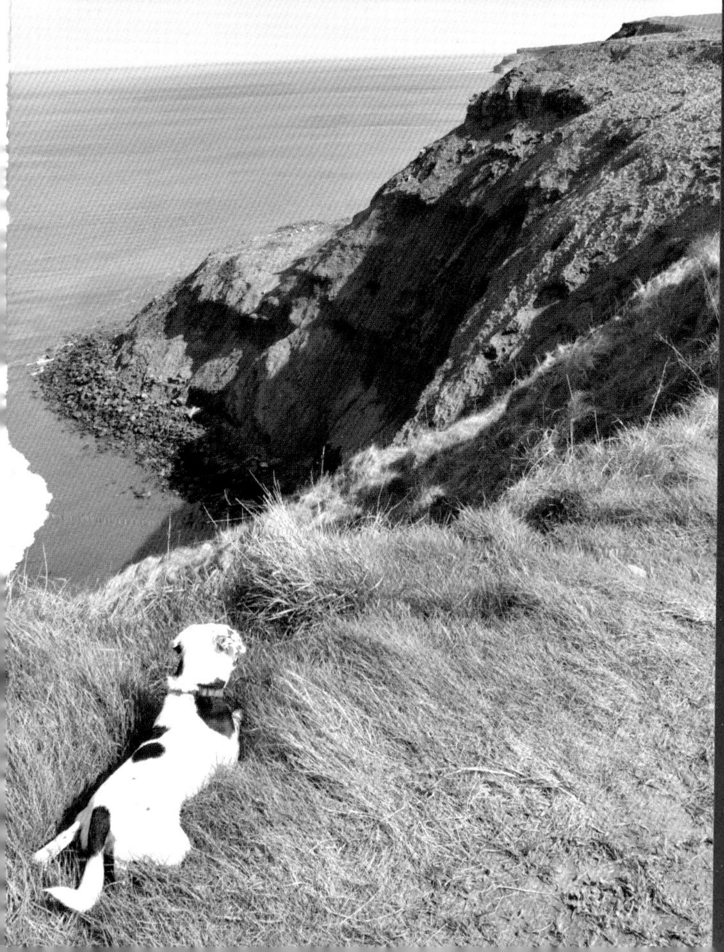

Author

Cleveland Way
First edition: 2019

Publisher: Trailblazer Publications
The Old Manse, Tower Rd, Hindhead, Surrey, GU26 6SU, UK
www.trailblazer-guides.com

British Library Cataloguing in Publication Data
A catalogue record for this book is available from the British Library

ISBN 978-1-905864-91-1

© **Trailblazer** 2019; Text and maps

Editor: Anna Jacomb-Hood; **Layout & Index**: Anna Jacomb-Hood
Proofreading: Jane Thomas; **Cartography**: Nick Hill
Photographs (flora and fauna): © Bryn Thomas (unless otherwise indicated)
Cover and main photographs: © Henry Stedman (unless otherwise indicated)

Acknowledgements

Thanks to everyone who helped with the research of this new guide. At Trailblazer, thanks
to: Anna Jacomb-Hood for her usual forensic approach to editing the text, Nick Hill for the
maps, Jane Thomas for proofreading and Bryn Thomas, as always, for keeping me busy.

A request

The authors and publisher have tried to ensure that this guide is as accurate and up to date
as possible. However, things change even on these well-worn routes. If you notice any
changes or omissions that should be included in the next edition of this guide, please email
or write to Trailblazer (address above). You can also contact us via the Trailblazer website
(💻 www.trailblazer-guides.com). Those persons making a significant contribution will be
rewarded with a free copy of the next edition.

Warning – hill walking can be dangerous

Please read the notes on when to go (pp14-16) and health & safety (pp72-4). Every effort
has been made by the author and publisher to ensure that the information contained herein
is as accurate and up to date as possible. However, they are unable to accept responsibility
for any inconvenience, loss or injury sustained by anyone as a result of the advice and information given in this guide.

Updated information will shortly be available on: 💻 **www.trailblazer-guides.com**

Photos – Front cover and this page: It's not just walkers who love the Cleveland Hills!
Here a paraglider rides the currents above Alex Falconer Seat, near the Lordstones Café.
Previous page: 'Pawsing' on the cliffs to admire the view between Staithes and Port
Mulgrave. **Overleaf**: The beach north of Skinningrove, below Cattersty Cliffs, is vast
and often empty.

Printed in China; print production by D'Print (☎ +65-6581 3832), Singapore

Cleveland Way

PLANNING – PLACES TO STAY – PLACES TO EAT

**48 large-scale walking maps and guides to
27 towns and villages**

NORTH YORK MOORS – HELMSLEY TO FILEY

HENRY STEDMAN

TRAILBLAZER PUBLICATIONS

INTRODUCTION

History of the path 7 – How difficult is the path? 12 – How long do you need? 13 – When to go 14

PART 1: PLANNING YOUR WALK

Practical information for the walker
Route-finding 17 – GPS 17 – Accommodation 19 – Food and drink 24 – Money 26 – Internet access & wi-fi 27 – Other services 27 – Walking companies 27 – Information for foreign visitors 28 – Walking with a dog 31

Budgeting 31

Itineraries
Which direction? 33 – Suggested itineraries 33 – Village and town facilities 34 – The best day loops and weekend walks 37

What to take
Packing light 39 – How to carry your luggage 39 – Footwear 40 Clothing 41 – Toiletries 42 – First-aid kit 42 – General items 42 Sleeping bag and camping gear 43 – Money 43 – Maps 43 Recommended reading 45 – Sources of further information 46

Getting to and from the Cleveland Way
Getting to Britain 48 – National transport 48 – Getting to and from Helmsley & Filey 50 – Local transport 51 – Bus services table 52

PART 2: THE ENVIRONMENT & NATURE

Conserving the Cleveland Way 55

Geology 57

Flora and fauna 50

PART 3: MINIMUM IMPACT & SAFETY

Minimum impact walking
Environmental impact 68 – Countryside code 70 – Access 71

Outdoor safety
Avoidance of hazards 72 – Dealing with an accident 72 – Blisters 73 Hypothermia 73 – Hyperthermia 73 – Sunburn 74 – Personal safety 74

PART 4: ROUTE GUIDE AND MAPS

APPENDICES

Contents

ABOUT THIS BOOK

This guidebook contains all the information you need. The hard work has been done for you so you can plan your trip without having to consult numerous websites and other books and maps. When you're all packed and ready to go, there's comprehensive public transport information to get you to and from the trail and detailed maps (1:20,000) to help you find your way along it. The guide includes:

● All standards of accommodation with reviews of campsites, bunkhouses, hostels, B&Bs, guesthouses and hotels
● Walking companies if you want an organised or self-guided tour and baggage-carrying services if you just want your luggage carried
● Itineraries for all levels of walkers
● Answers to all your questions: when to go, degree of difficulty, what to pack, and the approximate cost of the whole walking holiday
● Walking times in both directions
● Cafés, pubs, takeaways, restaurants and shops for supplies
● Rail, bus and taxi information for all villages and towns along the path
● Street maps of the 10 main towns and villages on or near the path
● Historical, cultural and geographical background information
● GPS waypoints

❏ **MINIMUM IMPACT FOR MAXIMUM INSIGHT**

Man has suffered in his separation from the soil and from other living creatures ... and as yet he must still, for security, look long at some portion of the earth as it was before he tampered with it.

Gavin Maxwell, *Ring of Bright Water*, **1960**

Why is walking in wild and solitary places so satisfying? Partly it is the sheer physical pleasure: sometimes pitting one's strength against the elements and the lie of the land. The beauty and wonder of the natural world and the fresh air restore our sense of proportion and the stresses and strains of everyday life slip away. Whatever the character of the countryside, walking in it benefits us mentally and physically, inducing a sense of well-being, an enrichment of life and an enhanced awareness of what lies around us.

All this the countryside gives us and the least we can do is to safeguard it by supporting rural economies, local businesses, and low-impact methods of farming and land-management, and by using environmentally sensitive forms of transport – walking being pre-eminent.

In this book there is a detailed chapter on the wildlife and conservation of the region and a chapter on minimum-impact walking, with ideas on how to tread lightly in this fragile environment; by following its principles we can help to preserve our natural heritage for future generations.

INTRODUCTION

To those who've never walked the Cleveland Way before, it might seem slightly strange to discover that this was one of the first long-distance paths to be designated a 'National Trail', having been bestowed that honour way back in 1969. Only the massive Pennine Way that strides confidently through the very centre of Britain is older, having been designated a National Trail four years previously.

How curious, you may think, that those good people at the National Trail office should follow up the mighty Pennine Way with what is, by comparison, a rather diminutive, horseshoe-shaped path huddled around one small corner of England. At **107.4 miles (172.9km)**, its length is less than half that of the Pennine Way (268 miles/431km). What's more, the Cleveland

> **The Cleveland Way was the second path in the country to be designated a National Trail**

Way is confined solely to one country, England, and indeed one *county*, Yorkshire, whereas the Pennine Way crosses Derbyshire, Yorkshire and Northumberland before breaching the border into Scotland; it also climbs to only 454m (1489ft) above sea level at its highest point at Urra Moor, as opposed to 893m at Cross Fell on the Pennine Way; focuses on only one National Park, the North Yorkshire Moors, where the Pennine Way visits *four*; and even today is visited by only ten thousand people per year – as opposed to the

Above: The picture-perfect village of Staithes (see p131) rises up the cliffside from the little port.

Pennine Way's fifteen thousand-plus. Given all the above, you may find yourself wondering why anybody would choose to walk the Cleveland Way at all. Because if the Pennine Way is a path that follows the very backbone of England, the Cleveland Way could be seen, geographically speaking, as nothing more than a stroll around its armpit.

And then you take your first few steps on the path itself – and it all begins to makes sense.

To paraphrase that old footballing cliché, this is a walk of two halves. The first section, from Helmsley to Saltburn, is 57 miles long and can be characterised by some breathtaking yomping through the windswept, heather-smoth-

ered expanses of North York Moors National Park – though this rather crude characterisation hides a wealth of subtle variations, including farmland, woodland, meadow and bog. Study the landscape closely and you'll see that this is a land of rarity, the home of several varieties of seldom-seen orchids and even scarcer **wildlife**. Take the tiny alcathoe bat, for example, which has been positively identified in only two places in the UK – one of which is on the moors; or the montagu harrier, of

This is a walk of two halves: the first characterised by the heather-smothered expanses of the North York Moors and the second half along the Yorkshire coast

which there are believed to be only four breeding pairs in the UK, yet which nested in these parts recently. Nor must we forget the ultra-elusive pine marten, first spotted in England in 2015 after more than a century, and filmed on the North York Moors as recently as 2017.

Seeing any of these rarities on your trek will be something of a miracle, of course, but take a step back to drink in the scenery as a whole and you'll find it just as rewarding. Within a dozen miles of the start of the trail you come to Sutton Bank, a place that famed Yorkshire vet and author James Herriot – a man who clearly knew a bit about the 'great outdoors' – described as having '**the finest view in England**'. Another writer who had also earned a bit of a reputation for his writings on nature, the poet William Wordsworth, was so moved by the same view that he paused to write a sonnet there – even though he was getting married later that day, so probably had other things on his mind at the time. And throughout this first half of the walk the path brings you to some spectacular panoramas over the nearby fells and valleys – and at times it's truly breathtaking.

The second half of the Cleveland Way takes you along the blustery shores of Yorkshire as you make your way from Saltburn to Filey – a distance of just over 50 miles. It's an endlessly spellbinding stroll along the shoreline, punctuated every few miles by cosy little fishing villages as well as

Left: Savouring the view over the tiny village of Newton-under-Roseberry (see p111) from just below Roseberry Topping.

larger towns, such as Whitby and Scarborough, that survive and thrive largely on the proceeds of the tourist industry. It's a fascinating walk and one that will leave you not knowing which way to turn: whether to look down at your feet to explore the rockpools, seek out jet (this stretch of coastline is the only place in country where you can find this black lignite stone), or hunt for fossils in the Jurassic geology of Robin Hood's Bay and Ravenscar; or should you instead look out to sea to spot seals, porpoises and even whales; not forgetting, of course, to gaze to the heavens every now and again to see the birdlife circling around, with the cliffs around Filey believed to be the home of the British mainland's largest seabird colony.

Such treats are not gained without some effort, however, and many veterans of the Cleveland Way think this latter half of the trail is the harder of the two as you negotiate the sizeable undulations of Yorkshire's east coast, including, most dramatically of all, the cliff at **Boulby** – at 210m (690ft), the highest point on England's east coast.

> **... you can hunt for fossils in the Jurassic geology of Robin Hood's Bay ... or look out to sea to spot seals, porpoises and even whales**

It may surprise you to discover that, for all these natural riches, the North York Moors are largely a man-made landscape. Archaeological discoveries such as pottery and crude stone tools tell us that man has been here since the Mesolithic period (8000BC), when Britain was still joined to Europe. By the Bronze Age the trees were being cleared by the settlers, allowing the heather to flourish, while during the Iron Age (from 600BC) the local inhabitants were reshaping the land for their own purposes, with the national park home to three prominent hill forts at Roulston Scar near Sutton Bank, Boltby Scar and atop Live Moor – all right on the trail. Even later, the Romans built signal stations along the coast at Filey, Scarborough and Ravenscar, and in the intervening two millennia since that time man has built **castles** (Helmsley and Scarborough), and **abbeys** (Rievaulx and Whitby), **alum quarries** (such as those near Ravenscar) and **ironstone mines** (near Skinningrove) – the ruins and remains of which add so much beauty and interest to the trail. In fact, the park as a whole has over 12,000 archaeological sites and features, of which 700 are scheduled ancient monuments, and quite a few of them lie right on the national trail. Small wonder, then, that the area has become a magnet for walkers, with other long-distance trails passing through the park including Lyke Wake Walk and the Coast to Coast path – both of which sometimes share the same path as the Cleveland Way.

So yes, it may be shorter, slightly younger and less famous than the Pennine Way; but boy, this path packs a lot into its 107.4 miles. So perhaps we shouldn't be asking why any-

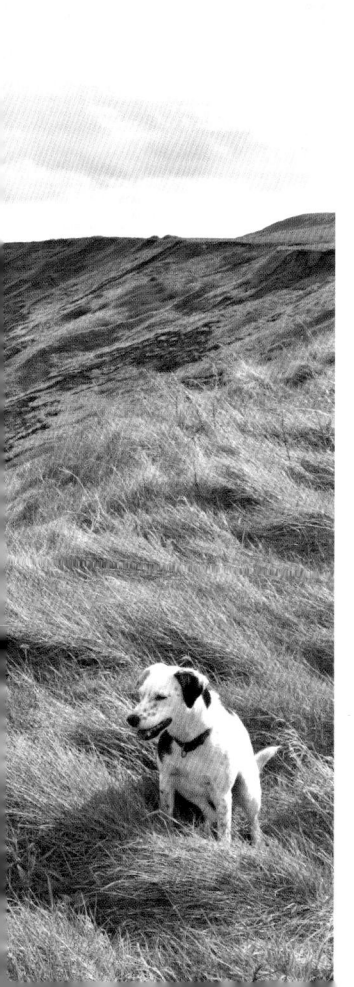

Left: One of the surprises of the Cleveland Way is the vast stretches of often empty sandy beaches, such as here below the clifftop path south of Saltburn.

one would want to walk the Cleveland Way; instead, maybe, it's time we started asking the exact opposite: Why *wouldn't* you want to?

How difficult is the path?

We think that the Cleveland Way is, in comparison with other long-distance trails in England, of a fairly medium difficulty. There's no problem with route finding – the path, like all national trails, is well furnished with signposts and there's only one place, through the pine plantations on the way down to Slapewath, where the signage can be confusing and people do sometimes get lost. Nor is it particularly remote. Sure, there are a couple of lonely sections on the first half of the walk, but in general there are enough B&Bs, campsites and eateries along the way to ensure that you're never too far from civilisation (and help, should you need it). Nor, for that matter, is it particularly long: at 107.4 miles, it's the ninth longest of the fifteen national trails.

The impressive ruins of Helmsley Castle are just a few hundred yards from the start of the trail.

Made it! Posing for photos on the commemorative bench at the end of the Cleveland Way

So the difficulty really lies only with the difficulty of the walking itself and how steep the gradients are. And yes, in places during the first half of the trail on the moors, such as the rollercoaster section between Osmotherley and Clay Bank Top, and Kildale and Slapewath, there are some particularly steep climbs that will leave you puffed-out and jelly-legged at the end – not to mention some equally steep descents too. And as for the second half of the walk, well coastal walking is usually a little bit arduous and the latter half of the Cleveland Way is no exception and includes one of the stiffest climbs on the whole walk,

See pp36-7 for some suggested itineraries covering different walking speeds

from Skinningrove at sea level to the top of Boulby Cliff, 203m (666ft) above it. But overall those of an average fitness, with a reasonable level of determination, stamina and luck, should finish the trail with little difficulty.

How long do you need?

Assuming you work, and this work takes place from a Monday to Friday, by taking a week off, and including in this vacation the weekends at either end (ie making nine days in total), you'll find that the Cleveland Way can be started and finished in one trip. This includes not only all the walking (assuming a reasonable 13-15 miles per day) but also a half-day or more to get to the trail at the start, and back home again at the end – with possibly enough time to take a break here and there on the trail too. Of course there's nothing to stop you going faster than this and finishing it all within seven days; but we think eight or nine days allows you more time to appreciate what you're seeing and to prevent it from being more than just an exhausting race to the finish.

Above: The famous Whalebone Arch on Whitby's West Cliff is actually the third set of bones to stand here, the first having been erected in 1853.
Below: The port at Whitby.

INTRODUCTION

❏ FESTIVALS AND ANNUAL EVENTS

The following list highlights just the main events taking place around the trail. The most famous are perhaps Whitby Goth Festival and the Tour de Yorkshire. If your trek coincides with a festival it's great to see a place when it's at its most lively but make sure you book accommodation beforehand – even if you plan to camp.

April/May

● **Books by the Beach** (🖳 booksbythebeach.co.uk) Scarborough's very own book festival, with events taking place around the town over a week in mid April.

● **Sci-Fi Scarborough** (🖳 scifiscarborough.co.uk) Now in its fifth year, this weekend-long sci-fi convention takes place in the Spa Complex. Dress appropriately.

● **Whitby Goth Weekend** (🖳 whitbygothweekend.co.uk) The first of two annual Goth weekends held in Whitby in April and October, a festival of music that's been going for 25 years now. Expect swathes of black clothing, lots of make-up and rubbish dancing. Alongside it is the Bizarre Bazaar Alternative Market.

● **Tour de Yorkshire** (🖳 letour.yorkshire.com) Four-day cycle race around the county held over the first May bank holiday; the exact course varies each year, though if it's coming near you, expect road closures, interrupted bus schedules and huge crowds.

June/July

● **Whitby SeaFest** (🖳 whitbyseafest.co.uk) Usually held over the first weekend in July, this festival started in the early '90s as the Captain Cook Fest, though these days has more of a general nautical theme, with balladeers, shantymen and folk musicians.

● **Robin Hood's Bay Folk Weekend** (🖳 folkweekend.rhbay.co.uk) A free weekend of relaxed music sessions and 'sing-arounds' in picturesque Robin Hood's Bay.

● **Scalby Fair** (🖳 scalbyfair.org.uk) Held in Scalby near Scarborough, this, one of the few remaining street fairs in the North, is a week-long festival of entertainment.

● **British Falconry Fair** (🖳 britishfalconryfair.com) Held towards the end of June at Helmsley's National Centre for Birds of Prey.

● **SeaFest Maritime Festival, Scarborough** (🖳 discoveryorkshirecoast.com/whatson Often held a few weeks after Whitby's version on the town's West Pier, the celebrations include a beer festival and live music all weekend.

● **Whitby Steampunk Weekend** (🖳 facebook.com/whitbysteampunkweekend) Alternative cultures get another look-in at Whitby at this weekend festival of flying goggles, pocket watches and moustache wax held over the last weekend of July at Whitby Ballroom and culminating in the Steampunk Ball.

● **MoorFest** (🖳 www.northyorkmoors.org.uk) A celebration of country life, culture and heritage on the moors, held at Sutton Bank on the last Sunday in July.

August/September

● **Tea on the Topping** (🖳 nationaltrust.org.uk/roseberry-topping) Have a cup of tea and a slice of cake on the top of Roseberry Topping – on the first Sunday in August.

● **Saltburn Folk Festival** (🖳 cuttywrenfolkclub.talktalk.net/SaltburnFF) Gigs all round the town, taking place over a weekend in August.

● **Whitby Regatta** (🖳 whitbyregatta.co.uk) Weekend of boat races, displays and fireworks, usually in August.

● **Whitby Folk Week** (🖳 whitbyfolk.co.uk) Week-long festival of music, dance and street entertainment usually held in the latter half of August.

● **Whitby Pirate Weekend** Held over the first weekend in September, a time for the locals to dress up as pirates for no reason whatsoever.

● **Staithes Festival of Arts & Heritage** (🖳 staithesfestival.com) Usually held over

When to go

SEASONS

As I write this in mid March there's a foot of snow outside our front door – something that few of us expected just a week or so ago when the birds were singing and a warm breeze was causing the daffodil flowers to bob in happy unison. The fact that those same daffodils are now struggling to poke their heads through the drifts is proof, I guess,

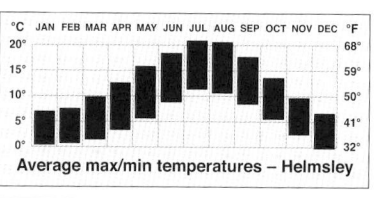

Average max/min temperatures – Helmsley

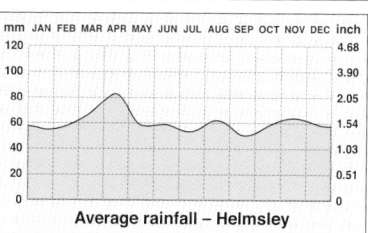

Average rainfall – Helmsley

that we humans aren't the only ones to be surprised by the weather. But while the English climate is hardly predictable, at least some generalisations can be made. Statistically, the months when the weather is least likely to be inclement are May to September. The air temperature at this time is generally at its warmest, with frosts unlikely from the end of May. Rain, though, is another factor. Some years can see continuous rain for several weeks, even in the height of summer, turning parts of the path into a quagmire. Conversely, April and October – months one associates with rain – often bring several days in a row that are bright and breezy, when the walking and the surroundings are at their best.

Spring

The weather in spring is as unpredictable as the rest of the year. In **April** it can be warm and sunny but conditions are more likely to be changeable, with blustery showers and cold spells reminding you that winter has only just passed. On the other hand, the days are long, and it may surprise you to discover that less rain falls on average in spring than at any other time of the year. This, combined with the milder weather of **May** and **June**, the proliferation of wild flowers that flourish early in the year and the long days, makes it one of the best times to walk.

Summer

July and **August** are the traditional holiday months and the conditions can be especially good for walking, with generally warm temperatures and many hours

the first weekend of September, when villagers open their cottage doors to the public as temporary galleries for works by resident and visiting artists.

October
● **Musicport Festival** (🖳 musicportfestival.com) Held at Whitby Pavilion over three days in mid October, this is the UK's biggest indoor world music festival.
● **Whitby Goth Weekend** See April above.

INTRODUCTION

of daylight. This is when the path is at its busiest and the seaside resorts such as Scarborough can suffocate with sun-seekers. Fortunately, the trail itself remains fairly quiet, with most people preferring to sit on the beach and develop their melanomas than stroll around the nearby cliffs, so you'll soon leave the hordes behind.

Autumn

Many connoisseurs consider autumn, especially early autumn, the best time of year for walking. **September** and **October** can be lovely months to get out on the trail, especially when the leaves begin to turn. That said, although the air temperature usually remains relatively mild, October can see the first frosts, and rain is an ever-present threat. The days are also getting quite short now, and once daylight saving time ends at the end of October, night falls at about 5.30pm.

Winter

Only the very hardiest of souls will attempt the Cleveland Way in winter. The days are shorter and you'll need to be at your destination by 4.30pm through November to March or risk walking in the dark. Cold weather, wind and driving rain are not the best recipe for a day's walking, although a crisp winter morning takes a lot of beating. Most campsites and some B&Bs and tearooms shut over winter, too, so if you are determined to walk at this time you need to plan carefully – because you really don't want to be sleeping rough on the moors in winter.

DAYLIGHT HOURS

When walking you should always keep half an eye on how much daylight you've got left. Less of an issue in the height of summer, of course: in mid to late June the sun rises at around 4.30am and doesn't set until after 9.40pm, plus you get

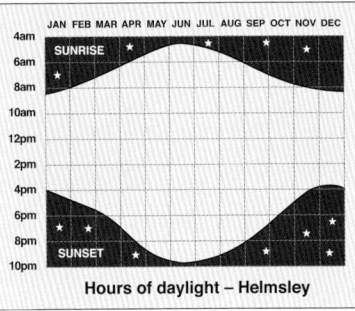

Hours of daylight – Helmsley

almost an hour's twilight after that, which should give you plenty of time to do as much walking as your little legs can manage in one day. But in autumn, winter or early spring, it's a different story and it will, of course, not be possible to cover as many miles or to be out for as long as you would in the summer. The table (above) gives the sunrise and sunset times for the middle of each month at latitude 54.5° North, which runs through the North York Moors, giving a reasonably accurate picture for daylight along the Cleveland Way.

Colour photos (following pages)
● **Opposite – Top**: 'The Circle' by Richard Farrington, at the top of the climb out of Saltburn. **Bottom**: The *Repus* sculpture (see p124), right by the path on the seafront at Skinningrove. ● **Overleaf, clockwise from top**: **1**. Taking a breather at the summit of Roseberry Topping. **2**. View from the Alex Falconer Seat (see p102). **3**. Saltburn Viaduct. **4**. Ancient standing stone near Urra Moor. **5**. Captain Cook Monument (see p112). **6**. Stepping stones near Noodle Hill.

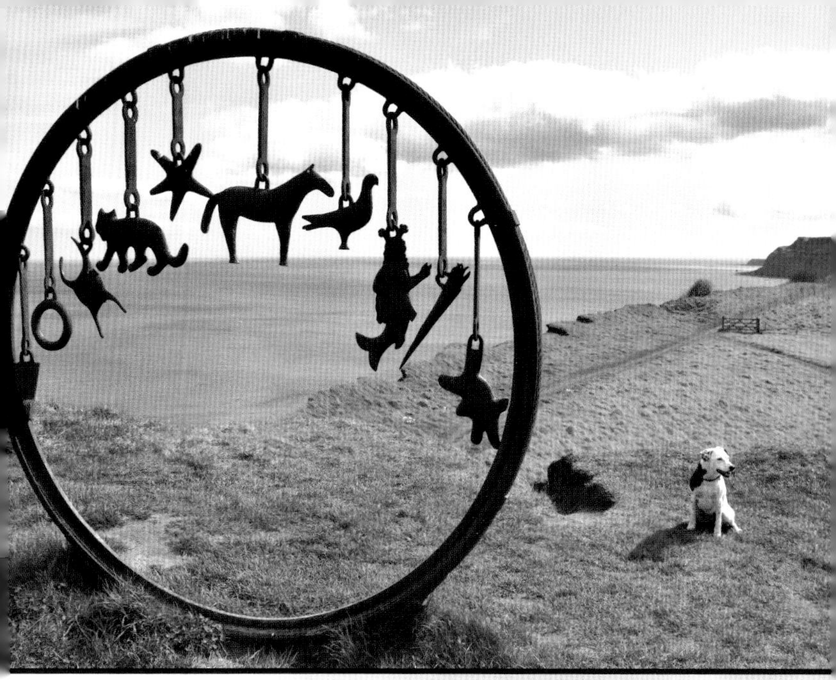

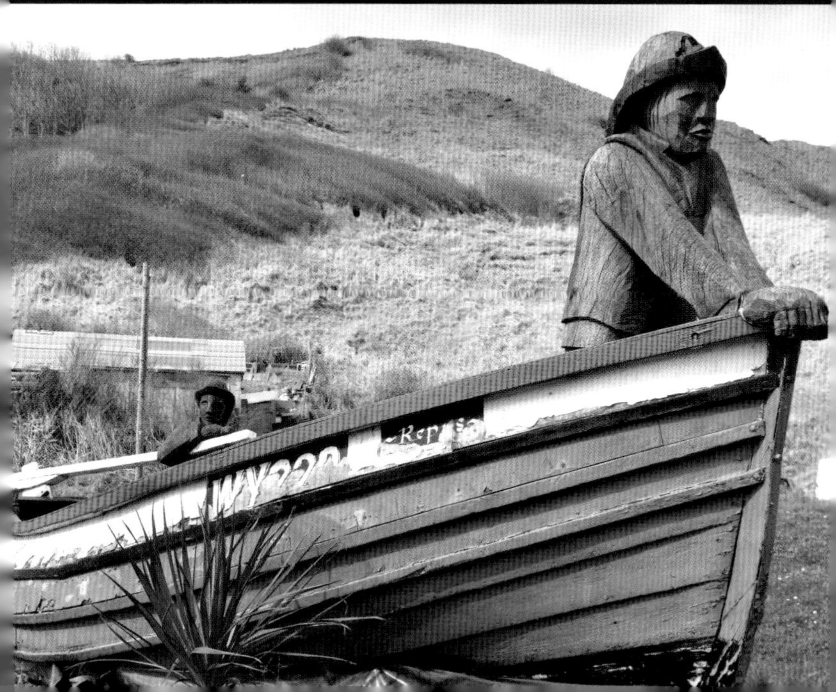

PLANNING YOUR WALK 1

Practical information for the walker

ROUTE FINDING

You shouldn't have much difficulty finding your way on the Cleveland Way. The signage is excellent throughout, with only one exception that comes to mind: as you leave the moors for the last time to head towards Slapewath, the Cleveland Way signs (which are usually distinguished by having an acorn symbol on them) suddenly dry up. This fact, combined with the myriad of alternative trails that suddenly present themselves, does make it a little tricky. But, suffice to say that when we first walked the trail, despite several times where we hesitated before choosing a path, and a couple of times where we just guessed what the right trail might be, at the end of that day we ended up exactly where we should have done, and appear, upon further investigation, to have taken the correct path to get there, too.

Apart from this small section, the first half of the walk is very well signposted and you shouldn't get lost, particularly if you follow the maps in Part 4 of this book. As for the latter half of the trail, past Saltburn, well you'll be walking by the coast from then on, so as long as you keep the sea to your left-hand side (assuming you are trekking in the direction given in this book) you shouldn't go too far wrong. The only time you may have difficulty is if coastal erosion has caused a temporary diversion; there was a big one when we researched this book, and which we've shown on Maps 40 and 41. The signage on these diversions is often less than exemplary, but again with a little bit of intuition and luck you shouldn't go too far wrong.

GPS

I never carried a compass, preferring to rely on a good sense of direction... I never bothered to understand how a compass works or what it is supposed to do... To me a compass is a gadget, and I don't get on well with gadgets of any sort. **Alfred Wainwright**

While Wainwright's acolytes may scoff, other walkers will accept GPS technology as an inexpensive, well-established if non-essential,

---

(Opposite) clockwise from bottom left: Scarborough(1-4) **1**. The Grand Hotel was at one time the biggest brick building in Europe. **2**. The graffiti covered Caravel Alley, just one of several surprises Scarborough springs on its visitors. **3**. South Beach. **4**. Scarborough is more famous for its beaches and bars than for its fishing harbour, though it sits right in the heart of the action. **5**. The evocative ruins of Whitby Abbey. **6**. Runswick Beach. **7**. Filey Brigg, at the end of the trail.

navigational aid. To cut a long story short, within a minute of being turned on and with a clear view of the sky, **GPS receivers** will establish your position as well as elevation in a variety of formats, including the British OS grid system to an accuracy of within a few metres. These days, most **smartphones** have a GPS receiver built in and mapping software available to run on them (see box on p44).

One thing must be understood however: **treating GPS as a replacement for maps, a compass and common sense is a big mistake**. Every electronic device is susceptible to battery failure or some electronic malfunction that might leave you in the dark. GPS is primarily a navigational aid or backup to conventional route finding and, in almost all cases, is best used in conjunction with a paper map. At its most basic level a GPS stops you exacerbating navigational errors and saves you time in correcting them. Newer units may come with some inbuilt mapping, but while it's possible to buy **digital mapping** (see box on p44) to import into a regular GPS unit with sufficient storage capacity, it might be considered as practical as having internet on a mobile phone – you still end up scrolling and zooming across a tiny screen.

Using GPS with this book – tracklog and waypoints

The easiest way to avoid getting lost is to install a **tracklog** of the route on either a GPS unit or a smartphone running GPS. A tracklog is a continuous line like a path that appears on your GPS screen; all you have to do is keep on that line. If you lose it on the screen you can zoom out until it reappears and walk towards it. To download the GPS tracklog on which this book's maps are based, see the Trailblazer website – 🖥 trailblazer-guides.com.

Where a tracklog is a continuous line, **waypoints** are single points like cairns. This book identifies key waypoints on the route maps. It's anticipated you won't tramp along day after day, ticking off the book's waypoints, transfixed by the screen on your GPS or smartphone; the route description and maps are more than adequate most of the time. Only when you're unsure of your position or which way to go might you feel the need to even turn on the unit for a quick affirmation.

The book's waypoints correlate to the list on pp182-3 which gives the OS grid reference and a description. You can either simply read off the nearest presumed waypoint from the list as and when the need arises and work out where you are in relation to it or, less confusingly, key it in as a new point and press 'go to'. As there will probably be only a handful of times you need to do this, for most that will suffice but, with less margin for keystroke error, you can download the complete list as a GPS-readable .gpx file of grid references (but with no descriptions) from 🖥 trailblazer-guides.com.

Using GPS with this book, be it a tracklog, all the waypoints or just the key waypoints, is *an option*. Without them you could find yourself staggering around a mist-clad moor, or ambling confidently down the wrong path. With GPS, when the need arises, you can reliably establish your position in relation to the path, or quickly find out how far and in what direction it is to a known point on the trail.

Bear in mind that the vast majority of people who tackle this path do so perfectly well without a GPS unit. Instead of rushing out to invest in one, consider putting the money towards good-quality footwear or waterproofs instead. However, correctly using this book's GPS data could get you back on track and dozing in front of the pub fireplace, or tucked up in bed, all the sooner.

For information on the trail maps, see pp75-6.

ACCOMMODATION

The route guide (Part 4) lists a fairly comprehensive selection of places to stay along the trail. The three main options are: camping; staying in hostels and/or camping/bunk barns (in which we have included the relatively new phenomenon of 'glamping'); or using B&B-style accommodation (B&Bs/pubs/guesthouses/hotels). Few people stick to just one of these the whole way, preferring, for example, to camp most of the time but spend every third night in a hostel, or perhaps take a hostel where possible but splash out on a B&B or hotel every once in a while.

The table on pp34-5 provides a snapshot of what type of accommodation and services are available in each of the towns and villages, while the tables on pp36-7 provide some suggested itineraries. The following is a brief introduction as to what to expect from each type of accommodation.

Camping

The Cleveland Way is wonderfully equipped for campers and, if you so desire, it's possible to camp for pretty much every night along the path. That said, few people will do so *every* night. You're almost bound to get at least one night where the rain falls relentlessly, sapping morale; it's then that most campers opt to spend the next night drying out in a hostel or B&B somewhere.

There are many advantages with camping. It's more economical, for a start, with most campsites charging somewhere between £5 and £10 per tent/pitch for up to two walkers, though it can climb to £23 (for example at Lord Stones) in high summer. Best of all there's **rarely any need to book**, except possibly in the very high season, and even then you'd be highly unlucky not to find somewhere, even if it means camping discreetly in the woods. The campsites vary and you get what you pay for: some are just pub gardens or a farmer's spare field with basic toilet/shower facilities; others are full-blown caravan sites with security access codes and sparkling ablutions blocks and a few spaces put aside for tents. Showers are usually available, occasionally for a fee, though more often than not for free. Note that the only (YHA) hostel on the Cleveland Way that still accepts campers is Helmsley. There are disadvantages too, of course. There aren't many campsites in town centres so your base for Scarborough or Whitby, for example, may be a couple of miles outside the town centre, though they may be less than that from the path.

Wild camping (ie camping not in a regular campsite; see p71) is illegal in England and Wales. If you do decide to err on the wrong side of the law, we've heard some people do wild camp on the Way and there are plenty of opportuni-

PLANNING YOUR WALK

ties to do so. However, please don't do so in a field without first gaining permission from the landowner.

Remember that camping, wild or 'tame', is not an easy option, especially for a solo walker. Walked continuously, the route is wearying enough without carrying the means to sleep and cook with you. Should you decide to camp at campsites, consider employing one of the baggage-transfer companies mentioned on pp28-9, though this does mean the loss of spontaneity which is, for many, the whole point of camping!

Camping/bunk barns, camping pods and 'glamping'

A **camping/bunk barn** is pretty much what it sounds like: an old barn in the corner of a farmer's field with a couple of wooden benches to sleep on; sleeping bags and sleeping mats are thus usually necessary. A camping/bunk barn is probably the nearest non-campers will get to sleeping outside, while at the same time providing shelter from the elements. Note also that these are sometimes booked for sole occupancy and thus it is essential to call in advance to check availability. There is a camping barn on the Cleveland Way at Kildale and at the time of writing a barn is being converted to a bunk barn at Urra.

❑ **Should you book your accommodation in advance?**
When walking the Cleveland Way, it's advisable to have your night's accommodation booked at least by the time you set off in the morning. Although it may compromise your spontaneity, nothing is more deflating than arriving at the end of a long day only to find that you've then got to walk another few miles or even take a detour off the route because everywhere is booked up. After all, what have you got to lose? Unless you have a real fear of telecommunications (a 'phonebia', perhaps?) it takes little effort and cost to call ahead and arrange your accommodation in advance of your arrival.

In the high season (**June to August**), unless camping, it's pretty much essential you have your night's accommodation secured, both during the first half of the walk, where accommodation is scarce, and on the second, coastal part of the trail where there is much more accommodation available but demand is also much higher as you stroll through the 'Yorkshire Riviera'. Outside the high season and away from weekends, as long as you're **flexible** and willing to take what's offered, you might get away with booking just a couple of weeks or even just days in advance. However, **weekends** are busy everywhere, so make sure you sort Friday and Saturday nights out well before you start your trek.

If you've left it too late and can only get accommodation for parts of the walk, **consider camping** to fill in the gaps. It's not to everyone's taste and it helps if you already own the gear, but it can save you money which you can lavish on yourself later without guilt and, if using a baggage service, they can cart the gear from door to door at no extra effort to yourself.

If you're planning on staying in hostels the same applies, though do be careful when travelling out of high season as many **hostels** close during the week and shut altogether from around November to February. Once again, it's well worth booking in advance. Campers, whatever time of year, should always be able to find somewhere to pitch their tent, though ringing in advance can't hurt and will at least confirm that the campsite is still open.

See also box p22.

Camping pods are a relatively new phenomenon that have appeared in the last few years as part of the craze for '**glamping**'. The specifications for a camping pod vary from site to site but essentially they are stand-alone pods set on a campsite; some are unfurnished, while others are well appointed affairs, such as those at Lord Stones which come with a bed, table and chairs, washroom, a small kitchenette and sometimes some outside seating too. They are undoubtedly novel and often quite charming: the wood-burning stove at Lord Stones, for example, is a nice touch. Then there are those at Middlewood Farm, Robin Hood's Bay, which are described as 'gypsy cabins' and include ovens, kettles, fridges and heaters – and are even insulated with sheep's wool! But don't be fooled into thinking that, because they have the word 'camping' in their name, they will be cheap. Like yurts, bell tents, shepherd's huts and all the other accommodation one usually associates with 'glamping', they cost as much as a room in a B&B, and often more. (A pod for two people in August at Lord Stones, for example, is £75 per night, and they'll usually only accept advance bookings for a minimum of two nights.) However, they are an experience.

Hostels

The Cleveland Way is fairly well served by hostels, with five belonging to the YHA. Indeed, if you're willing to stay in camping/bunk barns as well as hostels, and are prepared to walk from Helmsley to Osmotherley on the first day (a distance of 21.9 miles/35.2km), it's possible to stay in a hostel and/or camping/bunk barn for all but one night on the path. (The section from Kildale to Whitby, a distance of just 34.4 miles/55.5km, has no hostel so we advise you to book a B&B along this stretch instead. Alternatively if you're really determined to stay in a hostel every night you could walk to Staithes, a more manageable 23.3 miles/37.5km away, and catch a bus down to one of the hostels along the coast – Whitby would be the nearest – though by the time you factor in the return fare the saving you make when compared to staying in a B&B would be negligible.)

If you haven't visited a YHA hostel recently – and thus the words 'youth' and 'hostel' still conjure up images of strict curfews, draughty dorms, dreary food and severe staff – we advise you to take a second look; because hostels can offer some of the best-located and most interesting accommodation along the path. Despite the name, anyone of any age can join the YHA. This can be done at any hostel, or by contacting the **Youth Hostels Association of England and Wales** (☎ 01629-592700 or ☎ 0800 0191 700, 🖳 yha.org.uk). The cost of a year's membership is £20 for an adult (£15 if you pay by direct debit), £10/5 for anyone under 26. Having secured your membership, YHA hostels are easy to book, either online or by phone through the contact details above. Since non-members have to pay £3 more per night it is worth joining if you expect to stay in a YHA hostel for more than five nights in a year. You'll also get discounts at various outdoor shops (including Cotswold Outdoor and Go Outdoors) and up to 20% off Ordnance Survey maps – making this a very good deal.

Hostels come equipped with a whole range of facilities, from drying rooms to washing machines, televisions to pool tables and fully equipped kitchens. Some have a shop selling a selection of groceries, snacks and souvenirs and most have wi-fi in communal areas. Many offer breakfast and/or dinner (of varying quality) and a packed lunch; several have a licence to sell alcohol. They are also great places to meet fellow walkers, swap stories and compare blisters.

Weighed against these advantages is the fact that even though many hostels now have rooms with just 2-4 beds (which can be booked on a private basis), if you want a dorm bed you may still end up having to share your night with a heavy snorer. A couple of the hostels also suffer from uncomfortably small dorms when they're full. Some rooms now have en suite facilities but in others you have to share a shower room and in a couple of cases facilities may be limited.

If you're travelling out of the main season (particularly between November and February) you may find some hostels are shut to walkers during the week, or completely. Even in high season some are not staffed during the day and walkers may have to wait until 5pm before checking in, though you may be able to access the kitchen and leave luggage in a secure room before 5pm. And finally, the cost of staying in a hostel, once breakfast has been added on, is in many instances not that much cheaper (£14-30pp for YHA members) than staying in a B&B, especially if you're walking with someone.

Bed and breakfast-style accommodation

Bed and Breakfasts (B&Bs) are a great British institution and, as with many long-distance trails in the UK, are often a highlight of any trip, with properties sometimes three or four hundred years old. Older owners often treat you as surrogates for their long-departed offspring and enjoy nothing more than looking after you. As the name suggests, they provide you with a bed in a private room,

---

❏ **Rates and booking**
Rates in this guide start at around £20 per person (pp) for the most basic B&B accommodation and cost over £50pp for the most luxurious en suite places in a popular tourist haunt such as Whitby; most charge around £30-40pp. Rooms in pubs cost about the same amount but guesthouses and hotels are generally more expensive.

If you're travelling by yourself, try to find a place that has a single room; staying in a double or twin room by yourself and you'll often find that you have to pay the full room rate, particularly on the coast in summer, though outside the high season you may be able to negotiate a discount.

Many places have their own website and offer online/email **booking**; for some (particularly B&Bs), however, you will need to phone.

Most places ask for a **deposit** (about 50%) which is generally non-refundable if you cancel at short notice. Some places may charge 100% if the booking is for one night only. Always let the owner know as soon as possible if you have to cancel your booking so they can offer the bed to someone else. Guesthouses and hotels take credit or debit cards. Most smaller B&Bs accept only cheques by post or payments by bank transfer for the deposit; the balance can be settled with cash or a cheque.

See also box p20.

and breakfast – a hearty, British-style cooked one unless you specify otherwise beforehand – though they range in style enormously; see also p24.

Rooms usually contain either a double bed (known as a **double**), or two single beds (**twin room**); those can sleep three or four people (**triple** or **quad**) have either a double and a single, or a double beds with bunk beds, or three/four single beds. Few places have a **single** room with one bed for one person.

B&Bs have en suite rooms and/or rooms with either private or shared facilities. En suite facilities often mean a shower squeezed into a room but with private/shared facilities there may be a bath, which is what most walkers prefer at the end of a long day, and the bathroom is never more than a few feet away.

Solo trekkers should take note: single rooms are not so easy to find so you'll often end up occupying a double or twin room, for which you'll either have to pay a single occupancy supplement or the full room rate.

Some B&Bs, usually the more remote ones, provide an **evening meal** (around £8-15pp though you'll usually need to book in advance). If not, there's often a pub or sometimes a restaurant nearby or, if it's far, the owner may give you a lift to and from the nearest place with food (though do note that this may be a mile or two away and you may need to sort out getting back afterwards yourself). B&Bs in these more remote locations, especially away from the coast, may well offer a **packed lunch** too see p25. If being able to **smoke** is important for you see the notes in the box on p29.

Guesthouses, hotels, pubs and inns

Guesthouse provide bed and breakfast accommodation but should have a better class of décor and more facilities such as offering evening meals and a lounge for guests. However, they are unlikely to offer room service, unlike a hotel.

Pubs and inns may also offer bed and breakfast-style accommodation and tariffs are no more than in a regular B&B. However, you need to be prepared for a noisier environment, especially if your room is above the bar.

Hotels do usually cost more and some might be a little displeased by a bunch of muddy trekkers turning up. However, most places on the walk, particularly in the quieter towns and villages, are used to seeing trekkers, make a good living from them and welcome them warmly. Prices in hotels and pubs start from as little as £20pp (take a bow, Grand Hotel Scarborough) but are more usually around £35pp.

Airbnb

The rise and rise of Airbnb (🖳 airbnb.co.uk) has seen private homes and apartments opened up to overnight travellers on an informal basis. While accommodation is primarily based in cities, the concept is spreading to tourist hotspots in more rural areas, but do check thoroughly what you are getting and the precise location. While the first couple of options listed may be in the area you're after, others may be far too far afield for walkers. At its best, this is a great way to meet local people in a relatively unstructured environment, but do be aware that these places are not registered B&Bs, so standards may vary, yet prices may not necessarily be any lower than those of a regular B&B.

FOOD AND DRINK

Breakfast

Stay in a B&B/guesthouse/hotel and you'll be filled to the gills each morning with a cooked English breakfast. This can consist of a bowl of cereal followed by a plateful of eggs, bacon, sausages, mushrooms, tomatoes, and possibly baked beans or black pudding, with toast and butter, and all washed down with coffee, tea and/or juice. Enormously satisfying the first time you try it, by the fourth or fifth morning you may start to prefer the lighter continental breakfast or porridge, which most establishments now offer.

Alternatively, and especially if you're planning an early start, you might like to request a packed lunch instead of this filling breakfast and just have a cup of coffee before you leave.

The YHA hostels mentioned in this guide offer breakfast; usually it's a good meal but they charge an additional £5-6.

Lunch

By great good fortune, it's rare to spend a day on the trail without finding a place to eat en route. Even on the first half of the walk, from Helmsley to Saltburn, there is pretty much always a café conveniently located along the trail.

The longest section without any sort of eatery is from Kildale to Slapewath – a distance of over 10 miles – though even here, if you're truly famished, you can drop down from Roseberry Topping to the village below, Newton-under-Roseberry, about 15-20 minutes away, where there's a pub serving food all day.

❏ **Local foods**

Food in Yorkshire tends towards the hearty and tasty – which will be music to most trekkers' ears. The most famous local delicacy must be the **Yorkshire pudding**, a side dish usually accompanying a roast dinner (especially roast beef) and made of eggs, flour and milk or water. Though as I describe it as a side dish, often in Yorkshire it actually acts as the dish itself, with the rest of the main course – the meat, veg and gravy – placed inside one huge pudding.

As for cake, Yorkshire's best-known tea-time treat is **parkin**, a gingerbread cake traditionally made with oatmeal and black treacle that's eaten throughout the North of England, though which is particularly associated with God's Own County. You'll find it throughout your walk, though we found the best available in Helmsley, at either the deli, Hunters, or Auntie Anne's Bakery (see p80).

If there's one **cheese** that Yorkshire is famous for, it's Wensleydale. Originally produced by Cistercian monks in the vale of the same name, this crumbly hunk of creamy deliciousness received worldwide fame thanks to two of the county's most famous inhabitants, Wallace & Gromit. Once again, Hunters of Helmsley is a reliable place to pick up some.

Another local speciality is the **coble cake**, the ingredients of which include walnuts, cinnamon and apple, which is made in Sea Drift Café in Staithes.

It probably won't surprise you to discover that **fish and seafood** are the specialities of the North Yorkshire coast, especially Whitby crab; see the Route Guide for recommendations of restaurants where you can try out that day's catch.

❏ **Local beers**

With over 160 breweries and distilleries in North Yorkshire, it won't take you long to find a local tipple to your taste. Indeed, there's one right at the start of the walk: **Helmsley Brewing Company** (see p77) is well aware of its place on the Cleveland Way and brews a tipple called Striding the Riding. A percentage of the sales of this pale ale goes towards managing and promoting the trail.

Do also look out for the long-established **York Brewery's** Moor-ish Ale (geddit!), which uses heather from the national park's Levisham Estate; 2p from every pint sold now goes towards planting oaks on the estate.

Close to the trail in Stokesley and named after a feature on the Cleveland Way, **Wainstones Brewery** (🖥 stokesleybrewing.co.uk) offers just four beers, each named after the local geology such as the 4% Sandstone and 4,2% Ironstone.

More breweries can be found on the coast. **Whitby Brewery** (🖥 whitby-brewery.com) is a particular favourite of those who like their beers dark, with the tasty porter, Jet Black, and the delicious but strong stout, Black Death (5%), which was originally brewed for the town's Goth Weekend. Just down the coast, **Scarborough Brewery** (🖥 scarboroughbrewery.co.uk) currently produces a dozen beers including the sense-scrambling red ale, Phrenology (6.2%).

Perhaps most interesting of all is **Bay Town** (🖥 baytownrhb.com), which celebrates the smuggling heritage of Robin Hood's Bay (though it's actually based half a mile inland at Fylingthorpe) with beers such as Petticoat's Deceit, Revenue's Revenge and Squire's Connivance, as well as Zachariah Storm Gin and Lingers' Ghost Vodka. They even organise hour-long tours of Robin Hood's Bay's smuggling spots, finishing with a tasting of all seven of their beers.

If you're still worried that you'll be hungry on your walk, if arranged in advance your B&B host or YHA hostel can usually provide a packed lunch at an additional cost, or of course there's nothing to stop you preparing your own when there's a shop nearby.

Cream teas

Never miss a chance to avail yourself of the treats on offer in the tearooms and farmhouses of Yorkshire. I've never met a cream tea that I didn't like and though they may be more of a speciality of Devon and Cornwall, there are plenty of places that serve them up in Yorkshire too.

Nothing revives like a decent pot of tea, and the opportunity to accompany it with a scone served with jam and cream is one that should not be passed up, particularly when you consider that, given all the walking you're doing, this is one of the few times you can consume all these calories guilt-free!

Evening meals

If your B&B doesn't do an evening meal you may find that in many villages, the pub is the only place to eat out. **Pubs** are as much a feature of this walk as coastline and castles, old mines and moorland, and in some cases the pub is a tourist attraction as much as the finest ruined abbey. Most have become highly attuned to the needs of walkers and offer both lunch and evening meals (with often a few regional dishes and usually a couple of vegetarian options), some locally brewed beers, a garden to relax in on hot days and a roaring fire to huddle around on cold ones. The standard of the food varies widely, though portions are usually large – which is often just about all walkers care about at the end of a long day.

That other great British culinary tradition in the bigger towns is the **fish 'n' chip shop** which will deep fry your dinner and then slather it in a layer of mushy peas and brown sauce.

Larger towns also have **Chinese and Indian takeaways** and fast-food outlets serving **pizzas and kebabs**; a welcome change from too much pub food and usually the only places still serving food late in the evenings, with many staying open until at least 11pm.

Catering for yourself
Those looking to cook for themselves on their trek need to plan carefully. There's a couple of small supermarkets and the delis in Helmsley at the start of the walk, but the next place to buy provisions isn't until Osmotherley, over 21 miles/33km into your walk – and the next one after that isn't until Skelton, over 33 miles/53km further along. So make sure you carry enough food with you on these stretches. Once you hit the coast, however, things become a lot easier and there are supermarkets dotted fairly frequently along the shoreline.

Of course, food is only part of the equation; you'll also need fuel so you can cook it. Trekking shops in Helmsley, Whitby, Scarborough and Filey sell it, and some of the larger campsites (those with shops and who are used to dealing with backpackers) *may* have it, but this can't be relied upon.

Drinking water
Surprising as it may seem for such a soggy corner of this sceptred isle, it is possible to dehydrate on the Cleveland Way. The remoteness of the path on the first, 'inland', half of the trail, and the lack of both shelter and opportunities to pick up water en route, can mean that on a hot day it is possible to get dehydrated, which is at best highly unpleasant. Don't think you'll be able to collect water from the nearby streams either: for one thing, there aren't that many streams up on the moors, and any water you do find in channels or puddles is likely to be the colour of strong tea and possibly contaminated by chemicals or sheep shit.

Just remember to take plenty of water with you (2-3 litres should be enough) at the start of each day during the first half of the walk. Once you reach the coast there will be more opportunities to fill up as there are more towns and villages on the way – though again, don't be tempted to drink from the streams that cross the path – nor, of course, from the sea.

MONEY

The first thing to note is that most businesses accept **debit/credit card** payments these days – sometimes with the proviso that you spend a minimum amount – so **there shouldn't be too many cases when you'll require cash**. Sure, some B&Bs and campsites, and the odd café and shop do operate on a cash-only basis, but there aren't many and their numbers are dwindling all the time. This is good news, as there aren't many **banks or ATMs/cashpoints** on the Cleveland Way. Helmsley has one but then after that there isn't another until Skelton.

Post offices provide a useful service by allowing you to get cash (by debit card) for free at any post office counter if you bank with most UK banks or building societies. For a full list see ⌨ postoffice.co.uk and click on Products & Services and then Branch and banking services. Unfortunately, after Helmsley there aren't any 'fixed' post offices until Skelton either – the post office at Osmotherley only operates on a part-time basis in the village hall so it's uncertain whether they would offer this service.

Another option is to try getting cash via the **cashback** system: find a store that will accept a debit card and ask them to advance cash against the card. A number of the local village stores as well as some pubs will do this, though you'll usually have to spend a minimum of £5 with them first. It pays to ask.

Thus, despite the widespread acceptance of credit/debit cards, we still advise you to **carry some cash** (reckon on £100 per person, just to be safe).

INTERNET ACCESS AND WI-FI

Pretty much everywhere offers **wi-fi** free to visitors, though it's not 100% guaranteed in some of the more remote places on the route. Pubs in particular usually have a wi-fi connection, though this may in certain instances be only in the bar itself and not in the rooms. If an internet connection is vital to you, do ask beforehand to make sure your B&B is online.

OTHER SERVICES

Some villages have a **post office** that doubles as the local store and bank (see above), and sometimes nearby you'll find a **phone box**, though be warned that these are slowly being phased out. Where they do exist, some only accept cards (credit, debit, BT or prepaid). Calls from a phone box cost a minimum of 60p (including a 40p connection charge; thereafter 10p a minute).

There are **outdoor equipment shops** in Helmsley, Whitby, Scarborough and Filey, and **pharmacies** in these places, too, as well as in Skelton and Saltburn, and **tourist information centres/visitor centres** of varying degrees of helpfulness at Sutton Bank, Saltburn, Staithes, Whitby, Robin Hood's Bay, Ravenscar, Scarborough and Filey.

WALKING COMPANIES

It's possible to turn up with your boots and backpack at Helmsley and just start walking without planning much other than your accommodation (about which, see the box on p22). And indeed, for many that's all part of the challenge. The companies listed on pp29-31, however, are in the business of making your holiday as stress-free, effortless and enjoyable as possible – for a fee, of course. Most offer a range of itineraries but are always happy to tailor make a walk for you.

PLANNING YOUR WALK

Baggage transfer and accommodation booking

● **Brigantes Walking Holidays** (☎ 01756-770402, 🖳 brigantesenglishwalks .com; North Yorkshire) run a family operated **baggage-transfer** service which support trails across the north of England. They charge from £8.50 to £18 per person (minimum two people, each with one bag of no more than 17kg), depending on your itinerary and the number of people in your party. For their self-guided walks see p30.

● **Sherpa Van** (baggage line ☎ 01748-826917, 🖳 sherpavan.com; North Yorkshire) is a national organisation that runs a service from April to mid

❏ **Information for foreign visitors**

● **Currency** The British pound (£) comes in notes of £50, £20, £10 and £5, and coins of £2 and £1. The pound is divided into 100 pence (usually referred to as 'p', pronounced 'pee') which come in silver coins of 50p, 20p 10p and 5p and copper coins of 2p and 1p.

● **Money** Up-to-date **exchange rates** can be found at 🖳 xe.com/currencyconverter and at some post offices, or at any bank or travel agent.

● **Business hours** Most **shops** and main **post offices** are open at least from Monday to Friday 9am-5pm and Saturday 9am-12.30pm. Many choose longer hours and some open on Sundays as well. However, some also close early one day a week, often Wednesday or Thursday. **Banks** are usually open 10am-4pm Monday to Friday.

  Pub opening hours have become more flexible – up to 24 hours a day seven days a week – so each pub may have different times. However, most pubs on the Cleveland Way, save for those in Scarborough and Whitby, continue to follow the traditional Monday to Saturday 11am to 11pm, Sunday to 10.30pm, and some still close in the afternoon, particularly in the winter months.

● **National (Bank) holidays** Most offices are shut on 1 January, Good Friday and Easter Monday (March/April), the first and last Monday in May, the last Monday in August, 25 December and 26 December. Some shops and museums/galleries are also closed but pubs, restaurants and cafés are often open.

● **School holidays** School holiday periods in England are generally as follows: a one-week break late October, two weeks around Christmas, a week mid February, two weeks around Easter, a week in late May and from late July to early September.

● **Documents** If you are a member of a National Trust organisation in your country bring your membership card as you should be entitled to free entry to National Trust properties and sites in the UK. See also the box on p56.

● **Travel/medical insurance** The European Health Insurance Card (EHIC) entitles EU nationals (on production of the EHIC card) to necessary medical treatment under the UK's National Health Service while on a temporary visit here. However, this is not a substitute for proper medical cover on your travel insurance for unforeseen bills and for getting you home should that be necessary. Also consider cover for loss or theft of personal belongings, especially if you're camping or staying in hostels, as there will be times when you'll have to leave your luggage unattended. If you're walking the Cleveland Way any time after March 2019 do check, too, what the latest rules are, for the UK will have left the EU that March and you can expect some changes to the legislation.

● **Weights and measures** Britain's illogical mix of metric and imperial measures is undoubtedly a source of confusion for many visitors. For example, in Britain milk

October for many of Britain's walking and cycling trails including the Cleveland Way. They charge £8.50 a bag with a maximum weight of 20kg.

They also offer **accommodation booking** (☎ 01609-883731, 🖥 cleveland way.co.uk). From £30 per person they will book and confirm all your accommodation, and provide you with directions on how to reach it from the trail.

For their self-guided walks see Sherpa Expeditions on p30.

Self-guided holidays

Self-guided means that the company will organise accommodation, baggage transfer (some contracting out the work to other companies), transport to and

---

can be sold in pints (1 pint = 568ml), as can beer in pubs, though most other liquid including petrol (gasoline) and diesel is sold in litres. The population remains split, too, between those (mainly the older generation) who still use inches (1 inch = 2.5cm), feet (1ft = 0.3m) and yards and those who are happy with millimetres, centimetres and metres; you'll often be told that 'it's only a hundred yards or so' to somewhere, rather than a hundred metres or so. Distances on road and path signs are also given in miles (1 mile = 1.6km) rather than kilometres, and yards (1yd = 0.9m) rather than metres.

Most food is sold in metric weights (g and kg) but the imperial weights of pounds (lb: 1lb = 453g) and ounces (oz: 1oz = 28g) are often displayed too. The weather – a frequent topic of conversation – is also an issue: while most forecasts predict temperatures in centigrade (C), many people continue to think in terms of Fahrenheit (F; see temperature chart on p15 for conversions).

● **Time** During the winter the whole of Britain is on Greenwich Mean Time (GMT). The clocks move one hour forward on the last Sunday in March, remaining on British Summer Time (BST) until the last Sunday in October.

● **Smoking** Smoking in enclosed public places is banned. The ban relates not only to pubs and restaurants, but also to B&Bs, hostels and hotels. These latter have the right to designate one or more bedrooms where the occupants can smoke, but the ban is in force in all enclosed areas open to the public – even in a private home such as a B&B. Should you be foolhardy enough to light up in a no-smoking area, which includes pretty well any indoor public place, you could be fined £50, but it's the owners of the premises who suffer most if they fail to stop you, with a potential fine of £2500.

● **Telephones** From outside Britain the international country **access code** for Britain is ☎ 44 followed by the area code minus the first 0, and then the number you require.

Mobile (cell) phone reception is better than you think – despite the remoteness, you can get a signal along most of the Cleveland Way, though you may have trouble in the valleys that separate one moor from the next; Kildale, for example, can be a bit of a black spot. It's said the Vodaphone network works best across rural northern England followed by O2 and EE. If you're using a mobile phone that is registered overseas, consider buying a local SIM card to keep costs down.

● **Internet access and wi-fi** See p27.

● **Emergency services** For police, ambulance, fire and mountain rescue dial ☎ 999 (or the EU standard number ☎ 112); you should also dial ☎ 999 and ask for the Coastguard if you get into trouble on the coastal section of the trail.

PLANNING YOUR WALK

from the walk, and provide various maps and advice, but leave you on your own to actually walk the path and cover the cost of lunch and dinner.

- **Absolute Escapes** (☎ 0131-240 1210, 🖳 absoluteescapes.com; Edinburgh) Offer 4 itineraries: the whole trail in 9 and 10 days and two 'highlights' sections in 5 days/6 nights.
- **Brigantes Walking Holidays** (see p28) A wide range of itineraries from 5 days' walking/6 nights for about half the route and up to 11 days' walking/12 nights for the whole Way.
- **Celtic Trails** (☎ 01291-689774, 🖳 celtictrailswalkingholidays.co.uk; Wales) A family-run company (operating for over 20 years) with itineraries of 9 and 10 days' walking the whole trail.
- **Contours Walking Holidays** (☎ 01629-821900, 🖳 contours.co.uk; Derbyshire) Itineraries from 3 to 11 nights, with dog-friendly tours available on selected routes.
- **Discovery Travel** (☎ 01983-301133, 🖳 discoverytravel.co.uk; Isle of Wight) Offer a range of itineraries as required.
- **Freedom Walking Holidays** (☎ 07733-885390, 🖳 freedomwalkingholidays .co.uk; Goring-on-Thames) Has itineraries for the whole trail and in part.
- **Let's Go Walking** (☎ 01837-880075, 🖳 www.letsgowalking.com; Devon) Complete trail in 10 days' walking/11 nights and short breaks of 2 or 3 days.
- **Macs Adventure** (☎ 0141-530 8886, 🖳 macsadventure.com; Glasgow) Have itineraries of between 7 and 12 days.
- **Mickledore** (☎ 017687-72335, 🖳 mickledore.co.uk; Cumbria) Itineraries for the whole trail, moorland highlights, coastal highlights, and combined highlights.
- **Sherpa Expeditions** (☎ 020-8577 2717, 🖳 sherpaexpeditions.com; London) Offer a 12-day itinerary for the whole path.
- **The Walking Holiday Company** (☎ 01600-713008, 🖳 thewalkingholiday company.co.uk; Monmouth) Itinerary options of 5-10 walking days.
- **Wandering Aengus Treks** (☎ 016974-78443, 🖳 watreks.com; Cumbria) Options include 7-10 days for the entire route and one-week sections for the moor and coast.
- **Weather Goat Walks** (☎ 07483 870210, 🖳 kayamy.uwclub.net/wghome .htm; North Yorkshire) Based within sight of the Cleveland Way this small, specialist offers the whole path or sections as required.
- **Where2Walk** (☎ 07824 304060, 🖳 where2walk.co.uk; North Yorkshire) Offer the whole Way.

Group/guided walking tours

If you don't trust your navigational skills or simply prefer the company of other walkers as well as an experienced guide, the following companies will be of interest. Packages nearly always include all meals, accommodation, transport arrangements, minibus back-up and baggage transfer.

Look very carefully at each company's website before booking as each has its own speciality and it's important to choose one that's suitable for you.

- **HF Holidays** (☎ 0345 470 7558, 🖳 hfholidays.co.uk; Cumbria) The entire trail as an 8-day/7-night package from their base, Larpool Hall, near Whitby.

● **Ramblers Worldwide Holidays** (☎ 01707-331133, ⌨ ramblersholidays.co
.uk) Offers a 5-night exploration along the North Yorkshire coastline, between
Whitby and Scarborough, from their base in Ravenscar.

WALKING WITH A DOG   (see also pp183-5)

The Cleveland Way is a dog-friendly path and most cafés and pubs welcome
dogs, and many B&Bs do too. Nevertheless, it's extremely important that dog
owners behave in a responsible manner. Dogs should always be kept on leads
while on the footpath to avoid disturbing wildlife, livestock and other walkers.
Dog excrement should be cleaned up and not left to decorate the boots of other
walkers; take a pooper scooper or poo bag if you're walking with a dog.

   Note, too, that your dog needs to be extremely fit to complete the Cleveland
Way. You may not believe it when you watch it haring around the fields but they
do have a finite amount of energy, so make sure your dog is up to the task of
walking for 10-20 miles a day.

   For more information about long-distance walking with a dog see pp183-5.

Budgeting

England is not a cheap place to go travelling and, while the north may be one
of the less expensive regions, Yorkshire is a popular tourist destination and the
local businesses tend to charge accordingly. Sure, you may decide before you
set out that you're going to keep your budget to a minimum by camping every
night and cooking your own food but it's a rare trekker who sticks to this.
Besides, the B&Bs and pubs on the route are amongst the Cleveland Way's
major attractions and it would be a pity not to sample at least a couple of them
during your trek.

   If the only expenses of this walk were accommodation and food, budgeting
would be a piece of cake. Unfortunately, in addition to these there are all the little **extras** that push up the cost: for example beer, cream teas, buses or taxis,
baggage transfer, laundry, souvenirs – it's surprising how much these add up!

CAMPING

With campsites dotted along the trail, it is feasible to camp every night along
the trail. You can survive on less than £20 per person per day if you use the
cheapest campsites, don't visit a pub, avoid all the museums and tourist attractions in the towns, forage for or cook all your own food from staple ingredients
... and generally have a pretty miserable time of it. Even then, unforeseen
expenses will probably nudge your daily budget up. Include the occasional pint,
and perhaps a pub meal every now and then, and the figure will be nearer, or
over, £20pp per day.

HOSTELS, CAMPING/BUNK BARNS & 'GLAMPING'

The Cleveland Way is well served by the YHA, with five hostels on or very near the route. There are also establishments offering 'camping pods' or 'glamping' as well as a camping/bunk barn. All of which means you can stay at one of these for most of your nights on the trail.

The charge for staying in a hostel is £13-30pp per night – the glamping options are about the same and the camping barn at Kildale is from £10pp. Whack on another £6 for breakfast and £9-12 for an evening meal (though if staying in a YHA hostel you can use their self-catering facilities for both) and there's also lunch (a packed lunch at a YHA hostel costs about £5.50) to consider. This means that, overall, it will cost £30-50pp per day, or £60pp to live in a little more comfort, enjoy the odd beer and go out for the occasional meal.

B&BS, GUESTHOUSES AND HOTELS

You may still be able to find a B&B en route that charges less than £30pp but they're rarities these days. Add on the cost of food for lunch and dinner and you should reckon on about £50pp minimum per day. Staying in a guesthouse or hotel will generally cost more.

If you're walking alone, it's better if you can find a place with a single room; the alternative – single occupancy of a room – usually means paying either the full price of the room, or the room rate less only £10-20.

Itineraries

To help plan your walk look at the **planning maps** (see opposite inside back cover) and the **table of village/town facilities** (on pp34-5), which gives a rundown on the essential information you'll need regarding accommodation possibilities and services at the time of writing.

You could follow one of the **suggested itineraries** (see the boxes on pp36-7) which are based on preferred type of accommodation and walking speeds. Alternatively you could follow how the walk is arranged in the route guide; if this appeals see the box opposite for an explanation of how the coastal section of the Way is arranged as it is.

There's also a list of recommended linear **day and weekend walks** on pp37-8 which cover the best of the Cleveland Way, most of which are well served by public transport. The **bus services** table is on pp52-3 and **public transport map** on p54.

Once you have an idea of how you are going to approach your trek, turn to Part 4 for detailed information on accommodation, places to eat and other services in each village and town on the route. Also in Part 4 you will find summaries of the route to accompany the detailed trail maps.

> ❏ **Planning your itinerary along the coast**
> It should be noted that we chose the 'end point' of each stage along the coast (see pp119-77) largely on the basis that they happen to be a good day's walk from where we had started that day. There will be those, however, who will be gobsmacked that we chose to end one stage at Runswick Bay rather than Staithes, and that the next stage ends at Robin Hood's Bay rather than Whitby. And justifiably so, too, for Staithes is undoubtedly more charismatic than Runswick Bay and, while Robin Hood's Bay is charming, there are certainly more facilities and fun to be had in Whitby. But that is just one of the many joys of this latter half of the Cleveland Way – there are so many options when it comes to choosing somewhere to stay.
>
> All we can say is that we apologise if you disagree with our choice of destination for each stage, and to remind you that in the introduction to Part 4 (see p75) we do advise you that you can plan your itinerary however you wish – and the way we have divided the trail up is just one of many ways in which you can do so.

WHICH DIRECTION?

Most people begin their Cleveland Way odyssey in Helmsley and finish in Filey. Why? Well, following the first day that follows an east-to-west direction, the trail heads in an approximate easterly (usually either north-easterly or south-easterly) direction, thereby allowing trekkers to walk 'with the weather at their back'. That is to say; most of the time in the UK the prevailing winds blow off the Atlantic, so having got through this first day your chances of walking into a gale-force headwind are greatly reduced. For this reason we have written the guide section (Part 4) of this book beginning in Helmsley and ending in Filey, though there is of course nothing to stop you from tackling it in the opposite direction and using our guide 'backwards', ie starting at Filey, at the end of the guide, and working your way back to the start of Part 4 and Helmsley.

SUGGESTED ITINERARIES

The itineraries in the boxes on pp36-7 are based on different accommodation types; camping (not including wild camping which opens your options right out); hostels, camping or bunk barns & 'glamping'; and B&B-style accommodation – with each divided into three alternatives depending on your walking speed (relaxed, medium and fast). They are only suggestions so feel free to adapt them.

Don't forget to **add your travelling time** before and after the walk, in order to calculate the total time you need for your trip.

PLANNING YOUR WALK

VILLAGE AND

Place name (Places in **bold** are directly on the Cleveland Way) (see note below)	Distance from previous place approx miles	approx km	Cash Machine (ATM)/ Bank	Post Office	Tourist Information Centre (TIC)/ Point (TIP)/ Visitor Centre (VC)
Helmsley	0	0	✔	✔	TIP
Riveaulx Abbey	**3** (0.4)	**4.8** (0.7)			
Scawton	**0.8** (0.6)	**1.3** (1)			
Cold Kirby	2.2	3.5			
Kilburn	**2.9** (1.5)	**4.7** (2.4)			
Sutton Bank	1.4	2.3			VC
Boltby	**1.9** (1)	**3** (1.6)			
High Paradise Farm	2.3	3.7			
Osmotherley	7.4	11.9			✔(limited days/hours)
Carlton Bank	7.8	12.6			
Clay Bank Top	3.3	5.3			
Urra	(1)	(1.6)			
Chop Gate	(2.5)	(4)			
Great Broughton	(2.5)	(4)			
Kildale	9.1	14.6			
Newton-under-Roseberry	**4.2** (0.9)	**6.8** (1.4)			
Slapewath	6.1	9.8			
Skelton Green	2.1	3.4			
Skelton	0.4	0.6	✔	✔	
Saltburn-by-the-Sea	2.1	3.4	✔	✔	TIC
Skinningrove	3.6	5.8		✔	
Staithes	4.8	7.7	✔		TIC
Port Mulgrave	1.6	2.6			
Hinderwell	(0.8)	(1.3)			
Runswick Bay/Bank Top	1.8	2.9			
Lythe	**3.4** (1)	**5.5** (1.6)		✔	
Sandsend	1.6	2.6			
Whitby	2.8	4.5	✔	✔	TIC
Robin Hood's Bay	7.4	11.9		✔	VC
Boggle Hole	0.6	1			
Ravenscar	3.5	5.6			VC
Hayburn Wyke	**3.6** (0.3)	**5.8** (0.5)			
Scarborough	6.2	10	✔	✔	TIP
Cayton Bay	5.2	8.4			
Filey	4.3	6.9	✔	✔	TIP

Note: Places not in bold are a short distance from the path. Distances are given to the place on the path nearest to the village/town with the mileage from that point to the village/town in brackets

TOWN FACILITIES

Eating Place ✔ = one place ✔✔ = two ✔✔✔ = three +	Food Store	Campsite/ Camp/bunk barn (CB)/ Camping pod or glamping (P)	Hostels YHA	B&B-style accommodation ✔ = one place ✔✔ = two ✔✔✔ = three +	Place name (places in bold are directly on the Cleveland Way)
✔✔✔	✔	✔	✔	✔✔✔	**Helmsley**
✔					Riveaulx Abbey
		✔			Scawton
					Cold Kirby
✔				✔✔✔	Kilburn
✔				✔	**Sutton Bank**
				✔	Boltby
✔		✔		✔	**High Paradise Farm**
✔✔✔	✔	✔	✔	✔✔✔	**Osmotherley**
✔	✔	✔/P		✔*	**Carlton Bank**
					Clay Bank Top
		CB		✔	Urra
✔		✔		✔✔	Chop Gate
✔✔		✔		✔✔	Great Broughton
✔		✔/CB		✔	**Kildale**
✔				✔	Newton-under-Roseberry
✔		✔		✔	**Slapewath**
✔✔				✔	**Skelton Green**
✔✔✔	✔			✔	**Skelton**
✔✔✔	✔			✔✔✔	**Saltburn-by-the-Sea**
✔✔	✔			✔	**Skinningrove**
✔✔✔	✔			✔✔✔	**Staithes**
✔(limited days)					Port Mulgrave
✔✔✔		✔/P		✔✔	Hinderwell
✔✔		✔		✔✔✔	Runswick Bay/Bank Top
✔	✔	✔/P		✔	**Lythe**
✔✔✔	✔			✔✔✔	**Sandsend**
✔✔✔	✔	✔	✔	✔✔✔	**Whitby**
✔✔✔	✔	✔/P		✔✔✔	**Robin Hood's Bay**
✔			✔		**Boggle Hole**
✔✔✔		✔		✔✔✔	Ravenscar
✔				✔	Hayburn Wyke
✔✔✔	✔	✔	✔	✔✔✔	**Scarborough**
✔		✔			**Cayton Bay**
✔✔✔	✔	✔		✔✔✔	**Filey**

* 40 minutes along the trail east of Carlton Bank, at *Breakhills* (see p102)

CAMPING

Night	Relaxed Place	Approx distance miles	km	Medium Place	Approx distance miles	km	Fast Place	Approx distance miles	km
0	Helmsley			Helmsley			Helmsley		
1	Scawton	3.8	6.1	Sutton Bank*	10.3	16.6	Osmotherley	21.9	35.2
2	Sutton Bank*	6.5	10.5	Osmotherley	11.6	18.6	Kildale	20.2	32.5
3	Osmotherley	11.6	18.6	Kildale	20.2	32.5	Hinderwell	24.9	40.1
4	Carlton Bank	7.8	12.6	Slapewath	10.3	16.6	Ravenscar	21.1	34.0
5	Kildale	12.4	19.9	Hinderwell	14.6	23.5	Filey	19.3	31.0
6	Slapewath	10.3	16.6	R Hood's Bay	17.0	27.4			
7	Hinderwell	14.6	23.5	Scarborough	13.9	22.4			
8	Whitby	9.6	15.5	Filey	9.5	15.3			
9	Ravenscar	11.5	18.5						
10	Scarborough	9.8	15.8						
11	Filey	9.5	15.3						

* No campsites but other accommodation is available

Note
Distances given are to the nearest point on the trail to the campsite only. Please refer to the relevant place in the route guide to see how far you have to walk from there, or the Way, to the campsite.

STAYING IN HOSTELS, CAMPING BARNS & CAMPING PODS

Night	Relaxed Place	Approx distance miles	km	Medium Place	Approx distance miles	km	Fast Place	Approx distance miles	km
0	Helmsley			Helmsley			Helmsley		
1	Sutton Bank*	10.3	16.6	Sutton Bank*	10.3	16.6	Osmotherley	21.9	35.2
2	Osmotherley	11.6	18.6	Osmotherley	11.6	18.6	Kildale	20.2	32.5
3	Carlton Bank	7.8	12.6	Kildale	20.2	32.5	Staithes*	23.3	37.5
4	Kildale	12.4	19.9	Saltburn*	14.9	24.0	Boggle Hole	19.2	31.0
5	Slapewath*	10.3	16.6	R'wick Bay*#	11.8	19.0	Filey*	22.8	36.7
6	Lythe	19.8	31.9	R Hood's Bay	15.2	24.5			
7	Bogle Hole	12.4	20.0	Scarborough	13.9	22.4			
8	Scarborough	13.3	21.4	Filey*	9.5	15.3			
9	Filey*	9.5	15.3						

* No hostels, camping/bunk barns, or camping pods/'glamping' options, but other accommodation is available

R'wick Bay (Runswick Bay) refers to Runswick Bank Top

STAYING IN B&B-STYLE ACCOMMODATION

	Relaxed			Medium			Fast		
Place **Night**	**Approx distance** miles km		**Place**	**Approx distance** miles km		**Place**	**Approx distance** miles km		
0 Helmsley			Helmsley			Helmsley			
1 Sutton Bank	10.3	16.6	Sutton Bank	10.3	16.6	Osmotherley	21.9	35.2	
2 Osmotherley	11.6	18.6	Osmotherley	11.6	18.6	Kildale	20.2	32.5	
3 Clay Bank Top*	11.1	17.9	Clay Bank Top*	11.1	17.9	Staithes	23.3	37.5	
4 Kildale	9.1	14.6	Kildale	9.1	14.6	Ravenscar	22.7	36.6	
5 Slapewath	10.3	16.6	Saltburn	14.9	24.0	Filey	19.3	31.0	
6 Skinningrove	8.2	13.2	Runswick Bay#	11.8	19.0				
7 Runswick Bay#	8.2	13.2	R Hood's Bay	15.2	24.5				
8 Whitby	7.8	12.6	Scarborough	13.9	22.4				
9 Ravenscar	11.5	18.5	Filey	9.5	15.3				
10 Scarborough	9.8	15.8							
11 Filey	9.5	15.3							

* Nearest B&Bs are 1 mile south at Urra, 2½ miles south at Chop Gate and 2½ miles north at Great Broughton.

\# Runswick Bay refers to Runswick Bank Top

THE BEST DAY LOOPS & WEEKEND WALKS

The following trails are for those who don't want to tackle the entire path in one go or just want to get a flavour of the challenge before committing themselves. They are all described in more detail in Part 4.

Day walks bring you back to your starting point, either along other routes not mapped in this book or in some cases it is possible to use public transport. Where possible we've provided you with suggested public transport links (see pp52-3) back to the start of the walk. However, if there are two of you, you can shuttle with two cars as many walkers do.

Day walks
Helmsley to Sutton Bank   **10.3 miles/16.6km (pp82-8)**

Best done on a summer weekend, when you can get the X4 Moorsbus back to Helmsley at the end, this walk, uniquely for the Cleveland Way has neither moor nor coastline. What it does have, however, is an ancient abbey, a white horse – and the finest view in England.

Kildale to Newton-under-Roseberry   **10.2 miles/16.4km (pp110-11)**

This stage has some dramatic scenery, particularly the Captain Cook monument on Easby Moor and iconic Roseberry Topping. Stop for a break at Newton-under-Roseberry – then turn around and walk back the same way to Kildale.

Saltburn-by-the-Sea to Staithes 8.4 miles/13.5km (pp123-8)

A small walk but one that covers perhaps our favourite section of the trail, with sculptures aplenty and some breathtaking coastal strolling. The destination, too, is just wonderful. To get back to Saltburn take Arriva's X4 bus from the top of Staithes – but if the weather's good, why not walk back along the trail again for a total walk of 16.8 miles/27km.

Carlton Bank to Clay Bank Top 6.6 miles/10.6km (pp98-105)

A small amble but one that packs a punch or two, with several steep ascents as you cross Cringle Moor, Cold Moor and up to the Wain Stones. With great panoramas, a Bronze Age burial site, an old jet mine and, if the skies are clear, even a distant glimpse of the sea, this is a great day's meander. At Clay Bank Top you can either take exactly the same route back or, for a change of scenery, grab an OS map of the area and take the lower route home.

Whitby to Scarborough 21.1 miles/34km (pp149-64)

This very long walk between the trail's two biggest towns is packed full of interest, including lovely Robin Hood's Bay, the town-that-never-was, Ravenscar, and some excellent if exhausting clifftop hiking. Arriva's X93 bus will take you back to Whitby at the end of your trek.

WEEKEND WALKS

In addition to the walks described below, any of the contiguous day walks can be combined into a two-day trek.

Newton-under-Roseberry to Sutton Bank 36.9 miles/59.4km (pp88-112)

Starting beneath dramatic Roseberry Topping this lengthy yomp takes you across the toughest section on the entire Cleveland Way. But oh, what wonderful scenery and delightful walking too, and Sutton Bank is a suitably dramatic destination to finish. This is a walk that's best started on a Saturday, allowing you also to catch the summer weekend only M4 (Moorsbus) back from Sutton Bank at around 5pm on Sunday – which is why we've suggested you do this walk in the opposite direction to that described in the book, for the last bus back from Newton-under-Roseberry leaves just after midday.

Saltburn-by-the-Sea to Scarborough 40.6 miles/65.6km (pp123-64)

To put it simply, this is coastal walking at its best and if the weather's on your side this trail will stay with you for many years to come. A combination of Arriva's X93 and X4 buses will take you back to Saltburn (via Whitby) at the end of your trek – though note that you'll have to walk to the centre of Scarborough and its railway station to catch the X93.

What to take

PACKING LIGHT

The biggest mistake made by first-time trekkers is **taking too much**. Things that you are convinced are vital for the success of your trip can prove to be pretty much useless once you're out on the trail: indeed, worse than useless, for these items add to the weight of your pack and yet you're loath to get rid of them because of the amount they cost in the first place.

For this reason, experienced backpackers really do trim the contents of their backpack down to the absolute minimum. An unnecessarily heavy pack can exacerbate injuries and put excess strain on your already hard-pressed feet. Worst of all, it can make for a miserable trek too – which kind of negates the reason you took on this challenge in the first place! So our advice is if you are uncertain whether to take something or not, leave it at home. The Cleveland Way is not an expedition into the unknown and there are shops on the way should you find you've forgotten something that you really need. (It should be noted here, by the way, that we are assuming that you are carrying your own pack and aren't availing yourself of the various baggage-carrying services working on the Cleveland Way. If you do plan to take advantage of them, of course you can pack more into your bag – though our advice about carrying as little as possible on the trail still applies – and anyhow the baggage-transfer companies have weight limits.)

HOW TO CARRY YOUR LUGGAGE

Finally, at the age of 48 and after about 30 years of trekking, I think I've finally found a combination of backpack, clothes and camping/cooking equipment that I am happy with. The backpack is just 30 litres capacity and the tent/sleeping bag and sleeping mat are small enough that I can fit them all in (alongside my clothes, cooking equipment, supplies for the dog etc) and walk all day without any lasting injury or serious discomfort. The reason it's taken me so long to get this right, however, is because a) I'm not very bright; and b) the kind of equipment that is warm, waterproof and rugged enough to withstand the British climate, and yet is also lightweight and compact enough to fit in my small rucksack, is usually rather expensive – so it's taken me this long just to save up enough to afford it!

Unless you're willing to spend a medium-sized fortune on your equipment, however – which would be rather wasteful unless you plan to do lots of this sort of thing in the future – you'll probably need a pack of at least 60-litres' capacity if you're camping. Plan to stay in hostels instead and 40 litres should be ample; while for those eating out and staying in B&Bs a 20- to 30-litre pack should suffice; you could even get away with a daypack. Don't be tempted to buy a bag that's too big for your needs; you'll inevitably only fill it to capacity and thus increase the weight you're carrying on the trail.

Few backpacks these days claim to be waterproof, so use a waterproof **liner** or the elasticated backpack cover (that resembles an over-sized shower cap) that comes with some packs. It's also handy to **compartmentalise** the contents into smaller bags so you know what is where. Take a few (degradable) **plastic bags** for wet things, rubbish etc; they're always useful. Finally, pack intelligently with the most frequently used things readily accessible.

FOOTWEAR

Boots

A good pair of boots is vital. Scrimp on other gear if you must – you'll only use waterproofs some days but you'll be walking every mile on every day. Expect to spend up to £150 on quality, three-season items (though in the sales you should be able to buy a pair for less than three figures) which are light, breathable and waterproof, and have ankle support as well as flexible but thick **soles** to insulate your own pulverised soles. Don't buy by looks or price and avoid buying online until you've been to a shop and tried on an identical pair (and even this can backfire on you). The best tactic is to visit a big outdoor shop on a quiet weekday and spend an hour trying on everything they have in stock that appeals to you.

With modern fabric, the ancient tradition of **breaking in** a new pair of leather boots is largely a thing of the past. That said, arriving in Helmsley with an untried pair of boots is courting disaster. You must try them out beforehand, first round the house or office and then on a full day's walk or two. An old and trusted pair of boots can be resoled and transformed with shock-absorbing after-market **insoles**. Some of these can be thermally moulded to your foot in the shop, but the less expensive examples are also well worth the investment, even if the need for replacement by the end of the walk is likely. If you are using a baggage-carrying company it's conceivable you can pack some old trusted boots in your luggage in case your new footwear turns on you. Blisters are possible even with a much-loved boot if you walk long and hard enough; refer to p73 for blister-avoidance strategies.

Boots might be considered over the top for the Cleveland Way but we disagree. True, there are some long stretches where you'll be walking along wide, clear, flat, stone paths – the section around Bloworth Crossing springs to mind here. But there are also lengthy stretches – eg, the section from Osmotherley to Clay Bank Top – where the path, particularly the stone steps leading up to and down from the moors, can be treacherous when wet and only the grip provided by a decent walking boot will do. True, some will point to trail shoes as they are usually furnished with a similar sole to a trekking boot; but trail shoes won't last as long as boots, be as tough, or, crucially, have the height to keep your socks dry in the bogs and streams; nor do they provide much protection against turning an ankle. It's up to you, of course, and some will say that the nimbleness and greater comfort of a trail shoe will improve their walk, and will be willing to risk the extra danger to their ankles in order to achieve this. We just don't agree, that's all.

Socks

As with all outdoor gear, the humble sock has not escaped the technological revolution (with prices to match) so invest in two non-cotton pairs designed for walking. Although cushioning is desirable, avoid anything too thick which will reduce stability. A correctly sized boot with an anatomically shaped insole gives a sure-footed feel. As well as the obvious olfactory benefits, frequent washing will maintain the socks' springiness.

CLOTHES
Tops

The proven system of **layering** is a good principle to follow. A quick-drying synthetic – or a less odiferous merino wool – **base layer** transports sweat away from your skin; the mid-layer, typically a **fleece** or woollen jumper, keeps you warm; and when needed, an outer 'shell' or **jacket** protects you from the wind and rain.

Maintaining a comfortable temperature in all conditions is the key, and it pays to avoid getting too hot or cold; both can prematurely tire you. Trudging out of Scarborough on a sunny summer's day will soon have you down to your base layer, but sitting on Roseberry Topping when the wind gets up can freeze you to the marrow. Just be aware of how hot or cold you're feeling and adjust your clothing accordingly.

Avoid cotton; as well as being slow to dry, when soaked it saps away body heat but not the moisture – and you'll often be wet from sweat if not rain. Take a change of **base layers** (including underwear), a **fleece** suited to the season, and the best **breathable waterproof** you can afford. **Soft shells** are an alternative to walking in rustling nylon waterproofs when it's windy but not raining.

It's useful to have a **spare set of clothing** so you're able to get changed should you arrive chilled at your destination. Once indoors your body heat will quickly dry out a synthetic fleece and nylon leggings. However, always make sure you have a **dry base layer** in case you or someone you're with goes down with hypothermia; this is why a quality waterproof is important.

Leg wear

Your legs are doing all the work and don't generally get cold so your trousers can be light which will also mean quick-drying. Although they lack useful pockets, many 21st-century walkers find leg-hugging cycling polyester **leggings** very comfortable (eg Ron Hill Tracksters). If like me, however, you remain firmly fixed somewhere in the mid- to late 20th century – or the thought of catching yourself in the mirror in a pair of lurid lycra legwear is simply too ghastly to contemplate – then poly-cotton or microfibre trousers are excellent. Denim jeans are cotton and a disaster when wet.

If the weather's good, **shorts** are very agreeable to walk in, leaving a light pair of trousers clean for the evenings. It also means your lower legs get muddy and not the trousers. For this reason I prefer those trousers where you can detach the lower part of each leg with a zip to convert them into shorts. I like to think I am get two pairs of legwear for the price of one, which appeals to my penny-pinching character immensely – though my more fashion-conscious partner says that's pretty much the only thing that is appealing about them.

Given their extra weight, **waterproof trousers** are really advisable only for those people who really feel the cold or those walking out of season; most trekkers will find them unnecessary and awkward to put on and wear; quick drying, or minimal, legwear is better. **Gaiters** are a great idea; they also stop irritating pebbles dropping into your footwear.

Headwear and other clothing

Your head is both exposed to the sun and loses most of your body heat so, for warmth, carry a woolly **beany** that won't blow away and for UV protection a peaked cap; a bandana or microfibre buff makes a good back-up or sweat band too. Between them they'll conserve body heat and reduce the chances of dehydration. **Gloves** are a good idea in wintry conditions.

TOILETRIES

Besides **toothpaste**/brush, **liquid soap** can also be used for shaving and washing clothes, although a ziplock bag of **detergent** is better if you're laundering regularly. Carry **toilet paper** and a lightweight **trowel** to bury the results (see p71). Less obvious items include: **ear plugs** (very useful on noisy campsites); **sunscreen**; **moisturiser**; **insect repellent** (again, very useful if camping); and possibly a means of **water purification** – though, as we mention on p26, the water you find along the trail may well be contaminated by chemicals, which no purifier will be able to eradicate.

FIRST-AID KIT

Apart from aching limbs your most likely ailments will be blisters so a first-aid kit can be minimal. **Paracetamol** helps numb pain although rest of course is the only real cure. Both '**Compeed**', and '**Second Skin**' treat blisters.

An **elastic knee support** is a good precaution for a weak knee as are **walking poles**. A tube of Nuun tablets can flavour water and restore lost minerals on the march, and a few sachets of Dioralyte or Rehydrat powders will quickly remedy more serious dehydration.

Other items worth considering are: **plasters** for minor cuts; a small selection of different-sized **sterile dressings** for wounds; **porous adhesive tape**; **antiseptic wipes**; **antiseptic cream**; **safety pins**; **tweezers**; and **scissors**.

GENERAL ITEMS

Essential

Carry a **compass**, **whistle** and **mobile phone** as well as at least a one-litre **water bottle** or bag; an LED **headtorch**; **emergency snacks**, a **penknife** and a **watch**.

Useful

If you're not carrying a proper bivvy bag or tent, a compact foil **space blanket** is a good idea in the cooler seasons. Many people take a **camera**, **batteries** and **sunglasses**. A **book** is a good way to pass the evenings, especially in mid summer wild camps. A **vacuum flask**, for hot drinks or soup, is recommended if walking in a cooler season.

SLEEPING BAG & CAMPING GEAR

If you're camping you'll need a sleeping bag and a towel; you'll also need these for most 'glamping' options, or if staying in a camping/bunk barn, but some of these can provide bedding if requested and for an additional charge. All YHA hostels provide bedding and insist you use it.

A **two-season bag** will do for indoor use, but if you can afford it or anticipate outdoor use, go warmer. The choice over a **synthetic** or **down** filling is a debate without end. Year by year less expensive synthetic-filled bags (typically under £100) approach down's enviable qualities of good compressibility while expanding or 'lofting' fully once unpacked to create maximum warmth. But get a down bag wet (always a risk in the UK) and it clogs up and loses all its thermal qualities; and drying down bags takes half a day at the launderette.

If committed to the exposure of wild camping you'll need a **tent** you can rely on; light but able to withstand the rain and wind. In campsites you may just get away with a cheap tent. Otherwise, a good one-man tent suited to the wilds can cost under £120 and weigh just 1.5kg, with a sub-2kg two-man example costing around £250. An inflatable **sleeping mat** is worth many times its weight.

As for **cooking**, the extra weight of the pans, stove, cooking and cleaning utensils and cutlery, plus the extra hassle of buying provisions, means it's only really viable when shared by a group of two or more; otherwise get down the pub and help support the local economy.

MONEY

ATMs (cash machines) are infrequent along the first half of the Cleveland Way; once you leave Helmsley you won't find another until Skelton. Our advice, therefore, is to set off from Helmsley with £100 and a debit/credit card in your pocket, which should cover every eventuality. You could also ask for 'cash-back' when paying for items by debit card. Though they're seldom used by most people these days, a **cheque book** from a British bank could still be useful in those places where cards are not accepted. See also the table of village and town facilities on pp34-5. Crime on the trail is thankfully rare but it's always a good idea to carry your money in a **moneybelt**.

MAPS

The hand-drawn maps in this book cover the trail at a scale of just under 1:20,000: one mile equals $3^1/_8$ inches (1km = 5cm). At this generous scale, combined with the notes and tips written on the maps, and the waypoints, they

PLANNING YOUR WALK

should be enough to stop you losing your way as long as you don't stray too far off the route. That said, a supplementary map of the region – ie one with contours – can prove invaluable should you need to abandon the path and find the quickest route off high ground in bad weather. They also help you to identify local features and landmarks and devise possible side trips.

Thanks to the fact that the Cleveland Way is almost circular, so it actually encompasses quite a small area, only three Explorer maps, published by **Ordnance Survey** (🖳 ordnancesurvey.co.uk), are required to cover the whole trail. Those maps are: OL26 (North York Moors: western area), OL27 (North York Moors: eastern area) and 301 (Scarborough, Bridlington and Flimborough Head); get all three and you'll have the entire walk covered in 1:25,000 detail. While it may be extravagant to buy all these maps, members of Ramblers (see box on p47) can borrow up to 10 maps for free, paying only for return postage. Alternatively, if you are a member of a UK public library you may be able to borrow them from your local library.

❏ **Digital mapping**
There are several software packages on the market today that provide Ordnance Survey maps for a PC or smartphone. The two best known are Memory Map and Anquet. Maps are supplied electronically, on DVD, USB media, or by direct download over the internet. The maps are then loaded into an application, also available by download, from where you can view them, print them and create routes on them.

The real value of digital maps, though, is the ability to draw a route directly onto the map from your computer or smartphone. The map, or the appropriate sections of it, can then be printed with the route marked on it, so you no longer need the full versions of the OS maps. Additionally, the route can be viewed directly on your smartphone or uploaded to a GPS device. Most modern smartphones have a GPS chip so you will be able to see your position overlaid onto the digital map on your phone. Almost every device with built-in GPS functionality now has some mapping software available for it. One of the most popular manufacturers of dedicated handheld GPS devices is Garmin, who have an extensive range. Prices vary from around £100 to £600.

Smartphones and GPS devices should complement, not replace, the traditional method of navigation (a map and compass) as any electronic device can break or, if nothing else, run out of battery. Remember that the battery life of your phone will be significantly reduced, compared to normal usage, when you are using the built-in GPS and running the screen for long periods.

● **Anquet** (🖳 www.anquet.com) has the Cleveland Way from £13.17 using OS 1:25,000 mapping.
● **Ordnance Survey** (🖳 www.ordnancesurvey.co.uk) will let you download and then use their UK maps (1:25,000 scale) on a mobile or tablet without a data connection for a subscription of £3.99 for one month or £19.99 for a year (on their current offer).
● **Harvey** (🖳 www.harveymaps.co.uk) sell their Cleveland Way map (1:40,000 scale) as a download for £20.49 for use on any device.
● **Memory Map** (🖳 www.memory-map.co.uk) currently sell OS 1:25,000 mapping covering the whole of the UK for £45.

Stuart Greig

RECOMMENDED READING

Fiction

Perhaps the most famous book set in a place along the Cleveland Way is Bram Stoker's *Dracula* (Penguin Classics). In the story the Count, who was travelling from Russia to London, became shipwrecked off the coast of Whitby and much of the subsequent action takes place in the town. Stoker, who was staying in the town for a few days to recuperate from a gruelling tour of Scotland, was inspired by the wind-battered landscape and the ruins of the hill-top abbey. The book has become so intrinsically linked with Whitby that the town has Dracula Experience tours and holds a Goth Weekend twice a year (see pp14-15).

Not to be outdone, Scarborough has its own impressive literary connections. The youngest Brontë sister, Anne, set some of the key scenes of both her debut novel, *Agnes Grey* (Wordsworth Classics), and her second and last book, *The Tenant of Wildfell Hall* (Penguin English Library), in the seaside town of Scarborough. The first book follows the fortunes of the eponymous Agnes, who works as a governess for several families of the English gentry. The book is believed to be based on Anne's own experience as governess to Reverend Edmund Robinson and his wife Lydia; though they lived at Thorp Green, near York, they took their annual holidays at Scarborough and were obliged to take Anne with them. Indeed, Anne was buried at Scarborough following her premature death at the age of just 29 – the only one of her siblings not buried at their home at Haworth. (While we're on the subject of famous literary families, it should be noted that the celebrated poets and critics, the Sitwell siblings – Edith, Osbert and Sacheverell – were all raised at the grand house next to Scarborough Art Gallery, known as Wood End.)

As for 21st-century literature, Ross Raisin's debut novel *God's Own Country* (Penguin 2009) tells the story of Sam Marsdyke who, expelled from school, lives a lonely life on his parents' farm on the Yorkshire Moors with only his monosyllabic dad for company. Undoubtedly well written, it's also rather too dark for many people's tastes as Sam slowly slips into madness, paranoia and hallucinations.

Memoirs and other non-fiction

That archetypal Yorkshireman, James Alfred 'Alf' Wight, lived and practised as a vet in North Yorkshire; his series of books based on his experiences, written under the pseudonym James Herriot, went on to sell millions around the world and were subsequently made into both a highly successful TV series and two films. His actual surgery was in Thirsk (and now houses the James Herriot World attraction), just west of the trail, but many of his patients were farmers making a living on the moors and in the valleys that separate them. It was also he, of course, who described the view of Sutton Bank as the 'finest in England'. Sales of his first book in the series, *If Only They Could Talk* (Pan 1970), were initially slow but when the American publisher combined this with his second work, *It Shouldn't Happen to a Vet* (Pan 1972), into one volume and called it *All*

Creatures Great and Small, Wight's fortunes changed. (It should be pointed out that though Wight is seen as the quintessential Yorkshireman, he was in fact born in Sunderland, over the border in County Durham.)

Another memoir of appeal to those interested in the Yorkshire Moors is *Forty Years in a Moorland Parish; Reminiscences and Researches in Danby in Cleveland* (Macmillan & Co, 1892) by the Reverend John Christopher Atkinson. Published in 1891, the book is, to be honest, rather heavy-going and the writing style a little turgid; not, I suggest, a book to take with you on the trail if you're looking for a little light relief after a long-day's trekking. Despite the title, the book is actually largely a study of ancient folklore and superstition in the region, as well as an examination into the archaeology and geology of the area.

If it's a scientific study of the Moors that you're after, and in particular the botany, geology and zoology of the region, seek out *The Moorlands of North-Eastern Yorkshire: their Natural History and Origin* (A Brown & Sons 1912) by Frank Elgee. The author is also responsible, along with his wife Harriet Wragg Elgee, for *The Archaeology of Yorkshire* (Methuen & Co 1933) in which, once again, the moors feature prominently.

❏ SOURCES OF FURTHER INFORMATION

Online trail information
- 🖳 **nationaltrail.co.uk/cleveland-way** The official website of the Cleveland Way, crammed with info and includes a page dedicated to Google Trekker's imaging of the entire trail (🖳 **nationaltrail.co.uk/cleveland-way/google-trekker**)
- 🖳 **northyorkmoors.org.uk** Official website of the North York Moors National Park, refreshingly filled with useful information to help plan your visit.

Tourist information organisations
- **Tourist information centres (TICs)** The Cleveland Way isn't exactly awash with tourist offices. The first you encounter is halfway along the walk at Saltburn-by-the-Sea, in the library, and thereafter there's a volunteer-run one at the top of Staithes and one in Whitby, which is probably the best. Even that tourist Mecca, Scarborough, is bereft of one. Instead, they have **tourism information points** dotted about the town, which, in essence, are an unmanned collection of leaflets about the local area; one or two of these are equipped with a phone from which you can call someone sitting behind a desk in the town hall who has been paid to answer any questions you may have. Why they can't just take this person and his desk and stick them both in an office that's open to the public, so people can speak with him face to face, is beyond me, but that's the situation as it stands and doubtless has something to do with swingeing cuts and austerity. There's another of these tourist information points at Filey.

In addition to these offices there is also the impressive **National Park Centre** at **Sutton Bank** which can advise you on all things related to the North York Moors.

With information not easy to come by on the ground, you should perhaps look online. Most of the towns and villages have some sort of website dedicated to them, and in Part 4 (the Route guide section) we note those we've found.

Finally, for those with an interest in more prehistoric archaeology, the best book on the fossils that can be found on the coast is *Fossils of the Whitby Coast: A Photographic Guide* (Siri Scientific Press 2011) by Dean Lomax, with illustrations by Benjamin Hyde and Nobumichi Tamura.

Flora and fauna field guides

Collins *Bird Guide*, with its beautiful illustrations of British and European birds, continues to be the favourite field guide of both ornithologists and laymen alike.

For a guide to the flora you'll encounter on the Cleveland Way, *The Wild Flower Key* (Warne) by Francis Rose and Clare O'Reilly, is arranged to make it easy to identify unfamiliar flowers. Another in the Collins Gem series, *Wild Flowers*, is more pocket-sized and thus more suitable for walkers.

There are also several field guide **apps** for smartphones and tablets, including those that can aid in identifying birds by their song as well as by their appearance. One to consider is: 💻 merlin.allaboutbirds.org.

Getting to and from the Cleveland Way

NATIONAL TRANSPORT

Rail services
The main operators for services to places on the Cleveland Way are Northern Rail (which boasts an extensive regional network covering over 500 stations and serves Saltburn-by-the-Sea, Whitby, Scarborough & Filey), and Trans-Pennine Express which also serves Scarborough.

❏ **Getting to Britain**
● **By air** Leeds Bradford Airport (🖳 www.leedsbradfordairport.co.uk) is the nearest major international airport for the Cleveland Way but for most foreign visitors one of the London airports (or possibly Manchester) is likely to be their entry point to the country. But Leeds Bradford has direct flights to and from many European destinations as well as the occasional flight to New York so do check it out. From the airport the Flying Tiger bus service can take you to Leeds, from where you can catch a bus or train to York, then Transdev 31X service to Helmsley (see box on pp54-5) and the start of the walk.

    The closest airport to Helmsley is actually Durham Tees Valley Airport (🖳 durhamteesvalleyairport.com) though at time of writing that seems to receive flights mainly from Aberdeen, Amsterdam and Humberside. Humberside (🖳 humbersideairport.com) happens to be the closest airport to Filey, though again it serves nowhere near as many destinations as Leeds Bradford.

● **From Europe by train** Eurostar (🖳 eurostar.com) operates a high-speed passenger service via the Channel Tunnel between Paris, Brussels (and some other cities) and London St Pancras International – convenient for trains to York which leave from neighbouring King's Cross (see box opposite). For more information about rail services from Europe contact your national rail operator, or Railteam (🖳 railteam.eu).

● **From Europe by coach** Eurolines (🖳 eurolines.eu) have a huge network of long-distance coach services connecting over 600 destinations and 36 European countries (and Morocco) to London. Check carefully, however: once such expenses as food for the journey are taken into consideration, it often does not work out that much cheaper than taking a flight, particularly when compared to the fares for some budget airlines.

● **From Europe by ferry (with or without a car)** Numerous ferry companies operate routes between the major North Sea and Channel ports of mainland Europe and the ports on Britain's eastern and southern coasts as well as from Ireland to ports in both Wales and England. For the Cleveland Way, the most convenient crossing is the Hull–Rotterdam service run by P&O Ferries (🖳 poferries.com).

    For further information on all ferry crossings between the UK and Europe, see websites such as 🖳 directferries.com.

● **From Europe by car** Eurotunnel (🖳 www.eurotunnel.com) operates 'le shuttle' train service for vehicles via the Channel Tunnel between Calais and Folkestone taking one hour between the motorway in France and the motorway in Britain.

❏ Rail services & operators
Note: not all stops are listed

Northern Rail Ltd (🖳 northernrailway.co.uk)
● Hull to **Scarborough** via Beverley, Bridlington & **Filey**, approx 9/day
● Middlesbrough to **Whitby** via Great Ayton & **Kildale**, daily 4-5/day (this line is called Esk Valley Railway: 🖳 eskvalleyrailway.co.uk)
● Bishop Auckland to **Saltburn-by-the-Sea** via Darlington & Middlesbrough, daily 2/hr

Trans-Pennine Express (🖳 tpexpress.co.uk)
● Liverpool to **Scarborough** via Manchester Victoria, Leeds & York, daily 1/hr
● Manchester to Hull via Huddersfield & Leeds, daily 1/hr
● Manchester Airport to Middlesbrough via Manchester, Leeds & York, daily 1/hr
● Liverpool to Middlesbrough via Manchester Leeds, York & Darlington, daily 1/hr

London North Eastern Railway (🖳 lner.co.uk)
● London King's Cross to Edinburgh via York, Darlington & Newcastle, Mon-Sat 2/hr plus 1/hr to York, Sun 1-2/hr

Hull Trains (🖳 hulltrains.co.uk)
London King's Cross to Hull, Mon-Fri 7/day, Sat 6/day, Sun 5/day

Cross Country Trains (🖳 crosscountrytrains.co.uk)
● Reading to Newcastle via Birmingham, Derby, Sheffield, Doncaster, York, Darlington & Durham, daily approx 1/hr
● Plymouth to Glasgow via Exeter, Bristol, Birmingham, Leeds, York, Darlington, Durham, Newcastle & Edinburgh, daily approx 1/hr.

PLANNING YOUR WALK

Operators providing connecting services are London North Eastern Railway (which took over Virgin's East Coast service in 2018), Hull Trains and Cross Country Trains; see box above for details.

All **train timetable and fare information** can be found at National Rail Enquiries (☎ 03457-484950, 24hrs, 🖳 nationalrail.co.uk). Alternatively, you can look on the websites of the train companies concerned (see box above). Timetables and tickets are also available on 🖳 thetrainline.com and 🖳 qjump .co.uk.

Tickets can generally be bought from 12 weeks before departure and you are advised to book as far in advance as you can. Bought at Filey at the end of the walk, a ticket to London will cost over £120; if booked ahead it could cost about £32, depending on the day and time you travel. If your journey involves changes, it's worth checking which train company operates each leg of the journey – you may find you can save money by buying separate tickets for each train company rather than one through ticket for your whole journey.

(For details of North York Moors Railway tourist service see p146.)

Coach (long-distance bus) services
Coach travel is generally cheaper than train (though with the excellent advance-purchase rail fares that is not always true), but takes longer. **National Express**

(www.nationalexpress.com), the principal coach operator in Britain, operates direct services to Filey, Cayton Bay and Scarborough (for details see Filey opposite). For services to York for the start of the walk, see below.

Megabus (uk.megabus.com) serves Leeds from where you can get a connecting bus (see box pp54-5) to Whitby, Scarborough, or Filey. However, its services are usually cheaper (London to Scarborough via Leeds is typically about £15, for example).

GETTING TO AND FROM HELMSLEY & FILEY

Both Helmsley and Filey, the two towns that bookend the Cleveland Way, are reasonably well connected by public transport.

Helmsley

● **Train** (see box p49) Helmsley hasn't had a railway station since the mid 1960s but the town is well connected by bus to York, Pickering and Scarborough, all of which have some sort of rail service.

For most people, **York** will be the most convenient option; coming from London, an LNER train to York can cost as little as £13.10 if booked far enough in advance. Cross Country Trains and Transpennine Express also travel to York. Once in York, you'll have to rely on the local bus network to take you to Helmsley.

● **Coach** There is no direct National Express service to Helmsley but the NX563 (1/day) between London and Scarborough calls at York. Other options are: NX436 (London to Sunderland via Heathrow Airport via York, 1/day) and NX537 (Birmingham to Glasgow via York, 1/day). As for trains once in York you will need to change to the local bus network for Helmsley.

● **Bus** (see box pp54-5) From York Transdev's 31X bus runs to Helmsley. Note there is no direct bus service on Sunday, so it would be better to catch a train to

---

❏ **Car parking on the Way**

In Helmsley, you can leave your car in the long-stay car park (see box on p78) by the entrance to Helmsley Castle.

If you want to park elsewhere along the trail the National Park runs a similar scheme, charging £22.50 for seven days. The car parks under their management include those at Sutton Bank, Chop Gate, and Newton-under-Roseberry (at the foot of Roseberry Topping). You can buy these tickets from Sutton Bank National Park Centre and the National Park Office in Helmsley.

In Filey, £8 per day will secure you a permit that will allow you to keep your car in any of the (long-stay) car parks in the borough of Scarborough; this means not only in the public car parks in Filey, but also in Staithes, Runswick Bay, Sandsend, Whitby, Robin Hood's Bay and Scarborough. That said, many of these places also accept payment over the phone by credit/debit card (RingGO) and charge only £6 per day (though it's £9 in Scarborough and Whitby), so if you remember to update your ticket every day this method will save you a couple of quid per day. Filey also has plenty of free on-street parking (except in high summer when it gets very busy); towards the southern end of West Ave is a case in point.

Pickering or Scarborough and catch EYMS's 128 to Helmsley though this service only operates between Easter and the end of October.

● **Car** Helmsley lies on the A170 that connects Scarborough with Thirsk and skims the southern portion of North York Moors National Park. The road is believed to have existed since prehistoric times. West beyond Thirsk the A168 and A61 link with the A1M, an upgraded section of the A1 that runs north through the heart of England from London all the way to Edinburgh. Coming from the north, the A19, which separates off from the A1M above Newcastle, offers a more direct approach to Helmsley. See box opposite for parking details.

Filey

● **Train** (see also box on p49) Filey lies on Northern Rail's coastal line between Hull and Scarborough. Hull Trains provides the easiest way to get from London (King's Cross) to Hull as the services are direct but they are not necessarily the quickest way to reach Filey from London. Transpennine Express also operates services to Hull and Scarborough.

● **Coach** National Express's NX563 (1/day) service between London Victoria and Scarborough via Milton Keynes, Leeds, York & Bridlington calls in here, while the NX327 (1/day) between Bristol and Scarborough via Birmingham, Nottingham, Hull & Cayton Bay also drops by.

● **Car** The A64 connects Filey with York, Leeds and the A1M, though if you're coming from London and the South-East you should find turning off the A1M onto the M18 at Doncaster is a quicker alternative (this motorway being joined to Filey by the M62 and A614). See box opposite for parking details.

LOCAL TRANSPORT SERVICES

Public transport is limited along the Cleveland Way and to get between two places on the first, 'inland' half of the path will usually entail travelling to a third location first, then changing bus or train there in order to get to your final destination. That said, there is at least some sort of public transport to most of the settlements along the way, though these services may be irregular and often limited to just once or twice per day – or per week!

To check the current bus timetables, contact **traveline** (🖳 traveline.info), which has public transport information for the whole of the UK. This is usually easier than contacting the operator directly as many bus services are run by more than one operator.

❑ **Notes for bus services table (see pp54-5)**

● Service details were as accurate as possible at the time of writing but it is essential to check before travel

● Services on Bank Holiday Mondays are usually the same as Sunday services; services that operate Monday to Saturday generally don't operate on Bank Holiday Mondays

● Services generally operate at the same frequency in both directions

● In rural areas where there are no fixed bus stops it is usually possible to 'hail and ride' a passing bus though it is important to stand where visibility is good and also somewhere where it would be safe for the driver to stop.

❏ LOCAL BUS SERVICES

No	Operator	Route and frequency details
128	EYMS	**Scarborough** to **Helmsley** via Pickering, Mon-Sat approx 1/hr, Easter to end Oct Sun 6/day (Nov to Easter Sun Scarborough to Pickering only)
31X	TransDev*	York to **Helmsley** via Easingwold, Coxwold & Ampleforth, Mon-Sat 5/day
M1	Moorsbus	**Saltburn** to Guisborough via Marske & Redcar, late May-late Sep Sun & Bank Hols 1/day Guisborough to Redcar, late May-late Sep Sun 1/day
M2	Moorsbus	Darlington to Guisborough via Stockton & Middlesbrough, late May-late Sep Sun & Bank Hols 1/day
M3	Moorsbus	Guisborough to **Helmsley** via Danby, Blakey, Hutton le Hole & Kirkbymoorside, late May-late Sep Sat 1/day
M3	Moorsbus	Guisborough to Thornton Dale via Castleton, Danby, Blakey, Hutton le Hole, Kirkbymoorside & Pickering, late May-late Sep Sun & Bank Hols 2/day
M4	Moorsbus	Guisborough to **Helmsley** via Newton-under-Roseberry, Great Ayton, **Stokesley**, Great Broughton, **Chop Gate** & Riveaulx Abbey, late May-late Sep Sat 1/day
M4	Moorsbus	Guisborough to **Sutton Bank** via **Newton-under-Roseberry**, Great Ayton, Stokesley, Great Broughton, Chop Gate, Riveaulx Abbey & **Helmsley**, late May-late Sep Sun 2/day plus Rievaulx to Sutton Bank 2/day & Helmsley to Sutton Bank 1/day
M5	Moorsbus	Easingwold to **Helmsley** via Thirsk, Northallerton, Stokesley, Ingleby, back to Northallerton, Thirsk, Coxwold, Byland Abbey & Ampleforth, late May-Sep Sun & Bank Hols 1/day plus Thirsk to Helmsley, late May-late Sep Sun & Bank Hols 1-2/day
59	NYCC	Thirsk circular route via Bagby, Balk, Kilburn, Coxwold, Oulston & Husthwaite, Mon & Fri only 2/day
80	Abbott's	Stokesley to Northallerton via Ingleby Cross & **Osmotherley**, Mon-Sat 3/day
X80	Abbott's	Middlesbrough to Northallerton via Great Ayton & Stokesley, Mon-Sat 3/day
89	Abbott's	Stokesley to Northallerton via Great Broughton, Ingleby Cross & **Osmotherley**, Mon-Sat 3/day
X89	Abbott's	Stokesley to Northallerton via Great Broughton, **Osmotherley** & Ingleby Cross, Mon-Sat 1/day
81	Arriva	Marske to Stokesley via Redcar, Guisborough, **Newton-under-Roseberry** & Great Ayton, Mon-Sat approx 1/hr
81A	Arriva	Redcar to Guisborough, Sun 1/hr
5	Arriva	Middlesbrough to Easington via Guisborough, **Skelton**, **Skinningrove** (Mon-Sat 1/hr, Sun 5/day) & Loftus, daily 1-2/hr
5A	Arriva	Middlesbrough to Hollybush via Ormesby, Guisborough & **Skelton**, Mon-Sat 2/hr
28	Arriva	Middlesbrough to Lingdale via Guisborough, Mon-Sat 1/hr

28A	Arriva	Middlesbrough to Stokesley via Great Ayton, Mon-Sat 1/hr
X93	Arriva	Middlesbrough to **Scarborough** via Guisborough, **Slapewath (Charltons)**, **Whitby** & **Robin Hood's Bay**, summer Mon-Sat approx 1/hr, Sun 10/day but mostly in the morning (plus Whitby to Scarborough daily 2/hr), winter hours more limited
707	R & C	Redcar circular route to Guisborough, **Slapewath (Charltons)**, Lingdale, **Skelton** & **Skelton Green**, Mon-Sat 2/day plus 1/day from Guisborough but evening only
708	R & C	Liverton Mine to **Saltburn** circular route via Loftus, **Skinningrove** & **Skelton**, Mon-Sat 3/day but evening only
752	R & C	**Skelton** to Twizzlegill View circular route via **Skinningrove**, Loftus & Easington, Mon-Fri 3-4/day
3	Arriva	Lingdale to Redcar via **Skelton Green**, **Skelton**, **Saltburn** & Marske, Sun 1/hr
X3	Arriva	Lingdale to Middlesbrough via **Skelton Green**, **Skelton**, **Saltburn** & Redcar, Mon-Sat 1/hr,
X3A	Arriva	North Skelton to Middlesbrough via **Saltburn**, Marske & Redcar, Mon-Sat 1/hr
X4	Arriva	Middlesbrough to **Whitby** via Redcar, Marske, **Saltburn**, Brotton, Loftus, Easington, Boulby, **Staithes**, **Hinderwell**, **Runswick Bay**, **Lythe** & **Sandsend**, Mon-Sat 2/hr, Sun 1/hr plus 1/hr Redcar to Whitby
840	YC	Leeds to **Whitby** via York, Pickering & Thornton-le-Dale, Mon-Sat 4/day plus 3/day to Thornton-le-Dale, Sun 4/day
115	EYMS#	**Ravenscar** to **Scarborough**, Mon-Sat 2/day
X21	EYMS#	Hull to **Scarborough** via Beverley, Bridlington & **Filey**, late May to mid Sep, daily 1/day
12/13	EYMS#	Bridlington to **Scarborough** via **Filey** & **Cayton Bay**, early May to early Nov, daily 2/hr
555	SS	(Filey Flyer) **Scarborough** to **Filey** via **Cayton Bay**, Mon-Sat 7-8/day
843	Transdev	Leeds to **Scarborough** via York & Malton, Mon-Sat 10/day, Sun 8/day
X43	Transdev	Leeds to Bridlington via York, **Scarborough** & **Filey**, early July to mid Sep 1/day
X40	Transdev	Leeds to **Whitby** via York & Pickering, early July to mid Sep 1/day

Contacts Abbott's (Abbott's of Leeming; ☎ 01677-424987, 🖳 abbottscoaches.co.uk); **Arriva** (🖳 arrivabus.co.uk/north-east); **EYMS** (East Yorkshire Motor Services; ☎ 01482-592929, 🖳 eyms.co.uk); **Moorsbus** (🖳 moorsbus.org); **NYCC** (North Yorkshire County Council; 🖳 northyorks.gov.uk/bus-timetables); **R&C** (Redcar & Cleveland; 🖳 redcar-cleveland.gov.uk; click on 'P' for public transport); **SS** (Shoreline Suncruisers; ☎ 01723-360969, 🖳 shorelinesuncruisers.co.uk); **Transdev** (🖳 yorkbus.co.uk); **YC** (Yorkshire Coastliner; 🖳 yorkbus.co.uk)

Notes:

* Stephensons of Easingwold is part of TransDev York Bus

EYMS is the parent company of Scarborough & District (S&D); some buses may say Scarborough & District and some East Yorkshire.

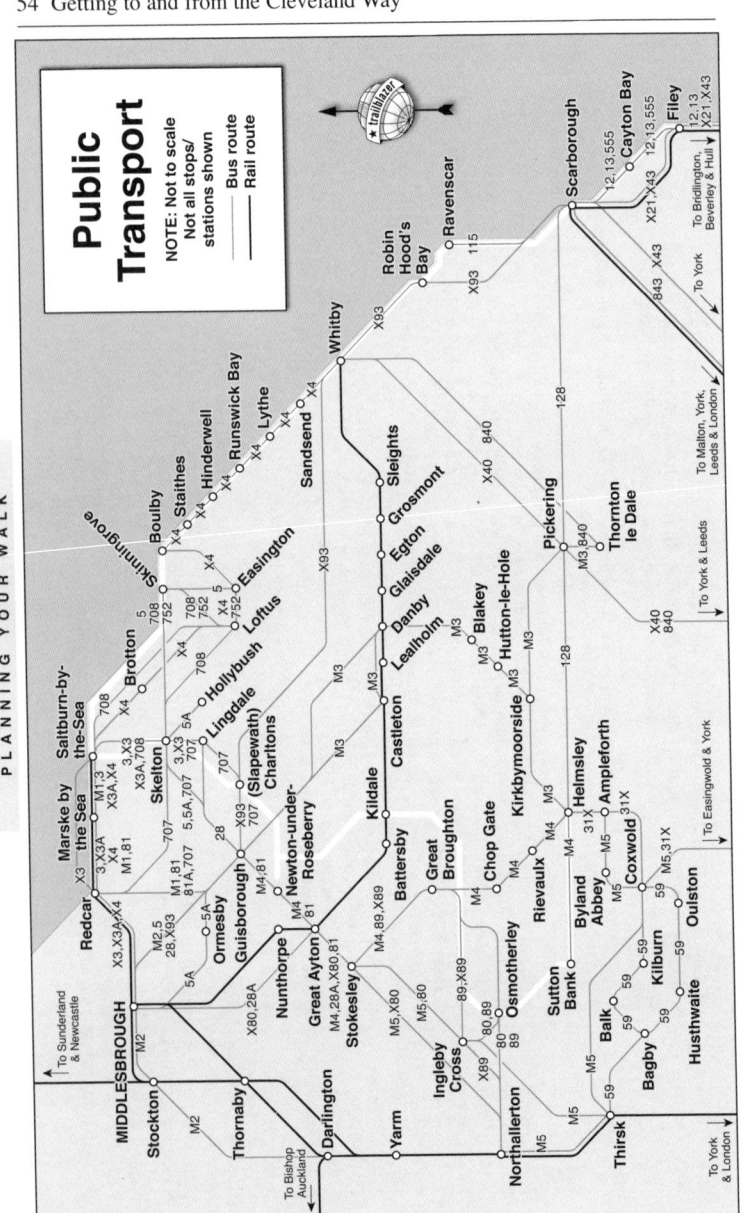

THE ENVIRONMENT & NATURE

2

Conserving the Cleveland Way

With a population of over 62 million, Britain is an overcrowded island, and England is the most densely populated part of it. As such, the English countryside has suffered – and continues to suffer – a great deal of pressure from both over-population and the activities of an ever more industrialised world. Thankfully, there is some enlightened legislation to protect the surviving pockets of forest and heathland.

In these enlightened times when environmental issues are quite rightly given more precedence, many endangered species, such as the otter, have increased in number thanks to the active work of voluntary conservation bodies. There are other reasons to be optimistic. The environment is no longer the least important issue in party politics and this reflects the opinions of everyday people who are concerned about issues such as conservation on both a global and local scale.

GOVERNMENT AGENCIES AND SCHEMES

Natural England
Natural England (🖥 gov.uk/government/organisations/natural-england) is responsible for enhancing biodiversity, landscape and wildlife in rural, urban, coastal and marine areas; promoting access, recreation and public well-being; and contributing to the way natural resources are managed. One of its roles is to identify, establish and manage: national trails, national parks, areas of outstanding natural beauty (AONBs), national nature reserves (NNRs), sites of special scientific interest (SSSIs), and special areas of conservation (SACs) and to enforce regulations relating to these sites.

The highest level of landscape protection is the designation of land as a **national park** which recognises the national importance of an area in terms of landscape, biodiversity and as a recreational resource. At the time of writing there were nine national parks in England (plus the Norfolk and Suffolk Broads which enjoy equivalent status and protection). Of interest to the Cleveland Way walker is, of course, the North York Moors National Park (🖥 northyork moors .org.uk), around which the path skirts. This designation does not signify national ownership and these are not uninhabited wildernesses, making conservation a knife-edged balance between protecting the environment and the rights and livelihoods of those living in the parks.

The second level of protection is **area of outstanding natural beauty** (AONB), though there aren't any on the Cleveland Way.

National nature reserves (NNRs) are places where the priority is protection of the wildlife habitats and geological formations. There are currently 224 NNRs in England. Again, none happens to lie on the Cleveland Way though Duncombe Park, near Helmsley, lies just to the south of the trail and was designated an NNR in the 1990s to protect its collection of ancient trees.

Local nature reserves (LNRs) are places with wildlife or geological features that are of special interest to local inhabitants. There are 17 in North Yorkshire and several on the Cleveland Way include Garbutt Wood near Sutton Bank; Hunt Cliff at Saltburn-by-the-Sea, a nationally important nesting site for kittiwakes; and two sites after Saltburn, the scrubland and grasslands of Cattersty Gill, before Skinningrove, and the beach and cliffs at Hummersea. The Yorkshire Wildlife Trust website (🖳 ywt.org.uk) has more details on these sites.

Sites of Special Scientific Interest (SSSIs) range in size from little pockets protecting wild flower meadows, important nesting sites or special geological features, to vast swathes of upland, moorland and wetland. SSSIs, of which there are over 4100 in England, are a particularly important designation as they

---

❏ **Campaigning/conservation organisations and charities**

These voluntary organisations started the conservation movement in the mid 19th century and are still at the forefront of developments. Independent of government but reliant on public support, they can concentrate their resources either on acquiring land which can then be managed purely for conservation purposes, or on influencing political decision-makers by lobbying and campaigning.

● **National Trust** (🖳 nationaltrust.org.uk) A charity with over two million members which aims to protect, through ownership, threatened coastline, countryside, historic houses, castles, gardens and archaeological remains for everybody to enjoy. Roseberry Topping (see p110) is managed by the National Trust, as are the ruins of the Peak Alum Works around Ravenscar (see p157) and Riveaulx Terrace (see p84).

● **Royal Society for the Protection of Birds** (RSPB; 🖳 rspb.org.uk) The largest voluntary conservation body in Europe with 150 reserves and over a million members.

● **The Wildlife Trusts** (🖳 wildlifetrusts.org) is the umbrella organisation for the 47 wildlife trusts in the UK. The relevant trust for the Cleveland Way is **The Yorkshire Wildlife Trust** (🖳 ywt.org.uk).

● **English Heritage** (🖳 english-heritage.org.uk) Charity which cares for over 400 historic buildings, monuments and sites with a central aim of ensuring that the historic environment of England is properly maintained. Helmsley and Scarborough castles and Whitby and Rievaulx abbeys are all part of their portfolio.

● **Butterfly Conservation** (🖳 butterfly-conservation.org) was formed in 1968 by some naturalists who were alarmed at the decline in the number of butterflies, and moths, and who aimed to reverse the situation. They now have 31 branches throughout the British Isles and operate 33 nature reserves and also sites where butterflies are likely to be found. For further information contact the **Yorkshire branch** (🖳 york shirebutterflies.org.uk).

have some legal standing. They are managed in partnership with the owners and occupiers of the land who must give written notice before initiating any operations likely to damage the site and who cannot proceed without consent from Natural England. Many SSSIs are also either a NNR or a LNR. The **North York Moors** is one big SSSI – one of the largest SSSIs in the country.

Special Area of Conservation (SAC) is an international designation which came into being as a result of the 1992 Earth Summit in Rio de Janeiro, Brazil. This European-wide network of sites is designed to promote the conservation of habitats, wild animals and plants, both on land and at sea. Every land SAC is also an SSSI. SACs on the Cleveland Way include Beast Cliff (Map 40) near Robin Hood's Bay.

Geology

There's a reason the North York Moors look the way they do and that reason lies right beneath your feet. This has not happened overnight, but is the work of 200 million years of changing land and climate. And while the southern coast of England from Exmouth, in Devon, to Studland Bay, in Dorset, may be better known for its Jurassic Coast – and is a UNESCO World Heritage Site to boot – the North York Moors does also have a decent claim to be England's very own Jurassic Park because the sheer number of dinosaur footprints and fossils found in and around the park is outstanding.

That there is so much evidence of dinosaurs in north-east Yorkshire is because most of the rocks were laid down during the Jurassic era, about 200 million years ago. The dark-coloured shale and limestone rocks at the bottom are the oldest, a period known as the **Lower Jurassic**. It was at this time that trees similar to today's monkey puzzle trees thrived, then died and decomposed in sea water. The result is **jet**, which is nothing more than fossilised wood that has decomposed under very high pressure in salt water.

These rocks of the Lower Jurassic period were in turn overlaid with the sandstone of the **Middle Jurassic** period (170 million years ago), a time when the seas receded and the land was characterised by river channels and swamps. It is this epoch that is more responsible than any other for how the North York Moors looks today, because the sandstone rocks of the Middle Jurassic form the main central 'slab' of the National Park. It is also this sandstone that provides much of the building material that gives the villages their distinctive look. Because sandstone is such a poor soil in which to grow plants it means that only a few of the hardier and more adaptable species can thrive – which is why the moors are today covered in heather and gorse. And it is in this sandstone that we find the **dinosaur footprints** and **fossilised skeletons** for which the region is famous.

Travel forward some 20 million years and we arrive at the **Upper Jurassic**, an epoch that saw the return of the ocean as sea levels rose. Within that seawater were marine organisms – coral, molluscs etc – whose skeletal fragments form the basis of limestone. Today this limestone is the major component of the Tabular Hills which fringe the park's southern edge. Incredible to think, isn't it, that when you stand atop **Sutton Bank**, you are actually standing atop a pile of billions of tiny skeletons. The hard limey gritstone that forms the uppermost strata of Sutton Bank was also formed at this time.

The above explains what the rocks of the region are and how they came to be here, but it doesn't go far in explaining the shape of the land and, in particular, its sometimes deep valleys and sheer-sided slopes. For this we must look back a mere 20,000 years, when huge ice sheets, many hundreds of metres thick, advanced and retreated across the land; where meltwater broke through the low points in the land it formed the **sheer-sided valleys** that are such a feature of parts of the moor today.

Meanwhile, on the park's north-western border, a combination of rain and river have slowly eroded the rocks from the Middle Jurassic epoch away. Underneath, of course, are the Lower Jurassic rocks that are much softer and so have also eroded away – which is why we get the steep escarpment on this north-western edge of the park. Curiously, there is one 'patch' on this north-western edge where the Middle Jurassic rocks have not been eroded; thus the rocks of the Lower Jurassic underneath have also been protected. This, of course, is **Roseberry Topping**, separated off from the rest of the escarpment by erosion but defiantly refusing to erode away itself.

For those with a particular interest in the geology of the region we urge you to pay a visit to Rotunda Museum in Scarborough (see p166), designed by William Smith, the so-called 'Father of English Geology', in the 19th century specifically to display the geological history of the Yorkshire coast. Whitby Museum (see p146) also has some impressive dinosaur skeletons found along this stretch of shoreline.

❏ **Just what and where is Cleveland?**
During your 107.4-mile ramble along some of the most picturesque parts of North Yorkshire, it may at some point occur to you to wonder just exactly what and where is this 'Cleveland' place after which the trail is named. After all, there's no county in modern Britain bearing this name, nor any town or settlement of any size on these shores. Indeed, for most people the most famous 'Cleveland' is the one in Ohio – which may well have been named after the UK version, but has little to do with it today.

Well, the name Cleveland actually comes from 'Cliff Land' and the earliest record of that name is in 1066, when Harald Hardrada, the last Viking king of Norway, landed on the coast of Yorkshire at a place called 'Cliffland' on his way to Stamford Bridge where he was defeated by Harold Godwinson (who then ran south to meet his own doom at the Battle of Hastings, at the hands of William the Conqueror). The name 'Cliff Land' is an apt one, of course, for during your semi-circumambulation of the North York Moor National Park you'll be walking on the edge of cliffs for most of the way, both along the coast and inland around Sutton Bank.

Flora and fauna

The landscape of the Cleveland Way can, rather clumsily, be divided into three categories: **coastal**, which covers almost exactly the entire last half of the trail; **heath and moorland**, which makes up about a third of the North York Moors National Park in total; and **woodland**, a category in which, for the purposes of expediency, we have also lumped meadows, farmland and anything else not in the above two groupings (we did warn you that the division was a clumsy one). Such a diverse terrain has resulted in a breadth of flora that is equally heterogenous – and, as a result, the creatures that live among (and often feed on) these plants are equally very varied.

FAUNA

As I write this, I am struggling to think of a long-distance path that has provided more encounters with some rarely seen fauna than the Cleveland Way. On my last walk I saw a stoat (living in a drystone wall on the coast near Kettleness) and deer (which I saw in several places, including just below Ravenscar's Visitor Centre), enjoyed the closest meeting with a seal that I've ever had, at Sandsend – plus, best of all, an encounter with an Eurasian eagle-owl on the Wain Stones that was just jaw-dropping – if a little too close for comfort.

Of course, I was lucky, and maybe the fact I was trekking by myself (and so was quieter than other trekkers), like to get up and set off early (when many animals are at their most active) and was walking early in the year (April) when there were few other trekkers on the path, all helped to contribute to my good fortune. But keep your eyes peeled and your ear to the ground and you never know…

Mammals and reptiles
Woodland, farmland, meadows and hedgerows The woodland patches of the North York Moors are where the greatest concentration of wildlife can be found. The mosses and acorns feed many rodents and other animals. Under the woodland canopy, however, you'll be very fortunate to see anything other than the ubiquitous grey squirrel (*Sciurus carolinensis*).

If you happen to be walking in late evening, however, you may just encounter the **badger** (*Meles meles*). Relatively common throughout the British Isles, these nocturnal mammals, with their distinctive black-and-white-striped muzzle, are sociable animals that live in large underground burrows called setts and appear after sunset to root for worms and slugs.

Another creature most often seen either early in the morning or in the crepuscular hours is the **roe deer** (*Capreolus capreolus*), a small native species that likes to inhabit woodland, though some can also be seen grazing in fields.

THE ENVIRONMENT & NATURE

One creature that you will see everywhere along the walk, nibbling on grass near hedgerows, is the **rabbit** (*Oryctolagus cuniculus*). Timid by nature, most of the time you'll have to make do with nothing more than a brief and distant glimpse of their white tails as they stampede for the nearest warren at the first sound of your footfall. Because they are so numerous, however, the laws of probability dictate that you will at some stage get close enough to observe them without being spotted; trying to take a decent photo of one, however, is a different matter. If you're lucky you may also come across **hares** (*Lepus europaeus*), often mistaken for rabbits but much larger, more elongated and with longer back legs and ears.

Both rabbits and hares form one of the main elements in the diet of the rural **fox** (*Vulpes vulpes*), one of the more adaptable of Britain's native species. Famous as the scourge of chicken coops, their reputation as indiscriminate killers is actually unjustified: though they will if left undisturbed kill all the chickens in a coop in what appears to be a mindless and frenzied attack, foxes will actually eat all their victims, carrying off and storing the carcasses in underground burrows for them and their families to eat at a later date. These days, however, you are far more likely to see foxes in towns, where they survive mostly on the scraps and leftovers of the human population, rather than in the country. While generally considered nocturnal, it's not unusual to encounter a fox during the day too, often lounging in the sun near its den.

In addition to the above, keep a look out for other fairly common but little-seen species such as the carnivorous **stoat** (*Mustela erminea*), its smaller cousin the **weasel** (*Mustela nivalis*), the **hedgehog** (*Erinaceus europaeus*) – these days, alas, most commonly seen as roadkill – and a number of species of **voles**, **mice** and **shrews**.

One of Britain's rarest creatures, the **otter** (*Lutra lutra*), is enjoying something of a renaissance thanks to concerted conservation efforts. Though more common in the south-west, otters are still present in the north of England. At home both in salt- and fresh-water, they are a good indicator of a healthy unpolluted environment; there are believed to be some resident on the River Esk, which empties into the North Sea at Whitby, and the River Derwent. Don't go to the north expecting otter sightings every day though. If you see one at all you should consider yourself *extremely* fortunate, for they remain rare and very elusive.

When it comes to rarity, however, even the otter must take a back seat when compared to the **alcathoe bat** (*Myotis alcathoe*), one of ten bat species that call the North York Moors National Park their home. Discovered in woodland in the National Park, it is thought that the alcathoe has probably been here for generations but, because of its similarity to other bats, was only identified as a separate species in 2010. The North York Moors is one of only two places in the UK where this tiny bat has so far been positively identified!

Amazingly, even the alcathoe bat is not the most difficult animal to see on the moors. That award must go to the **pine marten** (*Martes martes*). This solitary, shy, nocturnal creature was finally filmed in August 2017 on Forestry Commission land by a team that had been working for over four years to record one in the national park. Before this success, the last hard evidence of a pine marten in Yorkshire was back in 1993 when a skull was discovered outside the park. You can see the footage of the North York Moors pine marten at this address: ▢ naturespy.org/2017/08/naturespy-find-the-yorkshire-pine-marten.

Moorland Animals that call the moors their home tend to be rather diminutive in size, all the better for hiding in the low cover provided by the heathers. Mice, voles, lizards and other animals thrive, feeding on insects. These small animals are, in turn, prey for Britain's only venomous snake, the **adder** (*Vipera berus*), that stalks the heathers on the high ground. Recognisable by its zig-zag body pattern, they pose very little risk to walkers but dogs can get bitten when snakes come out of hibernation to warm themselves, often on a sunny path. They only bite when provoked, preferring to hide instead, and the venom is designed to kill small mammals such as mice, voles and shrews, so deaths in humans are very rare (ten have been attributed to adder bites in the last hundred years) but a bite can be extremely unpleasant and occasionally dangerous for children or the elderly.

The **common lizard** (*Lacerta vivipara*) may sometimes be seen basking in the sun on the moors and is harmless.

Coast There is so much wildlife to see off Yorkshire's east coast that there are even companies dedicated to providing whale-watching trips and safaris (see box p144). **Minke** (*Balaenoptera acutorostrata*), **pilot** (*Globicephala macrorhynchus*), **fin** (*Balaenoptera physalus*) and **sei** (*Balaenoptera borealis*) **whales** all swim just offshore in the North Sea and, while sightings from land are difficult, keep your eyes looking eastwards when you're walking along the cliffs during the summer months and you never know. **White-beaked dolphins** (*Lagenorhynchus albiros*) also make occasional guest appearances, following the shoals of mackerel and herring down from the Arctic.

The most commonly seen mammal in these parts, however, is the seal. There are two species along this stretch of the Yorkshire coast, the **common seal** (*Phoca vitulina*) and the **grey seal** (*Halichoerus grypus*, which roughly translates as hooked-nosed sea pig), and colonies of both can be seen beneath the cliffs at Ravenscar.

If sightings of any of the above elude you, you may have to content yourself with the inhabitants of the rockpools that dot the shoreline – though there's still plenty of variety here too, including the **blenny** (*Lipophrys pholis*), a small scaleless fish which is perhaps most famous for its ability to live out of water for many hours, and various shellfish such as **periwinkle** (*Littorina littorea*), **limpet**, **dog whelk** (*Nucella lapillus*), **mussel** and the occasional **edible crab** (*Cancer pagurus*) that can grow up to 25cm; needless to say, their claws can give you a nasty nip if provoked. Staying with shellfish, though moving inland, we should also point out that the River Esk, which empties into the sea at Whitby, is the only river in Yorkshire with a population of freshwater **pearl mussels** (*Margaritifera margaritifera*). These bivalve molluscs, which are thought to number no more than a thousand, can live for over a century and are a great indicator of the health of a river's ecosystem.

Butterflies, moths and other insects

● **Butterflies** Most of the more common UK butterfly species can be found in the national park, but it also plays host to a couple of rare ones too. The orange-and-black **pearl-bordered fritillary** (*Boloria euphrosyne*) loves the scrubland of the national park. It gets its name from the two large silver 'pearls' and row of seven outer 'pearls' on the underside hind wing. Once again, as with the park's other rarities, the exact location of their habitat is kept secret to help in their protection. The second rare species is the **Duke of Burgundy** (*Hamearis lucina*), of which a colony was discovered near Helmsley; the park can now boast that it holds almost 10% of the country's entire population.

Up above the rockpools on the clifftops the most eye-catching wildlife may well be the various butterfly species. The **painted lady** (*Vanessa cardui*) can, on first flutter, be mistaken for a **small tortoiseshell** (*Aglais urticae*) but look up close and you'll spot several differences to the markings including, most noticeably, the absence of a blue border at the bottom edge of its wings which is present on the tortoiseshell; the painted lady's story is significantly more interesting too as it will have migrated thousands of miles from North Africa to feed on the wildflowers of the Yorkshire clifftops in late summer. Another eye-catching butterfly is the **green hairstreak** (*Callophrys rubi*), though to fully appreciate its metallic green wings you need to see it at rest with its wings folded up; in flight it actually looks a fairly dull brown colour. Its relative, the **white-letter hairstreak** (*Satyrium w-album*), lives mainly in the treetops and thus is rarely seen and even harder to positively identify. Its main distinguishing characteristic is the white lines on its underwings that, when put together, spell out the letter 'w'.

● **Moths** Just as wondrous to behold as the butterflies are the local moths. There are two species in particular that catch the eye. The **emperor moth** (*Saturnia pavonia*) is a spectacular moor-dwelling moth that feeds on the heather. Both the brown hindwings and grey forewings have striking 'eye' markings on them, fooling the predators by making them think they are up against a much larger creature. The **eyed hawk-moth** (*Smerinthus ocellata*) is a fairly drab-looking moth most of the time but, if threatened, flashes its hindwings which, just like those of the emperor moth, are decorated with large eye markings.

● **Dragonflies** Another insect that causes trekkers to shout out 'What's that?' is the dragonfly, of which there are several species living in the park. The **golden-ringed dragonfly** (*Cordulegaster boltonii*) is a striking black insect with vivid yellow vertical bands all along its body. The female is the UK's longest dragonfly because of her long ovipositor (the tube through which she deposits her eggs). The **migrant hawker dragonfly** (*Aeshna mixta*) is similar but has pairs of blue spots down its length.

Avifauna

The seaside cliffs, woods, moorland and hedgerows encountered on the path provide homes for a wealth of different species.

Woodland, farmland, meadows and hedgerows In addition to those birds that are familiar to everyone – blackbirds, robins, song thrushes, **tits** (family *Paridae*, including blue, coal and great), sparrows etc – are several species that may be unfamiliar to those who haven't spent much time in the woods. On the trunks of trees look out for **treecreepers** (*Certhia familiaris*) hopping up the bark; if the bird can also head down the trunk head-first and has much brighter plumage it must be their relative the **nuthatch** (*Sitta europaea*). Both of these are members of the same family as the woodpecker, of which the **greater spotted** (*Dendrocopos major*) and **lesser spotted woodpecker** (*Dendrocopos minor*) and **green woodpecker** (*Picus viridis*) all thrive in the forest of the national park. While in the conifers watch out for **crossbills** (*Loxia curvirostra*) and **siskins** (*Carduelis spinus*).

Moorland Many bird species rely on the moors to nest, breed and feed. One of the most common birds seen on the path, particularly in the latter half of the walk, is the **pheasant** (*Phasianus colchicus*). Ubiquitous on the moors, the male is distinctive thanks to his beautiful long, barred tail feathers, brown body and glossy green-black head with red head-sides, while the female is a dull brown. An alternative way to distinguish them is by the distinctive strangulated hacking sound they make, together with the loud flapping of wings as they fly off. Another reasonably common sight on the moors of Yorkshire is the **lapwing** (*Vanellus vanellus*), also known as the peewit. Black and white with iridescent green upper parts and approximately the size of a pigeon or tern, the lapwing's most distinctive characteristic is the male's tumbling, diving, swooping flight pattern when disturbed, believed to be either a display to attract a female or an attempt to distract predators from its nest, which they build on the ground.

Less common but still seen by most walkers is the **curlew** (*Numenius arquata*), another bird that, like the lapwing, is associated with coastal and open fields, moors and bogs. With feathers uniformly streaked grey and brown, the easiest way to identify this bird is by its thin elongated, downward curling beak. Both the lapwing and the curlew are actually wading birds that nest on the moors in the spring, but which winter by the coast.

Other birds that make their nest on open moorland and in fields include the **redshank** (*Tringa totanus*), the rare **golden plover** (*Pluvialis apricaria*), **snipe** (*Gallinago gallinago*), **dunlin** (*Calidris alpina*) and **ring ouzel** (*Turdus torquatus*). There are **skylarks** (*Alauda arvensis*) aplenty, too, which you'll doubtless see performing a vertical lift-off from the moors as if powered, seemingly, by nothing but song. Somewhat ironically, these birds have benefited from the careful management of the moors which is mainly done to protect the populations of game birds: **red grouse** (*Lagopus lagopus*) and **black grouse** (*Tetrao tetrix*).

Birds of prey that may nest in the woodland but which you are probably more likely to see hunting in the skies above the moors include **kestrel** (*Falco tinnunculus*), **buzzard** (*Buteo buteo*), **barn owl** (*Tyto alba*), **short-eared owl** (*Asio flammeus*) and even **Eurasian eagle-owl** (*Bubo bubo*, from mainland Europe and Central Asia but since 2006 more than a dozen pairs now live here). The UK's smallest bird of prey, the endangered **merlin** (*Falco columbarius*),

THE ENVIRONMENT & NATURE

also likes to hunt on the moors and indeed roosts there too, but in winter will often drop to lower coastal areas. Even rarer, in 2010 a pair of **Montagu's harriers** (*Circus pygargus*) nested in the national park for the first time in half a century, where they raised three chicks. Unfortunately, the decline of the species has continued and there are now thought to be only four breeding pairs left in the UK and their whereabouts are kept secret from the public – so even if the harriers do return to the park, there's little chance that we'll know about it.

Coast   It's hard to over-state just how important the coast of North Yorkshire is for the birdlife of the British Isles. Indeed, the RSPB declared in 2017 that a 17-mile stretch of coast starting at Bridlington and stretching north past Filey (and thus including part of the Cleveland Way) is the largest mainland seabird colony in Britain. While bird populations elsewhere in the UK are declining, including those of seabirds at other colonies on our shores, the cliffs surrounding Filey are home to a staggering 298,054 breeding seabirds (apparently it took a team of RSPB experts 34 days to count them all, with much of that time spent on a boat bobbing up and down in the North Sea). And it's growing too, with populations of **gannets** (*Morus bassanus*) up from 2550 in 2000 to 13,400 pairs (a jump of over 400%), **guillemot** (*Uria aalge*) rising from 31,000 to more than 57,000 pairs, their close relatives the **razorbills** (*Alca torda*) up from 5700 to 19,000 pairs, and **kittiwakes** (*Rissa tridactyla*) increasing from 42,000 to 45,300 pairs. There's even a decent population of the nation's favourite seabird, the **puffins** (*Fratercula arctica*), with 1440 breeding pairs.

Terrifying these huge populations is the **peregrine falcon** (*Falco peregrinus*), which can famously reach speeds of 200mph as it plummets down to catch its prey. The clifftops near Staithes are popular nesting sites for the peregrine.

It's not just the cliffs that provide such good habitats for the local avifauna, either. The harbours and bays are home to large populations of **oystercatchers** (*Haematopus ostralegus*) that prey on the bivalves that live in the mudflats. Also present is the **cormorant** (*Phalacrocorax carbo*) and its diminutive lookalike the **shag** (*Phalacrocorax aristotelis*), various members of the **grebe** family (*Tachybaptus*), the starling-sized **little auk** (*Alle alle*) and both the **bar-tailed** (*Limosa lapponica*) and **black-tailed godwits** (*Limosa limosa*).

FLORA

Flowers, grasses, moss and fungi
Woodland, farmland, meadows and hedgerows   Spring is the time to come and see the rich displays of colour on the Cleveland Way. From March to May **bluebells** (*Hyacinthoides non-scripta*) proliferate on the woodland floor, forming large carpets of bright blue, bell-shaped flowers, particularly in the trees below Roseberry Topping. Other common spring woodland flowers are the pink-tinged **wood anemone** (*Anemone nemorosa*) – which often flower around the same time of year as the bluebell and can similarly carpet an entire woodland – while thriving near streams and rivers is the powerful-smelling white-petalled wild garlic (*Allium ursinum*), whose broad pointed leaves release

Above, clockwise from top: **1**. Red grouse on a drystone wall near Osmotherley (©HS). **2**. Eurasian eagle-owl (see p104, ©HS). **3**. Razorbill (©BT). **4 & 5**. A common seal emerges from the surf for a spot of sunbathing at Sandsend (©HS). **6**. Herring gull (©HS). **7**. Puffin (©BT).

Gorse
Ulex europaeus

Meadow Buttercup
Ranunculis acris

Marsh Marigold (Kingcup)
Caltha palustris

Bird's-foot trefoil
Lotus corniculatus

Honeysuckle
Lonicera periclymemum

Tormentil
Potentilla erecta

Primrose
Primula vulgaris

Ox-eye Daisy
Leucanthemum vulgare

Lousewort
Pedicularis sylvatica

Common Ragwort
Senecio jacobaea

Hemp-nettle
Galeopsis speciosa

Cowslip
Primula veris

Yellow Rattle
Rhinanthus minor

Meadow Cranesbill
Geranium pratense

Heartsease (Wild Pansy)
Viola tricolor

Scarlet Pimpernel
Anagallis arvensis

Rowan (tree)
Sorbus aucuparia

Thrift (Sea Pink)
Armeria maritima

Ramsons (Wild Garlic)
Allium ursinum

Common Hawthorn
Crataegus monogyna

Sea Campion
Silene maritima

Bluebell
Hyacinthoides non-scripta

Yarrow
Achillea millefolium

Hogweed
Heracleum sphondylium

Herb-Robert
Geranium robertianum

Dog Rose
Rosa canina

Forget-me-not
Myosotis arvensis

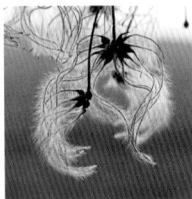

Travellers' Joy
Clematis vitalba

Red Campion
Silene dioica

Common Dog Violet
Viola riviniana

Germander Speedwell
Veronica chamaedrys

Heather (Ling)
Calluna vulgaris

Harebell
Campanula rotundifolia

Early Purple Orchid
Orchis mascula

Bell Heather
Erica cinerea

Foxglove
Digitalis purpurea

an onion bouquet when crushed. You may also see clumps of the cute yellow **primrose** (*Primula vulgaris*).

Moving out of the shade of the tree canopy and into the sunlight at the woodland's edge, the feathery **Travellers' Joy** (*Clematis vitalba*) twists through hedgerow and has pale-cream fluffy blooms in autumn – hence its other name of **old man's beard**. Another climber is the **honeysuckle** (*Lonicera periclymemum*), a valuable butterfly food plant.

At the woodland edge and in scrubland you will also find **bramble** (*Rubus fruticosus*), a common vigorous shrub; edible **blackberry** fruits ripen from late summer into autumn. They can be quite tart and very 'pippy' – but rather yummy too. Fairly common in scrubland and on woodland edges is the **dog rose** (*Rosa canina*) which has a large pink flower, the fruits or 'hips' of which are rich in Vitamin C and can be used to make the delicious rose-hip syrup.

A member of the carrot family, though not edible, is **Queen Anne's Lace** or **cow parsley** (*Anthriscus sylvestris*), with its white flowers covering banks and verges from early summer. **Red campion** (*Silene dioica*) is a decorative pinkish red flower with five petals and is common between March and October. The pretty pink geranium **herb robert** (*Geranium robertianum*) flowers through to September. Other flowering plants to look for in hedgerows and on the edge of the woods include the tall **foxglove** (*Digitalis purpurea*) with its trumpet-like flowers and **forget-me-not** (*Myosotis arvensis*) with tiny, delicate blue flowers.

But notwithstanding all the beauty of the flowers we've so far mentioned, it is the sight of an orchid that always excites people the most. The North York Moors can boast several species, including the most common **early purple orchid** (*Orchis mascula*), the **bee orchid** (*Ophrys apifera*) and the **pyramidal orchid** (*Anacamptis pyramidalis*). You'll occasionally come across them near the trail, particularly on roadside verges or anywhere where there's lots of sun. The bee orchid is perhaps the most striking, and has the best story; the bee-like flower is supposed to attract the attentions of a lustful young male, who lands on the flower's velvety lip in the hope of initiating sexual congress. In doing so, the pollen from the orchid sticks to the legs and body of the bee, who eventually flies off frustrated to try his luck elsewhere – thus spreading the pollen to another flower. That's the theory, at least, though in the UK the right type of bee doesn't actually exist, so the plant has to self-pollinate.

Heading back into the shade of the woods, come autumn the various species of **fungi** really start to come into their own. **Chicken of the wood** (*Laetiporus sulphureus*), also known as bracket fungus, is perhaps the easiest to spot as it clings to the side of old trees, often forming a series of horizontal shelves down the side of a trunk. It is well named, for this fungus is edible. Looking like a vivid yellow piece of coral that has somehow washed up in deep, dank forest, the radiant antlers of the **staghorn** (*Calocera viscosa*) fungus are nevertheless much harder to spot, preferring to grow on rotting pieces of wood buried under fallen leaves. A third common species and another woodland floor dweller, the **common earthball** (*Scleroderma citrinum*) is a dull, brown, round fungus that's similar in appearance to the edible puffball – which is perhaps why this mushroom is said to cause more poisonings than any other in the UK.

THE ENVIRONMENT & NATURE

Heath No plant is more closely associated with the Yorkshire moors than **heather** (*Calluna vulgaris*) and with good reason: the national park boasts the largest continuous tract of heather moorland in England and Wales. Taken in isolation, an individual heather plant can be considered an unremarkable evergreen shrub with small pink or purple flowers. But look across the vast expanse of moorland in late summer when the heather is in bloom and it can be quite breathtaking. There's a reason the plant grows in such huge quantities, the plants preferring to grow side-by-side to protect each other from the fierce winds that blow across the moor. For the same reason, the leaves are similarly thin and needle-like to prevent too much moisture being lost to the breeze. There are actually three types of heather on the moors of North Yorkshire, with the pink-flowered **ling** (*Calluna vulgaris*) by far the most common. If you're trekking in early summer, however, it may well be that **bell heather** (*Erica cinerea*) will be the most noticeable, its pink and purple flowers showing at this time while the flowers of the ling don't really appear until late summer. The third variety, **cross-leaved heath** (*Erica tetralix*), tends to prefer boggier ground; it, too, has pink flowers, bell-shaped, that are clustered at the end of long, branched stems.

But there's more to the moors than just heather. The acidic soil is also beloved by other species such as **wavy hair grass** (*Deschampsia flexuosa*), an attractive tall brown grass with delicate tufts of purplish spikelets at the tip of each stem. Another plant that manages to cling to survival on these sometimes-bleak moors is the **cloudberry** (*Rubus chamaemorus*), a low-lying plant with the thick fleshy evergreen leaves of a succulent, and distinctive black berries that are edible, though best eaten after cooking. The bogs that decorate the moors have their own ecosystems, of course, and thriving here you should spot varieties of **sphagnum moss**, while sitting amongst it is the carnivorous **sundew** (*Droseraceae*) waiting for its next unwitting victim to land. You may also spy other bog-dwellers including the white bobbing heads of **common cotton grass** (*Eriophorum angustifolium*) and perhaps even the yellow star-shaped flowers of the **bog asphodel** (*Narthecium ossifragum*).

As you drop down the slopes off the moors you'll doubtless end up walking through a band of **bracken** (*Pteridium aquilinum*) that beards the hills below the heather. In fact, it is estimated that about 20% of the national park is covered in bracken. Not the prettiest of plants, it nevertheless provides valuable habitat for birds such as the orange-breasted winchat.

Coastal flora With its coconut aroma, sharp spines and yellow blooms, **common gorse** (*Ulex europaeus*) is probably the most common – or at least noticeable – plant on the latter half of the Cleveland Way. Other plants that you may come across on the coast include **scurvy-grass** (*Cochlearia*), also called spoonwort, sea and bucks-horn plantains and the **harebell** (*Campanula rotundifolia*). The subject of much 19th-century poetry, the harebell or 'fairest flower' (according to Shakespeare) flowers in grassland from July to September and is one of the most fragile looking and beautiful of all our clifftop plants.

Trees

If you've never visited the North York Moors National Park before, it may surprise you to discover that about 22% of the land it covers is actually woodland. The traditional English broadleaf or mixed woodland makes up about a third of this total – or 100 sq km. The usual species thrive here – **oak** (*Quercus petraea*), **ash** (*Fraxinus excelsior*), **silver birch** (*Betula pendula*), **rowan** (*Sorbus aucuparia*), are easy to see, while **alder** (*Alnus glutinosa*) line the woodland rivers and streams.

Two tree-like shrubs, **hazel** (*Corylus avellana*) and **hawthorn** (*Crataegus monogyna*), add an understorey beneath the woodland canopy. The former has traditionally been used for coppicing. The trees are cut off at ground level every few years yielding many slender, straight and pliable branches used for making charcoal, fences, hurdles, bean poles, barrels and even as dowsing rods for water divining. As for the hardy hawthorn, its berries provide essential food for many of the woodland-dwelling birds. Solitary hawthorn trees are also associated with spirits and fairies.

The national park is also, rather magnificently, home to the largest concentration of **ancient trees** in northern England. (An ancient tree is any that is considered to have reached a great age for its species – which for an oak, for example, may be many hundreds of years old.) Many of these ancient trees can be found at Duncombe Park; the Cleveland Way skirts to the north of the park just after leaving Helmsley. Indeed, in 1994 over half the park was declared a National Nature Reserve (NNR) in order to preserve its many venerable trees.

The other two thirds of woodland in the national park are given over to **plantations**, usually coniferous woodland. It's easy to be sniffy about this sort of woodland; while it comes as quite a novelty to walk on the springy needle-covered carpet of a pine plantation floor, that novelty soon wears off after a few minutes and the next thing most walkers notice is the comparative lack of birdsong and other signs of life when compared to a traditional, thriving deciduous woodland. Add to this the relative lack of daylight that filters through to the floor in a pine forest, and the lack of available views too, and it's not uncommon for pine-plantation pedestrians to develop a feeling of boredom and a desire to exit onto sunnier, airier paths as soon as possible. But while this is entirely understandable, one should also recognise the fact that these plantations, for all their eerie silence, actually shelter many different creatures that prefer this sort of woodland to the traditional broadleaf variety. Rare species such as the crossbill (see p63), goshawk and nightjar all prefer to make their nests in coniferous woodland. Nevertheless, the biodiversity of a conifer plantation cannot compare to the richness of deciduous woodland. They also tend to be much younger, having been planted almost exclusively in the last 100 years. The main species are **Sitka spruce** (*Pinus sitchensis*), which accounts for about a fifth of all managed coniferous plantations in the park; **Scots pine** (*Pinus sylvestris*) and **Japanese** and **hybrid larch** (*Larix kaempferi* and *Larix leptolepis*). Only about a third of the trees in these plantations are over 60 years old, and it's doubtful that any are over 100.

THE ENVIRONMENT & NATURE

3 MINIMUM IMPACT & OUTDOOR SAFETY

Minimum impact walking

ENVIRONMENTAL IMPACT

A walking holiday in itself is an environmentally friendly approach to tourism. The following are some ideas on how you can go a few steps further in helping to minimise your impact on the environment while walking the Cleveland Way.

Use public transport whenever possible

The public transport network serving the Cleveland Way is, admittedly, not extensive, though most places have at least some sort of bus service and once you reach the coast you'll find getting around much easier. Public transport is always preferable to using private cars as it benefits everyone: visitors, locals and the environment.

Never leave litter

'Pack it in, pack it out'. Leaving litter is antisocial so carry a degradable plastic bag for all your rubbish, organic or otherwise and even other people's too, and pop it in a bin in the next village. Or better still, reduce the amount of litter you take with you by getting rid of packaging in advance.
● **Is it OK if it's biodegradable?** Not really. Apple cores, banana skins, orange peel and the like are unsightly, encourage flies, ants and wasps, and ruin a picnic spot for others; they can also take months to decompose. Either bury them or take them away with you.

Buy local

Look and ask for local produce to buy and eat. Not only does this cut down on the amount of pollution and congestion that the transportation of food creates, so-called 'food miles', it also ensures that you are supporting local farmers and producers.

Erosion

● **Stay on the main trail** The effect of your footsteps may seem minuscule but when they're multiplied by several thousand walkers each year they become rather more significant. Avoid taking shortcuts,

widening the trail or taking more than one path, especially across hay meadows and ploughed fields.

● **Consider walking out of season** Maximum disturbance by walkers coincides with the time of year when nature wants to do most of its growth and repair. Walking at less busy times eases this pressure while also generating year-round income for the local economy. Not only that, but it may make the walk a more relaxing experience with fewer people on the path and less competition for accommodation.

Respect all flora and fauna

Care for all wildlife you come across along the path; it has as much right to be there as you. Tempting as it may be to pick wild flowers, leave them so the next people who pass can enjoy them too. Don't break branches off trees. If you come across wildlife keep your distance and don't watch for too long. Your presence can cause considerable stress, particularly if the adults are with young, or in winter when the weather is harsh and food is scarce. Young animals are rarely abandoned; if you come across young birds keep away so that their mother can return.

The code of the outdoor loo

'Going' in the outdoors is a lost art worth reclaiming, for your sake and everyone else's. As more and more people discover the joys of the outdoors this is becoming an important issue. In some parts of the world where visitor pressure is higher than in Britain, walkers and climbers are required to pack out their excrement. This might one day be necessary here. Human excrement is not only offensive to our senses but, more importantly, can infect water sources.

● **Where to go** Wherever possible **use a toilet**. Public toilets are marked on the trail maps in this guide and you'll also find facilities in pubs and cafés along the path. If you do have to go outdoors, avoid ruins which can otherwise be welcome shelter for other walkers, as well as sites of historic or archaeological interest, and choose a place that is at least **30 metres away from running water**. Use a stick or trowel to **dig a small hole** about 15cm (6") deep to bury your excrement. It decomposes quicker when in contact with the top layer of soil or leaf mould. Stirring loose soil into your deposit speeds up decomposition. Do not squash it under rocks as this slows down the composting process. If you have to use rocks to cover it make sure they are not in contact with your faeces.

● **Toilet paper and tampons** Toilet paper takes a long time to decompose whether buried or not. It is easily dug up by animals and may then blow into water sources or onto the path.

The best method for dealing with it is to **pack it out**. Put the used paper inside a paper bag which you then place inside a plastic bag. Then simply empty the contents of the paper bag at the next toilet you come across and throw the bag away. If this is too much bother, light your used toilet paper and watch it burn until the flames are out – you don't want to start a wild fire. Pack out **tampons** and **sanitary towels**; they take years to decompose and may also be dug up and scattered about by animals.

❏ The Countryside Code

The Countryside Code, originally described in the 1950s as the Country Code, was revised and relaunched in 2004, in part because of the changes brought about by the CRoW Act (see opposite); it was updated again in 2012, 2014 and also 2016. The Code seems like common sense but sadly some people still appear to have no understanding of how to treat the countryside they walk in.

An adapted version of the 2016 Code, launched under the logo 'Respect. Protect. Enjoy.', is given below:

Respect other people

● **Consider the local community and other people enjoying the outdoors** Be sensitive to the needs and wishes of those who live and work there. If, for example, farm animals are being moved or gathered keep out of the way and follow the farmer's directions. Being courteous and friendly to those you meet will ensure a healthy future for all based on partnership and co-operation.

● **Leave gates and property as you find them and follow paths unless wider access is available** A farmer normally closes gates to keep farm animals in, but may sometimes leave them open so the animals can reach food and water. Leave gates as you find them or follow instructions on signs. When in a group, make sure the last person knows how to leave the gate. Follow paths unless wider access is available, such as on open country or registered common land (known as 'open access land'). Leave machinery and farm animals alone – if you think an animal is in distress try to alert the farmer instead. Use gates, stiles or gaps in field boundaries if you can – climbing over walls, hedges and fences can damage them and increase the risk of farm animals escaping. If you have to climb over a gate because you can't open it always do so at the hinged end. Also be careful not to disturb ruins and historic sites.

Stick to the official path across arable/pasture land. Minimise erosion by not cutting corners or widening the path.

Protect the natural environment

● **Leave no trace of your visit and take your litter home** Take special care not to damage, destroy or remove features such as rocks, plants and trees. Take your litter with you (see p68); litter and leftover food doesn't just spoil the beauty of the countryside, it can be dangerous to wildlife and farm animals.

Fires can be as devastating to wildlife and habitats as they are to people and property – so be careful with naked flames and cigarettes at any time of the year.

● **Keep dogs under effective control** This means that you should keep your dog on a lead or keep it in sight at all times, be aware of what it's doing and be confident it will return to you promptly on command.

Across farmland dogs should always be kept on a short lead. During lambing time they should not be taken with you at all. Always clean up after your dog and get rid of the mess responsibly – 'bag it and bin it'. (See also p31 and pp183-5).

Enjoy the outdoors

● **Plan ahead and be prepared** You're responsible for your own safety: be prepared for natural hazards, changes in weather and other events. Wild animals, farm animals and horses can behave unpredictably if you get too close, especially if they're with their young – so give them plenty of space.

● **Follow advice and local signs** In some areas there may be temporary diversions in place. Take notice of these and other local trail advice.

Wild camping

Wild camping is technically illegal in England (except, curiously, in parts of Dartmoor). This is a shame since wild camping is much more fulfilling than camping on a designated site. Living in the outdoors without any facilities provides a valuable lesson in simple, sustainable living where the results of all your actions, from going to the loo to washing your plates, can be seen. And there's no doubt that, illegal or not, plenty of people still indulge in the pastime. If you do want to wild camp **always ask the landowner** for permission. In most cases this is, of course, completely impractical so don't camp on farmland at all, but out on the uncultivated moors or in forests, and follow these suggestions:

● **Be discreet** Camp alone or in small groups, spend only one night in each place, pitch your tent late and leave early.
● **Never make or light a fire** Accidental fire is a great fear for farmers and foresters. Also the deep burn caused by camp fires, no matter how small, damages turf which can take years to recover; cook on a camp stove instead. Take any lit matches and cigarette butts out with you to dispose of safely.
● **Don't use soap or detergent** There is no need to use soap; even biodegradable soaps and detergents pollute streams. You won't be away from a shower for more than a couple of days. Wash up without detergent; use a plastic or metal scourer, or failing that, a handful of fine pebbles or some bracken or grass.
● **Leave no trace** Endeavour to leave no sign of having been there: no moved boulders, ripped up vegetation or dug drainage ditches. Make a final check of your campsite before departing; pick up any litter, leaving the place in the same state you found it in, or better.

ACCESS

Britain is a crowded island with few places where you can wander as you please. Most of the land is a patchwork of fields and agricultural land and the Cleveland Way has much of this, as well as moorland and coastline. This is fine, but what happens if you feel a little more adventurous and want to explore the moorland, woodland and hills that *aren't* on the walk?

Right to roam

The Countryside & Rights of Way Act 2000 (CRoW), or 'Right to Roam' as dubbed by walkers, came into effect in 2005 after a long campaign to allow greater public access to areas of countryside in England and Wales deemed to be uncultivated open country; this essentially means moorland, heathland, downland and upland areas. Some land is covered by restrictions (ie high-impact activities – such as driving a vehicle, cycling, horse-riding – are not permitted) and some land is excluded (such as gardens, parks and cultivated land). Full details are given on the Natural England website (see p55).

With more freedom in the countryside comes a need for more responsibility from the walker. Remember that wild open country is still the workplace of farmers and home to all sorts of wildlife. Have respect for both and avoid disturbing domestic and wild animals.

Outdoor safety

AVOIDANCE OF HAZARDS

With good planning and preparation most hazards can be avoided. This information is just as important for those out on a day walk on the moors as for those walking the entire Cleveland Way. Always make sure you have suitable **clothing** (see pp41-2) to keep warm and dry, whatever the conditions, and a change of inner clothes. Carrying plenty of food and water is vital too.

To ensure a safe and stress-free walk **follow the countryside code** (see box on p70) and:

● Check **weather forecasts** before you leave by listening to the radio or TV, or visit one of the online forecasts such as ⌨ bbc.co.uk/weather or ⌨ metoffice .gov.uk.

● Make sure that **somebody knows your plans** for every day you are on the trail. This could be a friend or relative whom you have promised to call every night, or whatever accommodation place you plan to stay in at the end of each day's walk. That way, if you fail to turn up or call that evening, they can raise the alarm.

● **Stick to the path** and avoid old quarries or taking shortcuts on steep sections of the escarpment.

● **Check your location** regularly on the map; it's unlikely that you'll lose your way but it'll save you missing a turning to a village and the frustration of retracing your steps at the end of a long day.

● Always fill your **water** bottles/pouches at every available opportunity and drink regularly.

● Make sure you have some **high-energy snacks** – fruit, nuts, or chocolate – to keep you going on the last few miles of a long day or in an emergency.

● Always carry a **torch** and **whistle** (see below for details about the international distress signal).

● Wear strong **boots** with good ankle support and a good grip, and have **suitable clothes** including wet-weather gear (see pp41-2).

● Be extra vigilant with **children** and/or **dogs** (see pp183-5).

DEALING WITH AN ACCIDENT

● Use basic first aid to treat the injury to the best of your ability.

● The **emergency signal** is six blasts on a whistle or six flashes with a torch, best done when you think someone might see or hear them.

● Work out exactly where you are. If possible leave someone with the casualty while others go to get help. If there are only two people, you have a dilemma. If you decide to get help, leave all spare clothing and food with the casualty.

● In an emergency dial ☎ 999 (or the EU standard number ☎ 112). Don't assume your mobile won't work up on some of the remoter corners of the moors.

BLISTERS

It is important to break in new boots before embarking on a long trek. Make sure the boots are comfortable and try to avoid getting them wet on the inside. Air your feet at lunchtime, keep them clean and change your socks regularly. If you feel any hot spots stop immediately and apply Compeed or Second Skin before the blister develops. Applied at the right time it's magic stuff. If you've left it too late, do not burst the blister as this can lead to infection; dress it with any blister kit to protect it from abrasion. If your skin is broken keep the area clean with antiseptic and cover with a non-adhesive dressing material held in place with tape.

HYPOTHERMIA

Also known as exposure, hypothermia occurs when the body can't generate enough heat to maintain its normal temperature, usually as a result of being wet, cold, unprotected from the wind, tired and hungry. It's usually more of a problem in upland areas such as on the moors or the coastal cliffs.

Hypothermia is easily avoided by wearing suitable clothing, carrying and consuming enough food and drink, being aware of the weather conditions and checking the morale of your companions. Early signs to watch for are feeling cold and tired with involuntary shivering. Find some shelter as soon as possible and warm the victim up with a hot drink and some chocolate or other high-energy food. If possible give them another warm layer of clothing and allow them to rest until feeling better.

If allowed to worsen, erratic behaviour, slurring of speech and poor co-ordination will become apparent and the victim can very soon progress into unconsciousness, followed by coma and death. Quickly get the victim out of wind and rain, improvising a shelter if necessary.

Rapid restoration of bodily warmth is essential and best achieved by bare-skin contact: someone should get into the same sleeping bag as the patient, both having stripped to the bare essentials, placing any spare clothing under or over them to build up heat. Send or call urgently for help.

HYPERTHERMIA

Not an ailment that you would normally associate with the north of England, hyperthermia (heat exhaustion and heatstroke) is a serious problem nonetheless.

Symptoms of **heat exhaustion** include thirst, fatigue, giddiness, a rapid pulse, raised body temperature, low urine output and, if not treated, delirium and finally a coma. The best cure is to drink plenty of water.

Heatstroke is another matter altogether, and even more serious. A high body temperature and an absence of sweating are early indications, followed by symptoms similar to hypothermia (see p73) such as a lack of co-ordination, convulsions and coma.

Death will follow if treatment is not given instantly. Sponge the victim down, wrap them in wet towels, fan them, and get help immediately.

SUNBURN

It can happen, even in northern England and even on overcast days. The only surefire way to avoid it is to stay wrapped up or smother yourself in sunscreen (with a minimum factor of 15) and apply it regularly throughout the day. Don't forget your lips, nose and the back of your neck.

PERSONAL SAFETY

The Cleveland Way is much safer than any city and you are more likely to twist an ankle and have to hobble painfully to the nearest village, than become a crime victim. However, if you do walk on your own it's all the more important to make sure someone knows your plans for the day (see p72), and take all the usual precautions such as keeping an eye on your belongings at all times.

OTHER USERS

Large chunks of the western portion of the Cleveland Way is bridleway, which means that on this part of your walk you may well be sharing the path with cyclists and horse-riders. Most horse-riders are a considerate bunch and it's usually the horse itself that's the problem, the riders grimly trying to control the equine equivalent of an F1 racing car. Just give them a wide berth and you'll be fine. As for cyclists, most are decent people though you always get the odd pillock who treats the trail as his own private race track (I say 'his' because the pillock in question is nearly always male). Again, just give them plenty of room and try to avoid any confrontations, no matter what you think of their behaviour, as that can ruin the entire day's walk.

ROUTE GUIDE & MAPS 4

Using this guide

This trail guide has been described from west to east and divided into 10 stages. Each stage is approximately a day's walk in length though that doesn't mean you have to divide the trail up this way; you can plan your walk however you wish, of course, and much will depend on the speed you walk at, your interests and where you stay. See pp36-7 for some suggested itineraries.

To enable you to plan your own itinerary, **practical information** is presented clearly on the trail maps. This includes walking times for both directions, places to stay, camp and eat, as well as shops where you can buy supplies. Further service **details** are given in the text under the entry for each place. For an overview of this information see the village and town facilities table on pp34-5.

For **map profiles** see the colour pages at the end of the book.

TRAIL MAPS

Scale and walking times
The trail maps are to a scale of 1:20,000 (1cm = 200m; 3¹/₈ inches = one mile). Walking times are given along the side of each map and the arrow shows the direction to which the time refers. Black triangles indicate the points between which the times have been taken. **See note on walking times in box below**. The times are there as an aid to planning your walk – not to judge your ability. There are many variables which will affect your speed including weather, ground conditions, whether you are walking alone or with company and how interesting you find parts of the landscape.

> ❏ **Important note – walking times**
> Unless otherwise specified, **all times in this book refer only to the time spent walking**. You will need to add 20-30% to allow for rests, photography, checking the map, drinking water etc. When planning the day's hike count on 5-7 hours' actual walking.
>
> To research this book I walked alone so kept a faster pace than if I were walking with companions. Most health and fitness professionals calculate the average walking speed for humans to be 2-3mph/3-5kph. After a few days you will hopefully know how fast you walk compared to the time bars and can plan your day more accurately.

Up or down?

Other than when on a track or bridleway the trail is shown as a dotted line. An arrow across the trail indicates the slope; two arrows show that it is steep. Note that the arrow points towards the higher part of the trail. If, for example, you are walking from A (at 80m) to B (at 200m) and the trail between the two is short and steep, it would be shown thus: A- – – – >>- – – -B. Reversed arrow heads indicate a downward gradient.

Other features

Features marked on the maps are pertinent to navigation but, to avoid clutter, not all features have been marked.

ACCOMMODATION

The accommodation included in the book is either on the trail or within easy reach of it and details of each place are given in the accompanying text. The number and type of rooms is given: **S** = single bed, **D** = double bed, **T** = twin beds (two single beds), **Tr/Qd** = rooms that can sleep three/four people, but note that this often means two people sharing a double bed and the other(s) in bunk beds; however, these rooms can also be used as doubles or twins. Some places have rooms that can sleep more than two people but only children, not adults.

Rates given are **per person (pp)** based on two people sharing a room for a one-night stay – rates are almost always discounted for a longer stay. Where a single room (**sgl**) is available the rate for that is quoted if different from the per person rate. The rate for single occupancy (**sgl occ**) of a double/twin is generally higher, and the per person rate for three or more sharing a room may be lower. Unless specified, rates are for B&B. At some places the only option is a room rate; this will be the same whether one or two people share. Don't bank on a discount in the off-season; year-round demand from business travellers, holidaymakers and weekenders for accommodation along and near the Cleveland Way keeps prices high. Note that many places, particularly hotels and YHA hostels, have rates that vary from one night to the next according to demand; in this case we've just asked the proprietors to provide us with an approximate rate. Note, too, that some hotels have different rates advertised on booking agency websites. In this case, it's usually best to contact the hotel or B&B as it's often cheaper to book direct with them. See also pp22-3.

The text also mentions whether a **bath** is available (☛) in, or for, at least one room; and whether **dogs** (🐾) are welcome. Most places will not take more than one dog in a room and also only accept them subject to prior arrangement. Some make an additional charge (usually per night but occasionally per stay) while others may require a deposit which is refundable if the dog doesn't make a mess. See also pp183-5.

Some owners are prepared to collect walkers from points on the trail where the accommodation is a mile or two off the path and take them back the next morning – it is worth asking if this is possible when booking. Often this service is free but any offer to pay petrol money will generally be appreciated.

The route guide

HELMSLEY [map p79]

The only market town in the North York Moors National Park, Helmsley has plenty of charm and is handsome in an affluent but unostentatious sort of way.

Given that even the greater Helmsley ward has a population that only just creeps over the 3000 mark, it's also fair to say that the town punches well above its weight: not only can it boast of having its own castle, church, arts centre and brewery, but in the past few years the centre of Helmsley has also been awarded the title of Britain's 'Best Market Town High Street', and the local deli, Hunters (see Services), has been crowned Britain's best small shop! There are certainly enough facilities and sights in Helmsley to make you miss it when you're walking on the bleak and lonely moors; but, by the same token, there's probably not enough here to force you to delay your departure to any significant degree – and as such, it's the perfect place from which to start a long-distance walk.

What to see and do

Helmsley's most prominent attraction is its **castle** (Apr-Sep daily 10am-6pm, Oct to 5pm, Nov-mid Feb Sat & Sun 10am-4pm, mid Feb-Mar Fri-Sun 10am-4pm; £6.80, EH members free), situated just outside the centre to the west of town and best reached by taking the pedestrian-only cul-de-sac past Castlegate Tearooms and the allotments, turning right at the end to arrive at the entrance. Now run by English Heritage, there's actually not a huge amount to see, the ravages of 900 years of history having left little of this medieval fortress save the East Tower, though the outlines of several other rooms – the kitchen, pantry, buttery etc – can all be traced on the ground. The original castle was constructed in wood in around 1120 on the orders of Walter Espec, better known as 'Walter the Woodpecker', the man who also founded nearby Rievaulx

Abbey and Kirkham Priory. Little remains of Walter's construction save for the defensive ditches surrounding the site. Converted entirely to stone before the end of the 12th century, half the original keep was blown away by Cromwell's men following a three-month siege during the Civil War. The Tudor Mansion that was built on the grounds prior to the Civil War *did* survive, however, and remains in a much more complete condition to this day, with highlights including the wood panelling and plasterwork on the walls and ceiling of the dining room.

Behind the castle and just off the Cleveland Way itself is the gorgeous **Helmsley Walled Garden** (Map 1; ⌨ helmsleywalledgarden.org.uk; Apr-Oct daily 10am-5pm; £7.50; 🐕 on leads), a 250-year-old 5-acre site lovingly restored back to full health over the past 20 years.

In the late 17th century the castle was bought by Charles Duncombe, whose son-in-law ordered the building of nearby Duncombe Park, now home to the **National Centre for Birds of Prey** (☎ 0844 742 2035, ⌨ ncbp.co.uk; daily 10am-5.30pm or to dusk, late Jan to late Dec; £9). The highlights of any visit here are the thrice-daily flying demonstrations. The centre lies about a mile (1.5km) south-west of town though the walk through parkland is a pleasant one.

Finally, if all this sightseeing sounds a bit too worthy, you can opt instead to visit **Helmsley Brewing Company** (⌨ helmsleybrewingco.co.uk; see box p25). Tours of the brewery are held every Wednesday between 10am and noon and cost £8, which includes a free pint at the end.

Services

Most services are huddled around the main square, Market Place.

There is no longer a **tourist office** but at several points about town you'll find leaflets that you can pick up which contain a map and a brief introduction to the attractions in town. You may also want to check out the website: 💻 visithelmsley.co.uk.

As for facilities that *do* still exist, on the main square is the **trekking shop** Helmsley Outdoors (Mon-Sat 10am-5pm, Sun to 4.30pm), Co-op **supermarket** (daily 7am-10pm) and, to the south on Bridge St, a Costcutter (Mon-Sat 8am-9pm, Sun 9am-8pm), which also plays host to the town's **post office** (same hours as shop). There is also an **ATM** near the church.

Helmsley Pharmacy (Mon-Fri 9am-5.30pm) is at the Medical Centre on Carlton Rd, opposite the YHA hostel.

Transport
There's no railway station in Helmsley, of course, but several **bus services** call at Market Place (the two benches by Lord Faversham Monument that face the road or opposite, between The Feathers and the Co-op). The most frequent services are EYMS's No 128 and Transdev's No 31X. The seasonal and infrequent buses operated by Moorsbus (M3, M4 & M5) also stop at the monument. See box pp52-3 for more details.

For a **taxi** try Ryedale's Comfy Cars & Taxis (☎ 01439-377277, 💻 ryedalescomfy cars.co.uk), or RED's (☎ 0709-330 2585).

Where to stay
The only **camping** (Mar-Oct) in the town centre is provided by *YHA Helmsley* (☎ 0345-371 9638, 💻 yha.org.uk/hostel/yha-helmsley; 1 x 2-, 1 x 3-, 1 x 4, 1 x 5- with double bed, 4 x 6-bed rooms; some en suite;

WI-FI; Mar-end Oct weekends and daily in school holidays), a modern purpose-built **hostel** to the north-east of the town centre on Carlton Lane. The hostel's connection with the Cleveland Way is deep, for it was here that the official opening ceremony for the Cleveland Way was conducted in 1969. Be warned that it is only open at certain times for individual bookings, though if the hostel has not been booked by a group less than three months in advance there may be more availability. Even when it is open you can't check in before 5pm, though otherwise this place is fine. Meals are available but the hostel also has a good self-catering kitchen and a pleasant conservatory and patio. There are also laundry and drying facilities. Rates start at £13pp for a dorm bed (though £18-23pp is more common in summer) and from £25 for a private room sleeping up to two people (around £49.50 in summer), with camping from £10pp (£12-15pp in summer). Campers can use all the hostel's facilities and they can have a dog as long as it is on a lead. (Note, too, that there's a very good site at Scawton, see p82, that's just a couple of miles outside town and only a few minutes from the trail.)

For **B&B** accommodation, *Carlton Lodge* (☎ 01439-770557, 💻 carlton-lodge .com; 1S/1T/3D/2Tr, all en suite, 1D private bathroom; 🐾; WI-FI) on Bondgate, lies about 350m from the town centre and has been going under the same ownership for over a quarter of a century now. It charges from £47.50pp (sgl/sgl occ from £58/75), though the prices approximately double for

---

❏ Long-stay parking in Helmsley
You can buy a week-long parking ticket for £22 from the Helmsley Castle reception, run by English Heritage. The ticket is valid in the neighbouring car park and if you think you are going to stay for longer than seven days you can buy two tickets and ask the receptionist to make sure they run consecutively.

Incidentally, **if you have arrived in a campervan or mobile home**, you are allowed to sleep in it overnight (ie between 6pm and 9am) **for free** in the car park next door (though do note that regular parking charges apply during the daytime). Though probably of limited use to Cleveland Way walkers, it's nevertheless rare and wonderful to see a town that's happy to let people sleep in their vehicles without fining them or moving them on – and another example of the warm welcome Helmsley typically extends to visitors.

ROUTE GUIDE AND MAPS

Helmsley

Where to eat and drink

1 Feversham Arms
2 Black Swan Tearoom
3 Thomas the Baker
4 Sugared Butterfly
5 Mannion & Co
6 Cocoa
7 Sweet Corner
8 Auntie Anne's Bakery
9 Castlegate Tearooms
10 Royal Oak
11 Hunters of Helmsley
12 Crema
13 Barkers
14 Gepetto's
15 Scott's Fish & Chips
16 Nice Things
17 Porters
18 Helmsley Spice
19 The Feathers
20 Helmsley Fish Shop

YHA Helmsley
Carlton Rd
Pharmacy & Medical Centre
Carlton Lodge
To High Rigg
Bondgate
Carlton Lane
A170
Pottergate
Sawmill Lane
100m
50
0
Market Cross (Official start of the Cleveland Way)
Bus stop
The Feathers
Lord Feversham Monument (Alternative start to the Cleveland Way)
Co-op
Costcutter & Post Office
Bridge St
A170
Helmsley Brewery
Elmslac Close
Market Place
Borogate
Bridge St
Canons Garth Lane
Black Swan Hotel
ATM
Royal Oak
Helmsley Outdoors
Castlegate
Helmsley Church
Stillworth House
Allotments
To National Centre for Birds of Prey, 1 mile/1.6km
Beckdale Rd
Feversham Arms
Auntie Anne's Bakery
Cleveland Way
Toilets
Helmsley Castle entrance (place to buy 7-day parking permits)
Carved seat
Overnight car park
Helmsley Castle
B1257
Church St

single-night bookings on Friday or Saturday nights. However, do note, too, that they have long-term parking for those setting off on the Cleveland Way but this is subject to prior arrangement as they have limited spaces. When you think that the alternative is to spend £22 at the public car park in town, this could make a stay here a very good deal indeed.

The Georgian *Stilworth House* (☎ 01439-771072, 🖳 stilworth.co.uk; 2D/1T, all en suite; WI-FI but intermittent) is situated just off the main square at 1 Church St, with views of Helmsley Castle from the back; they charge £45-50pp (sgl occ from £70).

High Rigg (☎ 01439-770209, 🖳 high rigg.net; 2D, both en suite; ➤; WI-FI; 🐾 but in separate building only) is about three miles out of town but as they offer a lift to the start of the trail, their inclusion in this guide is easily justified. With walkers welcomed warmly every time, treated to a hearty breakfast and encouraged to take fruit from their garden, this is a lovely way to start your trip. Rates are £37.50-42.50pp (sgl occ room rate).

The **pubs** all offer accommodation as well, and rather smart some of them are too. Best value is on Market Place where the *Royal Oak* (☎ 01439-770450, 🖳 royaloak hotelhelmsley.com; 3D/1D or T/1Qd, all en suite; ➤; WI-FI; 🌓; 🐾) provides facility-filled rooms for around £45-50pp (sgl occ from £65-75). Also facing the main square, both *The Feathers* (☎ 01439-770275, 🖳 feathershotelhelmsley.co.uk; 1S/13D/2D or T/5T/3Tr/1Qd, all en suite; ➤; WI-FI; 🌓; 🐾) and *Black Swan* (☎ 01439-770466, 🖳 blackswan-helmsley.co.uk; 1S/27D/21T, all en suite; ➤; WI-FI; 🌓; 🐾) have prices that vary according to demand and thus can change every day. Suffice to say that at The Feathers, which was only converted into a hotel in the 1950s from two neighbouring houses that had been knocked together, you can still pick up a room for £35pp (sgl occ from £70); while at the older, slightly smarter Black Swan – which is actually made up of three separate houses, including one Georgian and one Elizabethan – doubles start at £65pp (sgl occ from £100). Four of the rooms at the Black Swan can sleep adults with up to two children. The

owners of the Black Swan also run the even more upmarket *Feversham Arms* (☎ 01439-772935, 🖳 fevershamarmshotel .com; 22D/11D or T, all en suite; ➤; WI-FI; 🌓; 🐾), on the corner of Canons Garth Lane and the B1257, which has its own spa including heated outdoor pool, Jacuzzi, foot spa, salt inhalation room and monsoon shower; though we can't be 100% sure what each of these facilities and treatments is, we are fairly certain that this looks like the sort of place you should be staying in *after* your trek rather than before it. Rack rates start at a reasonable £60pp (sgl occ rates on request) rising to a less reasonable £215pp for a poolside suite (complete with log-burning stove), though you can find lower prices online.

Where to eat and drink

You won't go hungry or thirsty in Helmsley; there are cafés and eateries galore, of which the following is just a selection.

For early risers, the first place to throw open its doors is *Thomas the Baker* (🖳 www.thomasthebaker.co.uk; Mon-Sat 7am-5pm, Sun 9am-4.30pm), right on Market Place and very good value, with a hot bacon or sausage sarnie plus a drink for £2.90. *Auntie Anne's Bakery* (🖳 auntieannescast legatebakery.co.uk; Mon-Sat 8am-4pm, Sun 10am-5pm), down the pedestrian-only cul-de-sac leading to Helmsley Castle, is another early option and again, very good value; though it, too, is takeaway only, the pastries and pasties are great (eg pork pie £1.55), very cheap – and the hot drinks are only £1-1.20. For packed lunch ingredients you can't do better than *Hunters of Helmsley* (🖳 huntersofhelmsley.com; Sun-Thur 9am-4.30pm, Fri & Sat 8am-5.30pm), the award-winning deli that is also on Market Place.

If you want to sit down and eat you'll have to wait for the 'regular' cafés to open. For those who like a traditional tearoom you need look no further than *Nice Things* (Mon-Sat 9am-5pm, Sun 10.30am-4.30pm), on the southern side of Market Place, with an uncomplicated menu of jacket potatoes (£5.60-6.10), toasted sandwiches (£5.75-6.10) and breakfasts (up to £8.95). On the western side of the square, *Sugared Butterfly* (daily 9.30am-4pm) is more up-to-date in terms of décor and style – the food is often served on wooden boards, for example, rather than crockery – but the menu is still fairly traditional. Nothing wrong with that, however, for this is a fine and very good-value place with a fair choice of breakfasts (from £2.50 for toast up to £8.25 for the Full English), sandwiches (£5.95-6.95) and paninis. We also really like **Crema** (🖳 www.cremacof feehouse.co.uk; Mon-Sat 9.30am-4.30pm, Sun 10am-4.30pm, winter daily 10am-4pm), just off the main square below Hunters at 2 & 3 Borogate. It's a friendly place that tries very hard to cater for its customers' requirements with an extensive menu of breakfasts (£4.60-7), lunches (largely sandwiches and toasties including a decent Welsh rarebit for £7.50) and a vast array of cakes (£2.75-3.25). All in all, a top place.

Moving away from the main square, **Porters** (daily 8am-5pm) offers sandwiches (from £4.50) and jacket potatoes (from £4.95) but is most notable for its wide array of cakes. Porters does have an outside seating area where dogs can sit (they can also sit at the back of the café inside) but if it's a lovely day the nicest option for al-fresco eating is **Barkers** (daily 9.30am-5.30pm), set in a nice little sun-trap courtyard away from traffic, where you can share a platter (£15-19 for two), bruschetta (£3.70-4.30), or their all-day breakfast rolls (ciabatta filled with two rashers, two sausages, tomatoes, beans & mushrooms for £6.50). As you'd expect given the name, they're also dog friendly. We really like this place; however, the eatery that receives the most recommendations from locals is **Vine House Café** (Map 1; 🖳 vinehousecafehelmsley.co .uk; daily 10am-5pm) in the Walled Garden. It's certainly a novel and pretty place to eat, and we like the fact they take a lot of ingredients from the garden. But we found the 'greenhouse' setting too hot and too bright and the menu – a few 'open sandwiches' for £7.50 and salads (£8.50) as well as an (albeit frequently changing) specials board – too limited and overpriced to really win us over. Still, they do dish out free dog biscuits, a policy of which we heartily approve, and we do seem to be one lone voice of dissatisfaction standing against a chorus of positive online reviews, so maybe we were just not in a good mood when we visited because the only scones they had were fruit ones (£3).

As for the knot of eateries on the way to the castle, our favourite is **The Cocoa Tree** (Fri-Wed 10am-5pm, winter to 4.30pm), with a varied menu including something called a Discovery Cake (a rich apricot and ginger fruit cake made with a drop of brandy and served with Wensleydale cheese; £3.50).

When it comes to **evening dining**, for traditional pub food we really like the unpretentious fare on offer at the **Royal Oak** (see Where to stay; Mon-Fri noon-2.30pm & 5-8.30pm, Sat noon-3pm & 5-8.30pm, Sun noon-3pm) which is undoubtedly the best value. The menu is largely filled with pub classics (starting at £7.95 for the vegetable lasagne and with nothing over £11) and pizzas (from £8.50) but the food was tasty, the prices very reasonable and the place buzzing. Opposite, the dishes at **The Feathers** (see Where to stay; food served daily noon-9pm) are about a fiver more expensive than their Royal Oak counterparts (mains around £13-16), though we thought their lamb's liver with mash potato, veg and gravy was smashing.

Other options for evening dining include the Italian, **Gepetto's** (🖳 fatchef company.co.uk/gepetto-s; Tue-Sat 5-9pm), which has been serving pizzas (from £8.80) and authentic Italian fare (pasta dishes from £10.80 up to £14 for the fettuccine with prawns, king prawns and scallops, served in a brandy & creamy tomato sauce) to the locals of Helmsley for over two decades now; and the Indian **Helmsley Spice** (☎ 01439-771777; daily 5-11pm; cash only) with mains from £5.95 for the chicken tikka. There are also two chip shops, **Scott's** (🖳 scottsfishandchips.co.uk; Sun-Wed 11.30am-6.30pm, Thur to 7pm, Fri to 9pm & Sat to 8pm), and the more humble **Helmsley Fish Shop** (Tue-Thur 4.30-7.30pm, Fri & Sat 11.30am-1.30pm & 4.30-7.30pm).

Food is also available at **Feversham Arms** and **Black Swan** (see Where to stay) as well as **Mannion & Co**, **Sweet Corner** & **Castlegate Tearooms**.

HELMSLEY TO SUTTON BANK   [MAPS 1-4]

This **10.3-mile/16.6km stage** (**3hrs 10mins to 4hrs**) first stage provides an enjoyable and undemanding introduction to the Cleveland Way – though also rather an atypical one. There's little in the way of actual moorland here – which, given that it's a path that walks around the North York Moors National Park, you'd expect there would be – and, of course, no coastline, which characterises the entire last half of the trek. But it's an agreeable way to begin a long-distance footpath nevertheless with plenty to see, including farmyards and fir forests, an ancient abbey, a Victorian White Horse plus, of course, a panorama at the very end of this stage that is said to be 'the finest view in England'. Of course there are many rivals for this award – but certainly the view from near Sutton Bank over the vales of York and Mowbray, with the Pennines brooding in the distance, is vast and verdant enough to be a contender – and a great way to finish this first stage.

Everybody seems to have their own starting point for the Cleveland Way. The *official* start is the **Market Cross** on Helmsley's main square. Many people, however, prefer to start from the **monument to Lord Feversham**, perhaps because a) this is the more obvious landmark in the centre of Helmsley and b) this is where the buses pull in too.

There's also a third option, namely the commemorative **carved seat** by the overnight car park on the edge of Helmsley, which is certainly where many people have their 'before' photos taken (and at the end of the Cleveland Way you'll find a similar seat to mark the trail's end).

Wherever you choose to kick off the trail, it won't be long before you leave the hubbub of the Helmsley hordes behind, entering instead a tranquil realm where the only sound to be heard is the mellifluous song of the skylark and the gentle baa-ing of the local sheep – though this is occasionally interrupted by the ear-melting scream of fighter jets on manoeuvres.

After a stretch of woodland the path emerges at 19th-century **Griff Lodge**, standing guard over one of the entrances to nearby Duncombe Park. From here the path drops through yet more woodland, passing a couple of ancient quarries that were used in the construction of the nearby abbey, to a quiet country lane leading to **Rievaulx Bridge** (Map 2), with the **abbey** (see box p84) after which it is named 500m away on your right. (And in case you're wondering, it's pronounced 'Ree-voh'.)

Back at the bridge, the trail continues along the road for just over half a mile. (Incidentally, it is on this stretch of road that the body of a woman was discovered in 1981 following an anonymous tip-off. Despite an extensive investigation, including the exhumation of the 'Sutton Bank Body' in 2013 so it could undergo further forensic tests and DNA profiling, the woman, who was over 35 years old when she died and was the mother to at least two children, has never been identified.)

Arriving at a junction, the trail continues on your right, skirting between the base of **Noodle Hill** and a series of small fish ponds, while straight ahead is **Scawton** where, if you're planning on **camping** during your trek, *Bungdale Head Farm Camping* (☎ 01439-770589, ☐ bungdaleheadcamping.co.uk; 🐾)

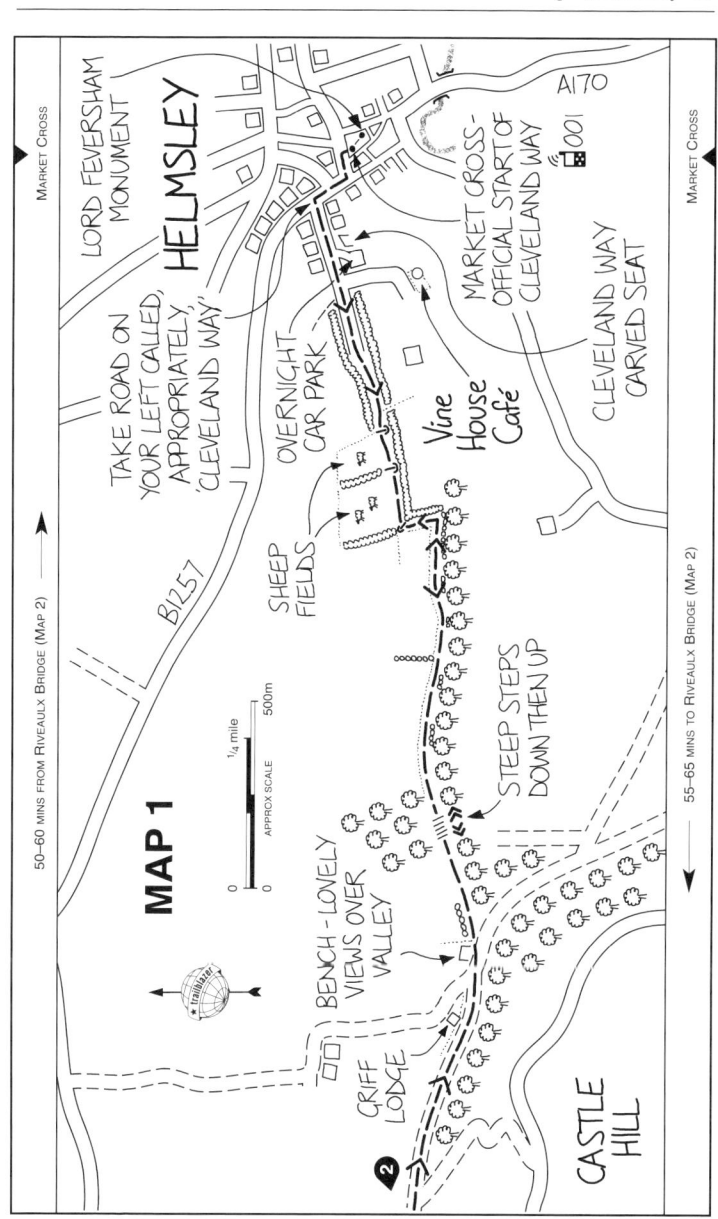

50–60 MINS FROM RIVEAULX BRIDGE (MAP 2)

MARKET CROSS

LORD FEVERSHAM MONUMENT

HELMSLEY

A170

TAKE ROAD ON YOUR LEFT CALLED, APPROPRIATELY, 'CLEVELAND WAY'

MARKET CROSS–OFFICIAL START OF CLEVELAND WAY

B1257

OVERNIGHT CAR PARK

Vine House Café

CLEVELAND WAY CARVED SEAT

SHEEP FIELDS

MAP 1

¼ mile

500m

0

0

APPROX SCALE

BENCH – LONELY VIEWS OVER VALLEY

STEEP STEPS DOWN THEN UP

GRIFF LODGE

CASTLE HILL

2

55–65 MINS TO RIVEAULX BRIDGE (MAP 2)

MARKET CROSS

ROUTE GUIDE AND MAPS

❑ **Rievaulx Abbey & Terrace**

Ruin though it may be, the **remains of Rievaulx Abbey** (Nov-mid Feb Sat, Sun & School hols 10am-4pm, mid Feb-Mar Wed-Sun 10am-4pm, Apr-Sep daily 10am-6pm, Oct to 5pm; £8.90; EH members free) are still fairly captivating, particularly when seen from the Cleveland Way, nestling at the foot of the wooded slopes of Ryedale.

Founded by 12 Cistercian monks in 1132, its remote location was a deliberate choice, all the better for the order to be able to conduct their strict, simple life of prayer and self-sufficiency, away from the temptations of the nearby towns. Yet in spite of their reluctance to communicate with the outside world, the abbey grew to be one of the wealthiest and most successful as the monks built up profitable businesses mining lead and iron, rearing sheep and selling wool. This, of course, all came to an end when Henry VIII got his hands on it during the dissolution of the monasteries in 1538, rendering the buildings uninhabitable and stripping away the abbey's wealth. The ruin eventually passed into the hands of the Duncombe family in the 18th century, who in turn gave it to English Heritage to run and maintain. Now open to the public, dogs are allowed to visit if kept on a lead and even if you've no interest in the ruins, the visitor centre at the front does have a *café* – the only place to get food hereabouts.

The Duncombes were also responsible for constructing the sinuous, grass-covered terrace that sits above the abbey, and which provides a bird's-eye view over the ruins for those with the necessary stamina to climb up the steep slope. This is **Rievaulx Terrace**, built in the 1750s and adorned with a Greek-style 'temple' at either end. Now owned by the National Trust, the terrace is open to the public (May-Sep 10am-5pm, Oct 10am-4pm; £5.95, NT members free), with the temples now used to house exhibitions.

is as good a place as any to start. This busy farm is located just a few minutes from the trail and boasts glorious views over the surrounding moors. It also has a very welcoming basic charm that's light years away from the facility-filled family campsites further along the trail – but none the worse for that. Rates are good too, starting at £6.50pp. Note, however, that you'll have to be self sufficient as there's no reasonable options for food near here.

After the fishing lakes the trail crosses a stream on **stepping stones**, eventually joining a track through cultivated fields to **Cold Kirby** (Maps 3 & 4) and the austere St Michael's Church, built in the 19th century though still housing the font from the original 12th-century church that stood here before it. You'll discover little else of interest in the village itself as you make your way past the large front gardens of the properties here, turning off down a 4WD track (Map 4) after the last house on the left to arrive, eventually, by stables. This area was, after all, once the location of Hambleton Racecourse, which for over 200 years was a major venue for horse-racing, second only in importance in England to Newmarket.

At the end of the **gallops** is a junction: turn right and you end up at *High House Farm* (☎ 01845-597557; 1D or T, not en suite; ☞; WI-FI), with just one room for which they charge £46pp (sgl occ from £48). Go straight ahead and there's a short-cut leading directly to Sutton Bank; but those trekkers with any integrity will continue on the Cleveland Way by turning left and crossing the

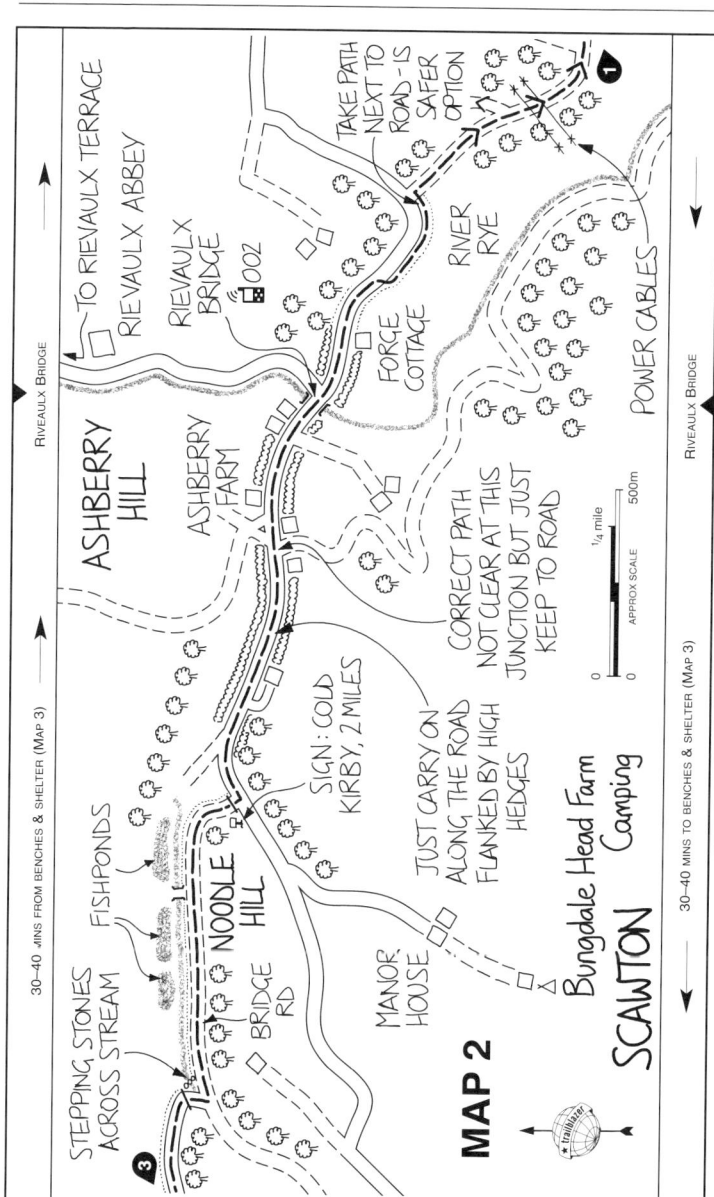

A170 to the **Kilburn White Horse** (see box below). Though you may not realise it, by walking along the edge of these cliffs you are actually tracing the defensive walls of Roulston Scar **Iron Age hill-fort**. Dating back to 400BC, this

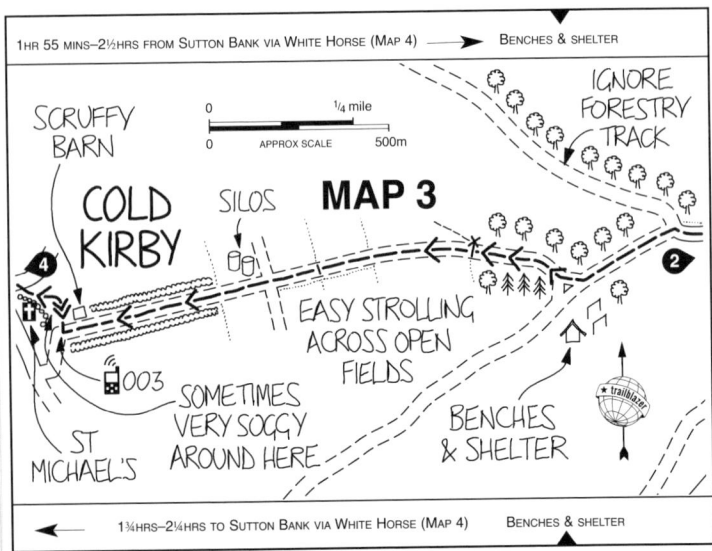

1HR 55 MINS–2½HRS FROM SUTTON BANK VIA WHITE HORSE (MAP 4) ⟶ BENCHES & SHELTER

IGNORE FORESTRY TRACK

SCRUFFY BARN

COLD KIRBY SILOS **MAP 3**

0   ¼ mile
0 APPROX SCALE 500m

EASY STROLLING ACROSS OPEN FIELDS

☎003 SOMETIMES VERY SOGGY AROUND HERE

ST MICHAEL'S

BENCHES & SHELTER

★ trailblazer

1¾HRS–2¼HRS TO SUTTON BANK VIA WHITE HORSE (MAP 4) BENCHES & SHELTER

❏ Kilburn White Horse

Designed and financed by Thomas Taylor in 1857, and built using labour from local schoolchildren under the tutelage of schoolmaster John Hodgson, this giant white horse was inspired by the ancient chalk horses of Wiltshire and elsewhere in southern England. Unfortunately, whereas those ancient equines were cut into chalk hills and thus are naturally white, the hill onto which the Kilburn White Horse was carved is made of a limestone that is more grey in colour. The horse thus has to be artificially whitened, which was originally done using whitewash, though nowadays they use chalk chippings from the Yorkshire Wolds.

At over 95m (314ft) long and 69m (228ft) high, there's no doubting the impressive scale of the figure. Indeed, it's said that 20 people can stand on the grass 'island' that makes the horse's eye – though walking on the horse these days is discouraged so we'll just have to take their word for it.

Alas, the point where the Cleveland Way meets the horse does not provide the best vantage point, the steepness of the slope meaning that little of the horse is actually visible and that which you can see is difficult to interpret due to the steep perspective. Those with the necessary enthusiasm and gumption can take the steps down past the horse's backside to the car park below, which at least allows you a clear sight of the body of the horse. To see the horse in its entirety, however, you probably need to hire a light aircraft or hot-air balloon – perhaps it's no coincidence that the top of the hill on which the horse has been constructed is home to Yorkshire Gliding Club.

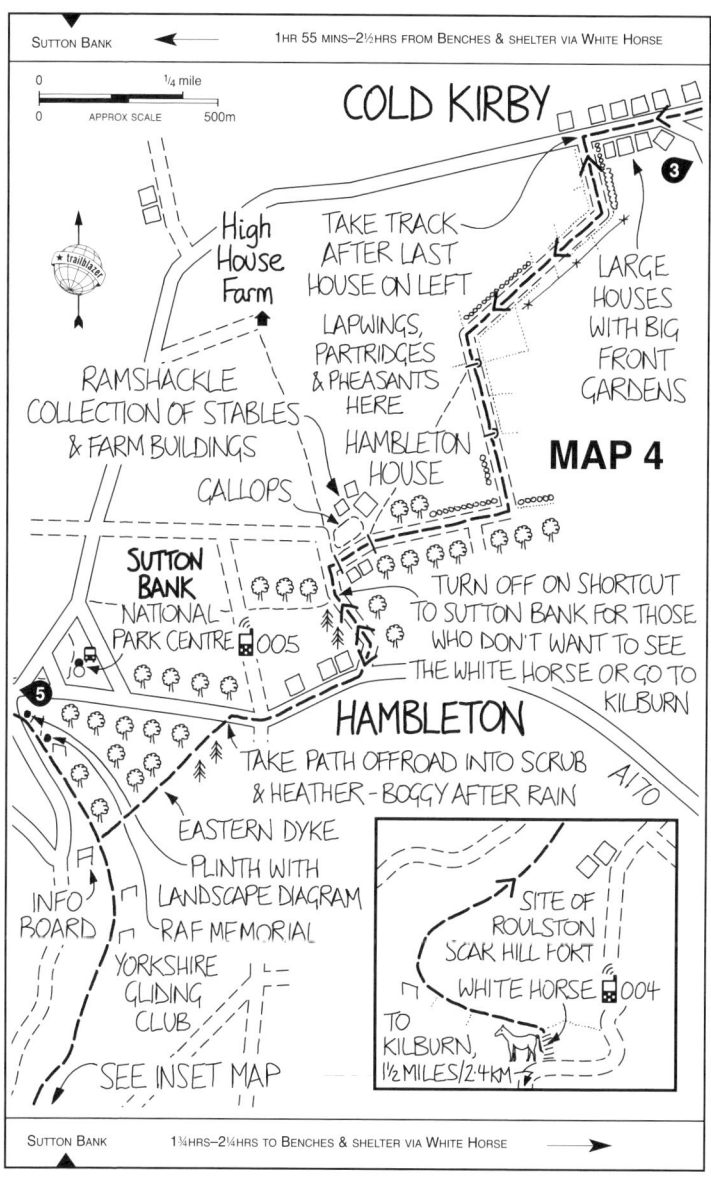

0 ¼ mile

0 APPROX SCALE 500m

★ traiblazer

COLD KIRBY

High House Farm

TAKE TRACK AFTER LAST HOUSE ON LEFT

❸

LARGE HOUSES WITH BIG FRONT GARDENS

RAMSHACKLE COLLECTION OF STABLES & FARM BUILDINGS

LAPWINGS, PARTRIDGES & PHEASANTS HERE

HAMBLETON HOUSE

MAP 4

GALLOPS

SUTTON BANK NATIONAL PARK CENTRE 005

TURN OFF ON SHORTCUT TO SUTTON BANK FOR THOSE WHO DON'T WANT TO SEE THE WHITE HORSE OR GO TO KILBURN

❺

HAMBLETON

A170

TAKE PATH OFFROAD INTO SCRUB & HEATHER – BOGGY AFTER RAIN

EASTERN DYKE

PLINTH WITH LANDSCAPE DIAGRAM

INFO BOARD

RAF MEMORIAL

YORKSHIRE GLIDING CLUB

SEE INSET MAP

SITE OF ROULSTON SCAR HILL FORT

WHITE HORSE 004

TO KILBURN, 1½ MILES/2.4KM

ROUTE GUIDE AND MAPS

is one of the biggest prehistoric forts found in England; it is believed the defensive ramparts would have enclosed the entire 53-acre (21-hectare) promontory and are estimated to have measured around 1.3 miles (2km) in length. With views to your right stretching across the Vale of York, it's clear why early Britons would have chosen this site.

KILBURN [off MAP 4, p87]

There's not much in the way of accommodation on Sutton Bank, but from the White Horse you can roll down the hill for about 1½ miles (2.4km) to Kilburn where three options await. The local inn, *The Forresters Arms* (☎ 01347-868386, ☐ for restersarms.com; 7D/1T/1Tr/1Qd, all en suite; ♥; WI-FI most rooms; ①; ⅋) is a handsome country pub with a lovely roaring fire going most of the time. Rates are from £45pp (sgl occ from £70). This is also the place to get **food** (Mon-Fri noon-3pm & 6-9pm, Sat noon-9pm, Sun noon-8pm).

Church Farm (☎ 01347-868318, ☐ churchfarmkilburn.co.uk; 1Tr en suite, 1Qd

private bathroom; ♥; WI-FI; ①; ⅋) stands only 100m from the pub. With services hard to come by on the trail, you may want to take advantage of their packed lunch (though you need to request one in advance). Rates are from £35pp (sgl occ from £40). A couple of hundred metres away is cute *Village Farm* (☎ 01347-868562, ☐ villagefarmkilburn.co.uk; 1Qd en suite, 1D private bathroom; ♥; WI-FI; ①); rates here are also start from £35pp (sgl occ from £40).

Kilburn is served by NYCC's No 59 **bus** (Friday only 2/day) between Thirsk and Coxwold; see box pp52-3 for details.

Having hit the horse, the trail then obliges walkers to retrace their steps back, nimbly tiptoeing along the edge of the escarpment to recross the A170 and arrive at **Sutton Bank National Park Centre**.

SUTTON BANK [MAP 4, p87]

It's probably no accident that the National Park chose to locate their **visitor centre** (☎ 01845-597426, ☐ northyorkmoors.org.uk/ suttonbank; Apr-Jul & Sep-Oct daily 10am-5pm, Aug 9.30am-5.30pm, Nov, Dec & mid Feb to end Mar daily 10.30am-4pm, Jan-mid Feb Sat & Sun 10.30-4pm) at Sutton Bank. After all, the view from here

is so breathtaking that at one time or another it caused artist JMW Turner to stop on his travels and sketch, and poet William Wordsworth to pause to sit and pen *'Composed After a Journey Across the Hambleton Hills, Yorkshire'*. The local author James Herriot summed it up neatly when he described the panorama from

---

> ### ❏ The dark skies of North York Moors
>
> The joys of the North York Moors National Park are not confined to ground level. The lack of towns and cities within its borders means that there is little light pollution and clear horizons, so allowing those who look skyward to see up to two thousand stars at any one time. Three places in particular have been designated as being of particular interest to stargazers: Danby, Dalby Forest and Sutton Bank. These have been given the title **Dark Sky Discovery Sites** (Milky Way class), so-called because you can see our own galaxy, the Milky Way, with the naked eye.
>
> The national park celebrates their 'dark skies' by organising a three-week festival in February/March including night zips, wildlife and ghost walks, starlight runs and bike rides as well as simple stargazing. Rievaulx Terrace, too, is another great place, and the National Trust sometimes offers night walks and other stargazing events.

Sutton Bank as 'the finest view in England'. It's certainly extensive: stand on the escarpment, with Gormire Lake glistening to your right and the rocks of Roulston Scar on your left with the conical mound of Hood Hill nearby, and you may just be able to make out the tower of York Minster over 20 miles away, and even the Pennines beyond; see also box opposite.

There is a *café* (open same times as the Visitor Centre) here; note that the toilets here are also only open when the centre is open. The nearest (B&B) **accommodation** is at High House Farm, back along the trail; see p84.

Moorsbus M4 & M5 **bus** services call here in front of the centre but the service is limited; see box pp52-3 for details.

SUTTON BANK TO OSMOTHERLEY   [MAPS 4-10]

This **11.6-mile/18.6km stage (3hrs 40mins to 4hrs 40mins)** second stage is a lovely and fairly untaxing hike with plenty of interest. It also provides Cleveland Way walkers with their first proper taste of moorland, so much of this day will be spent to the accompaniment of grouse bickering, panicking pheasants chuntering and lapwings making their usual whoops, squeaks and whistles.

The day begins by continuing northwards along the western edge of the North York Moors National Park, whose border is delineated, by and large, by the sheer escarpment on your left. Passing above **Gormire Lake** (Map 5), the path mooches above steep **Garbutt Woods** and then **South Woods** to a junction with the path to **Boltby**, about a mile away (1.6km) down the slope.

BOLTBY   [off MAP 5, p90]

There are a couple of B&Bs down in Boltby that could be useful if other places nearer the trail are full. *Willow Tree Cottage* (☎ 01845-537406, 🖳 willowtree cottageboltby.co.uk; 2Tr, both en suite; 🛏; WI-FI; ⓛ; 🐾 free but in studio room only) has a B&B room and a studio room over the garage which also boasts a kitchenette so guests can cook their own dinner; alternatively a simple dinner (pie, mashed potatoes with veg and apple crumble to follow is the example they gave us; £12.50) can be ordered in advance, or they'll drive you to the nearest pub, two miles away, so you can eat there. Rates are from £35pp in the Studio

(plus £10pp for breakfast; sgl occ room rate plus £10), from £40pp in the B&B including breakfast (sgl occ from £70).

Town Pasture Farm (☎ 01845-537298, 🖳 townpasturefarm.co.uk; 1Tr/1T, both en suite; 🛏; WI-FI; ⓛ; 🐾; May-Oct) is one mile from the path but they'll give you a lift back to it the next day. It's a working farm – indeed, author James Herriot (see pp45-6) used to be their vet – and their oak-beamed rooms boast lovely views over the surrounding farmland. B&B costs from £37.50pp (sgl occ from £50). The proprietor doesn't offer an evening meal but is happy to take guests to the local pub.

Just after the junction with the path to Boltby is the site of an old Iron Age **hill fort** – the second on the trail, of course (and you've barely even gone 10 miles since Helmsley!) though you'll need the eyes of an expert to discern which of the various bumps in the ground are actually part of it.   *(cont'd on p92)*

(cont'd on p92)

❑ **Important note – walking times**
Unless otherwise specified, **all times in this book refer only to the time spent walking**. You will need to add 20-30% to allow for rests, photography, checking the map, drinking water etc. When planning the day's hike count on 5-7 hours' actual walking.

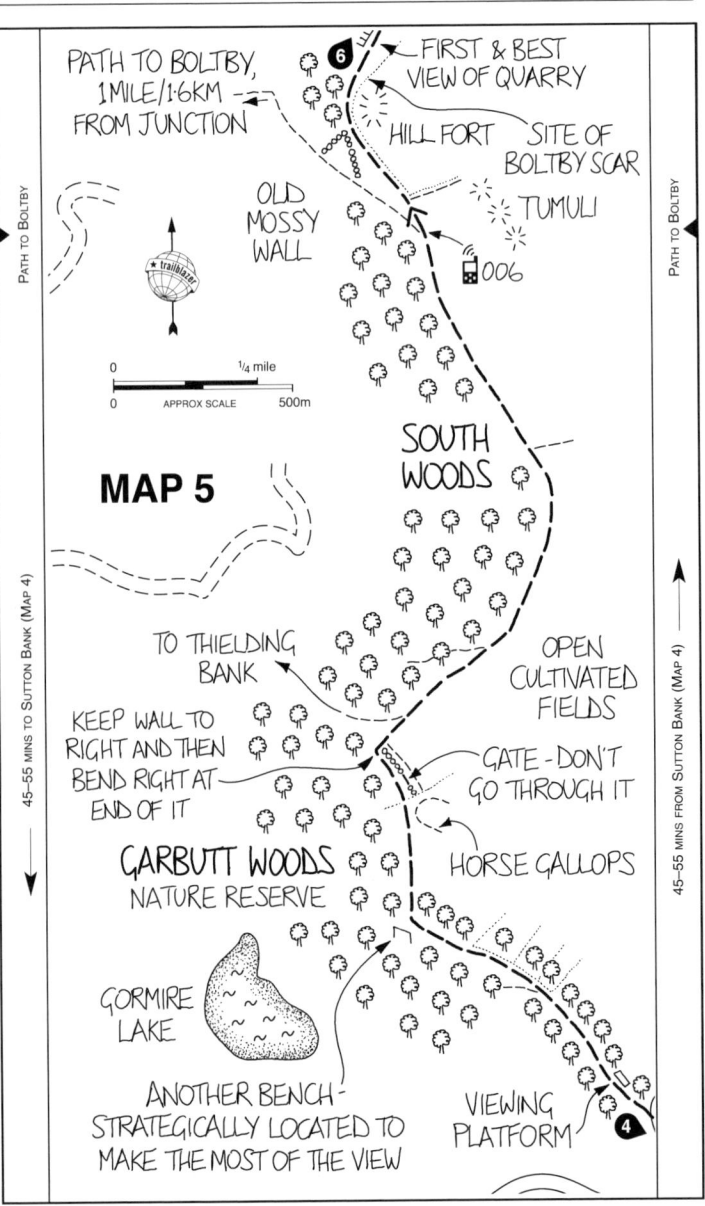

PATH TO BOLTBY, 1 MILE/1·6KM FROM JUNCTION

6

FIRST & BEST VIEW OF QUARRY

HILL FORT

SITE OF BOLTBY SCAR

TUMULI

006

PATH TO BOLTBY

OLD MOSSY WALL

trailblazer

0 — ¼ mile
0 — APPROX SCALE — 500m

MAP 5

SOUTH WOODS

PATH TO BOLTBY

45–55 MINS TO SUTTON BANK (MAP 4)

45–55 MINS FROM SUTTON BANK (MAP 4)

TO THIELDING BANK

KEEP WALL TO RIGHT AND THEN BEND RIGHT AT END OF IT

OPEN CULTIVATED FIELDS

GATE - DON'T GO THROUGH IT

GARBUTT WOODS NATURE RESERVE

HORSE GALLOPS

GORMIRE LAKE

ANOTHER BENCH - STRATEGICALLY LOCATED TO MAKE THE MOST OF THE VIEW

VIEWING PLATFORM

4

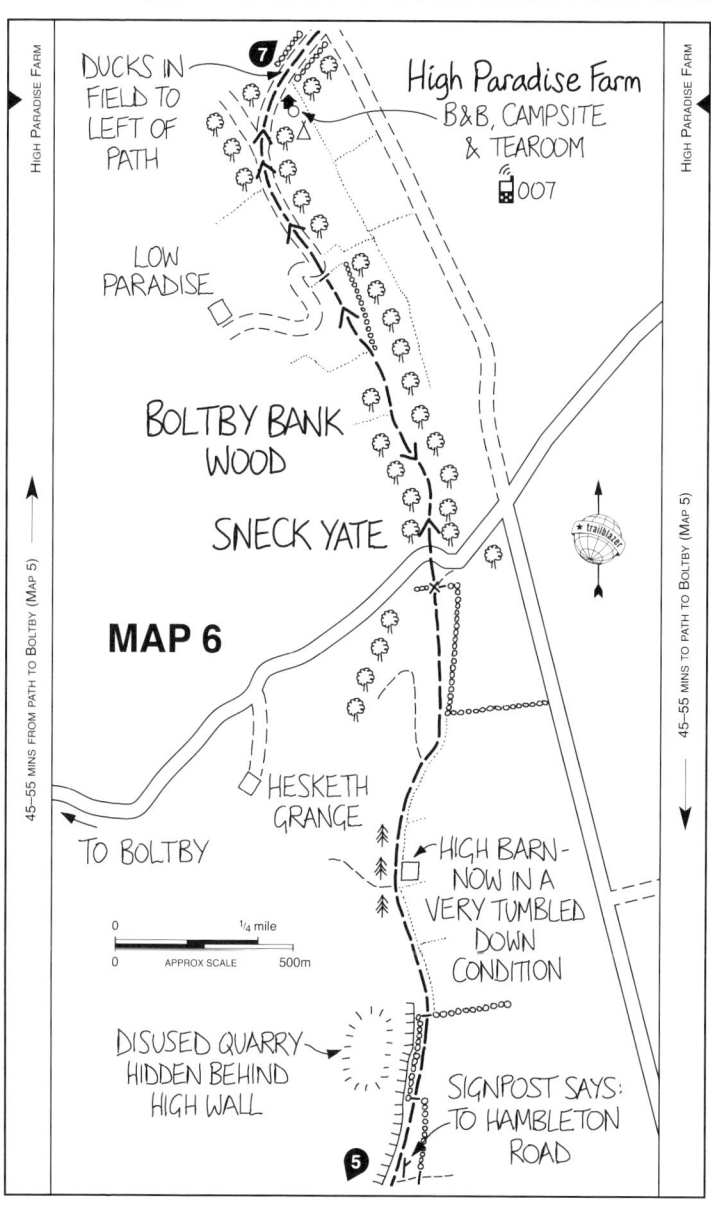

DUCKS IN
FIELD TO
LEFT OF
PATH

7

High Paradise Farm
B&B, CAMPSITE
& TEAROOM

📱007

LOW
PARADISE

BOLTBY BANK
WOOD

SNECK YATE

MAP 6

trailblazer

HESKETH
GRANGE

TO BOLTBY

HIGH BARN-
NOW IN A
VERY TUMBLED
DOWN
CONDITION

0   ¼ mile

0   APPROX SCALE   500m

DISUSED QUARRY
HIDDEN BEHIND
HIGH WALL

SIGNPOST SAYS:
TO HAMBLETON
ROAD

5

45–55 MINS FROM PATH TO BOLTBY (MAP 5)

45–55 MINS TO PATH TO BOLTBY (MAP 5)

ROUTE GUIDE AND MAPS

(cont'd from p89) From here you meander by an abandoned and lonely old **barn** (Map 6) to the hamlet of **Sneck Yate**. It's an unusual name and yet a typically Yorkshire one; the 'yate' (pronounced 'yat') means gate and the 'sneck' is a local term meaning latch.

Continuing on through the woods of **Boltby Bank**, it's not long before you find yourself in Paradise: boasting the ideal location – right on the trail and just over 14 miles (22.7km) from Helmsley, which many trekkers will consider a good distance for a first day's walk – ***High Paradise Farm*** (☎ 07739 498255, 💻 highparadise.co.uk) cleverly exploits its position by offering most things a walker would want, including both self-catering **rooms** (1D/1Tr/3Qd, all en suite; ▼; WI-FI; Ⓛ; 🐕; from £42.50pp, sgl occ from £70; breakfast available) and a basic **campsite** (£5pp; running water available and access to a toilet but little else; 🐕; generally Mar-Dec but weather dependent). They also offer evening meals (£8.50-20) for guests staying in the rooms – which, given that the nearest pub is four miles away, is a bit of a godsend. (Campers will either have to be self-sufficient, turn up before the tearoom closes, or contact the proprietor in advance to request something.) They also have an excellent ***tearoom*** (Mar-Sep Mon-Tue & Thur-Fri 10am-4pm, Sat & Sun to 5pm, Oct-Dec Sat & Sun only 11am-5pm, however the hours are variable depending on the weather and how busy they are).

Tearing yourself away from the scones of Paradise, within a few hundred metres the path joins the ancient track known as **Hambleton Street** or **Hambleton Road** (Map 7). In his 1771 book *Rural Economy of Yorkshire* Arthur Young describes this thoroughfare thus:

> *'You are obliged to cross the moors they call Black Hambleton, over which the road runs in narrow hollows that admit a south country chaise (Cart) with some difficulty, that I reckon this part of the journey made a hazard of my neck. The going down into Cleveland is beyond all description, terrible, you go through such steep, rough, narrow, rock precipices, that I would sincerely advise you to go a hundred miles to escape it.'*

Strange how, these days, Cleveland Way trekkers have often travelled hundreds of miles in order to walk *on* that very same drover's road rather than escape it! The road originally dates back to the Bronze Age, with much of the traffic down the centuries being Highland and Galloway cattle, having been driven down from Scotland on their way to the markets of Malton, York and Thirsk. Many drovers would have stopped off at the inn known as **Old Limekiln House**, which used to stand by the side of the track a little further along the trail, though little remains today save for a plaque that marks its location. The inn's name also hints at another industry that was popular hereabouts, and there are several old quarries nearby, with the limestone used in mortar and as agricultural lime as well as in drystone walls.

Dropping off this ancient track, the Way now descends steeply on slippery stones to **Oakdale Upper Reservoir** (Map 9), and from there skips merrily across road and bridge to the happy, attractive village of **Osmotherley**.

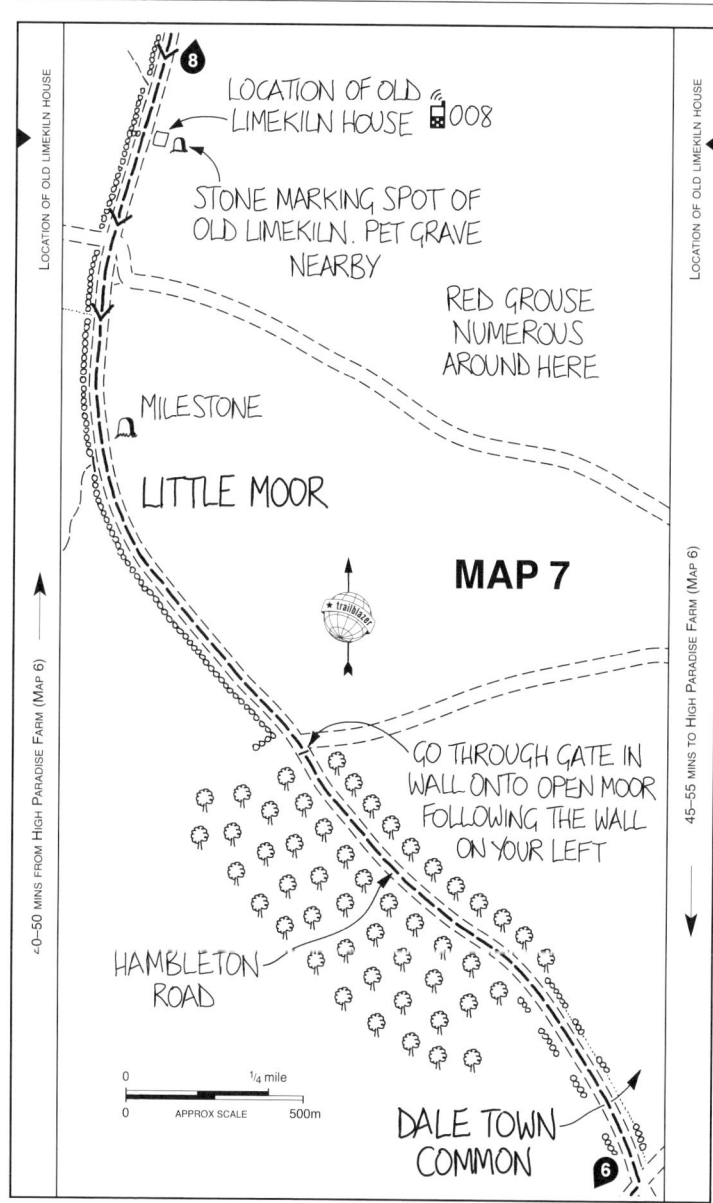

LOCATION OF OLD LIMEKILN HOUSE

LOCATION OF OLD LIMEKILN HOUSE

LOCATION OF OLD
LIMEKILN HOUSE 008

STONE MARKING SPOT OF
OLD LIMEKILN. PET GRAVE
NEARBY

RED GROUSE
NUMEROUS
AROUND HERE

MILESTONE

LITTLE MOOR

MAP 7

trailblazer

GO THROUGH GATE IN
WALL ONTO OPEN MOOR
FOLLOWING THE WALL
ON YOUR LEFT

HAMBLETON
ROAD

←0-50 MINS FROM HIGH PARADISE FARM (MAP 6)

45-55 MINS TO HIGH PARADISE FARM (MAP 6)

ROUTE GUIDE AND MAPS

0   ¼ mile

0   APPROX SCALE   500m

DALE TOWN
COMMON

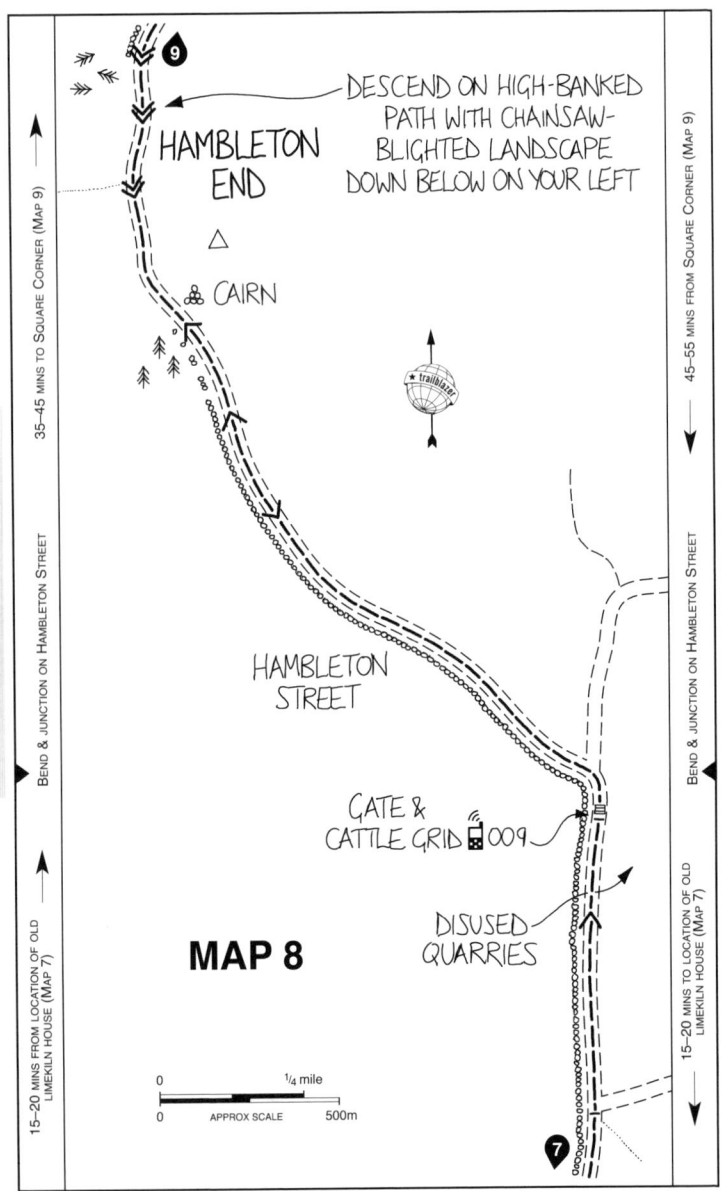

DESCEND ON HIGH-BANKED PATH WITH CHAINSAW-BLIGHTED LANDSCAPE DOWN BELOW ON YOUR LEFT

HAMBLETON END

△

♣ CAIRN

★ trailblazer

HAMBLETON STREET

GATE & CATTLE GRID 🔋009

DISUSED QUARRIES

MAP 8

0   ¼ mile

0   500m
APPROX SCALE

35–45 MINS TO SQUARE CORNER (MAP 9)

BEND & JUNCTION ON HAMBLETON STREET

15–20 MINS FROM LOCATION OF OLD LIMEKILN HOUSE (MAP 7)

ROUTE GUIDE AND MAPS

45–55 MINS FROM SQUARE CORNER (MAP 9)

BEND & JUNCTION ON HAMBLETON STREET

15–20 MINS TO LOCATION OF OLD LIMEKILN HOUSE (MAP 7)

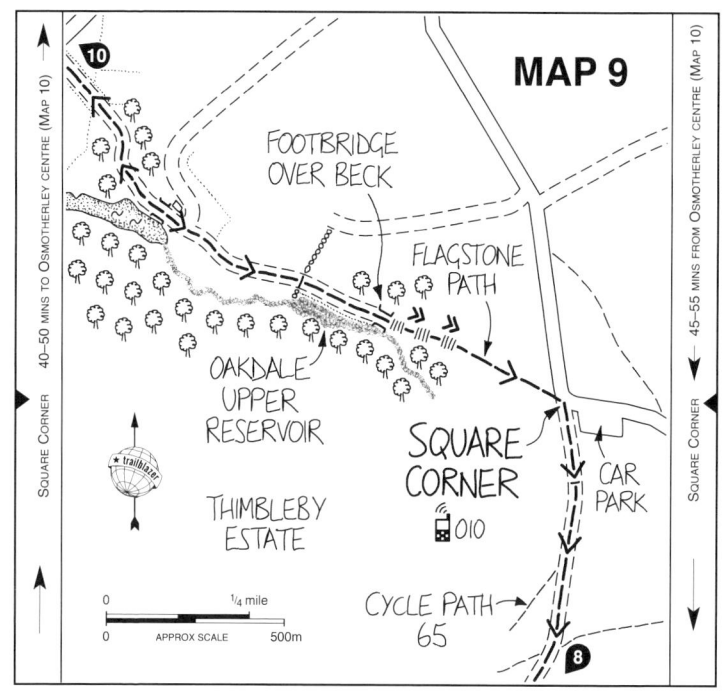

MAP 9

SQUARE CORNER (MAP 10) ← 40–50 MINS TO OSMOTHERLEY CENTRE (MAP 10)

45–55 MINS FROM OSMOTHERLEY CENTRE (MAP 10) → SQUARE CORNER

FOOTBRIDGE OVER BECK

FLAGSTONE PATH

OAKDALE UPPER RESERVOIR

★ trailblazer

THIMBLEBY ESTATE

SQUARE CORNER

☎ 010

CAR PARK

CYCLE PATH 65

0 — ¼ mile
APPROX SCALE
0 — 500m

ROUTE GUIDE AND MAPS

OSMOTHERLEY [map p96]

Osmotherley is a small, unassuming delight. There's not much to see here by way of tourist attractions, though there are a couple of minor diversions. In the centre stands a **market cross** and a **barter table**, believed to be the same one from which John Wesley preached. Indeed, in Chapel Yard you can find what's believed to be Britain's oldest practising **Methodist chapel**, constructed in 1754. There's also the church, **St Peter's**, built on Saxon foundations.

The most distinctive things about Osmotherley, however, are its beautiful, **stone terraced cottages**, built for the workers who laboured at the flax mill that now houses the hostel.

Services and transport

In the village there's an 'outreach' **post office** (Mon & Tue 9am-noon, Wed 1-4pm)

inside the village hall and the small **village store** (Mon-Sat 8.30am-5.30pm, Sun 9am-5pm) where they sell basic provisions and sandwiches.

Abbott's **bus** services (see box pp52-3) – called, variously, 80, 89 and X89 – call in at Osmotherley every day except Sunday.

Where to stay

Cote Ghyll Mill Caravan Park (☎ 01609 883425, 🖥 www.coteghyll.com; WI-FI; 🐕 on leads; Mar-end Oct) has **camping** for £9.50-11pp (inc use of toilet/shower facilities). As its name suggests, its main business is caravans and during the school holidays it can be crammed with sugar-high kids (so book in advance in summer), though they do have a few places to pitch a tent on the far side of the site. However, they now also have **hostel-type** accommodation (2-, 4- &

6-bed rooms; all en suite; WI-FI; Ⓛ); they charge from £26pp for a bed in a shared room, from £59 for two sharing a private room. There are kitchens for self-catering but meals can be provided at an additional charge.

A little further on from the campsite but part of the same complex, *YHA Osmotherley* (☎ 0345-260 2870, 🖳 yha.org .uk/hostel/yha-osmotherley; 4 x 2-, 6 x 4- & 4 x 6-bed rooms, all en suite; WI-FI; Ⓛ; Feb to end Oct) is housed in a converted linen mill and, rarely for a YHA, all rooms are en suite. Private rooms start from £51 for up to two sharing; otherwise, you can expect to pay around the £30pp mark for a bed in a dorm. Meals are available and there's a licensed bar too as well as laundry facilities and a drying room. Note that check in is from 5pm. It is possible to contact the hostel through Cote Ghyll's landline (see p95).

Simple, friendly accommodation can be found at *32 South End* (☎ 01609-883320, 🖳 diswales1@gmail.com; 1T, en suite; WI-FI) with B&B from £35pp (sgl occ from £40).

Of the **pubs**, *Queen Catherine Hotel* (☎ 01609-883209, 🖳 queencatherinehotel .co.uk; 1S/1D/2T, all en suite; WI-FI; Ⓛ; 🐾), 4 West End, charges from £42.50pp (sgl from £45, sgl occ rates on request) for B&B. The pub is actually named after Henry VIII's wife, Catherine of Aragon, who is believed to have sheltered with monks at nearby Mount Grace Priory. It is, surprisingly, the only pub in England named after her. Further up the hill a little way is charming *Vane House* (☎ 01609-883406, 🖳 vanehouse.co.uk; 3T/3D/1Qd, all en suite; ➳; WI-FI; Ⓛ; 🐾), 11A North End, with B&B from £50pp (sgl occ from £70).

The Three Tuns (☎ 01609-883301, 🖳 threetunsrestaurant.co.uk; 3D/1T, all en suite; ➳; 🐾) is a restaurant (see Where to

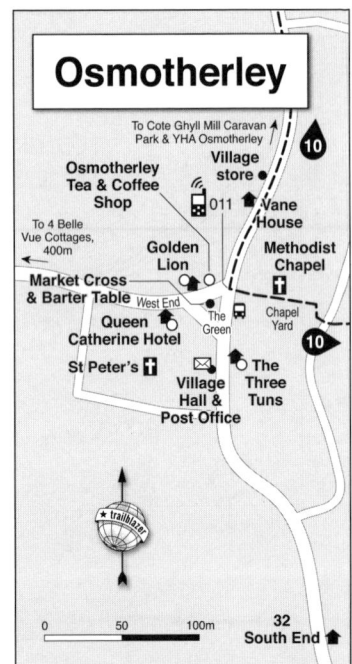

eat) that offers pleasant rooms. B&B starts at £50pp (sgl occ from £75).

The Golden Lion (☎ 01609-883526, 🖳 goldenlionosmotherley.co.uk; 5D or T/ 2D, all en suite; WI-FI; Ⓛ; 🐾) charges from £47.50pp (sgl occ from £75) for B&B.

Finally, there's also *4 Belle Vue Cottages* (☎ 01609-883435; 1S/1T shared bathroom; ➳; Ⓛ; Apr-Sep), which charges just £30pp (sgl occ from £30.

Where to eat and drink

We've had good reports about the food at *The Golden Lion* (see Where to stay; food

---

> ❏ **Where to stay: the details**
> In the descriptions of accommodation in this book: ➳ means at least one room has a bath; Ⓛ means a packed lunch can be prepared if arranged in advance; 🐾 signifies that dogs are welcome in at least one room but also subject to prior arrangement, an additional charge may also be payable; WI-FI means wi-fi is available. See also p76.

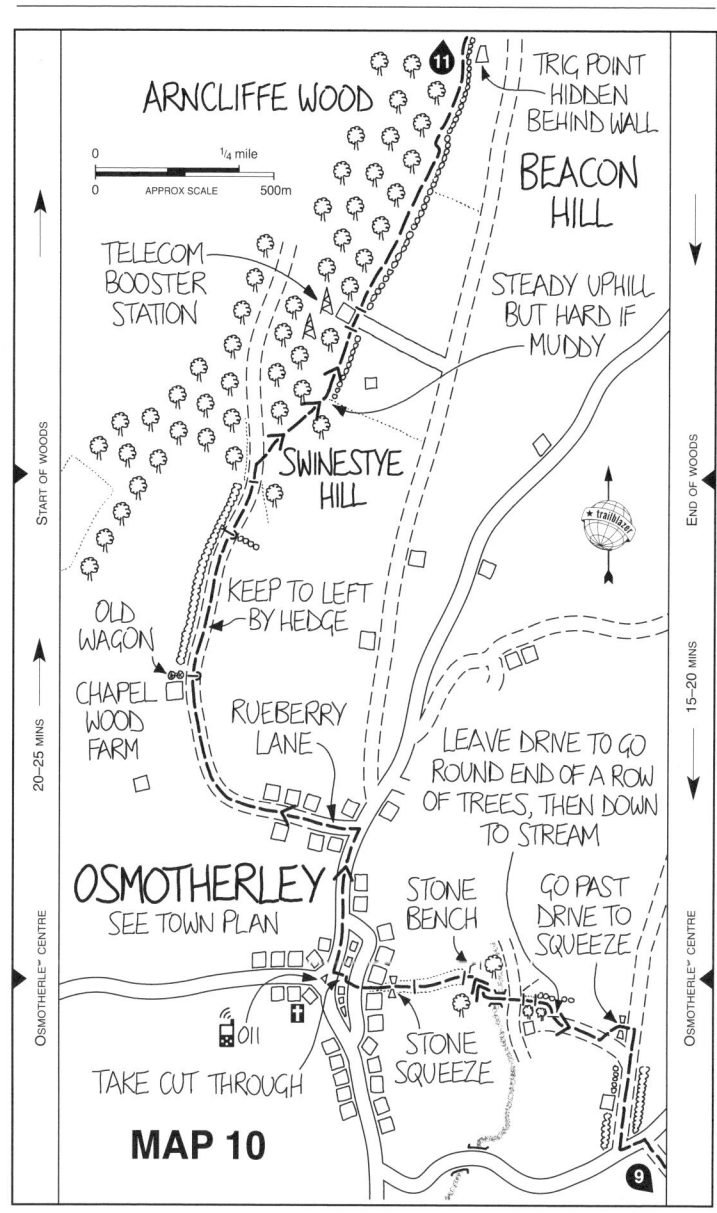

served Mon-Tue 6-9pm, Wed-Sun noon-2.30pm & 6-9pm). Mains start at £12.95; if it is on the menu look out for the spicy lentil chillada.

Queen Catherine Hotel (see Where to stay) has the most popular bar in town and serves up some great homemade meals (Mon-Sat noon-2.30pm & 6-9pm, Sun noon-4pm), with mains from £9.95 up to £17.95 for the 10oz sirloin.

The Three Tuns (see Where to stay; food served Mon-Sat noon-2.30pm & 5.30-9.30pm, Sun noon-6pm), opposite The Green, is a surprisingly smart establishment with starters from around £5.95 and mains from £10.50 for the braised rabbit short-crust pie.

For something lighter try *Osmotherley Tea & Coffee Shop* (☎ 01609-883419, 🖳 ossytc.co.uk; Easter-early Sep Wed-Sun 10am-4pm, Mon to 3pm, mid Feb-Easter & early Sep-Nov Fri-Sun 10am-4pm, Mon to 3pm; WI-FI; 🐾), a pleasant little café with a nice line in warm-filled rolls (£4.25-4.85) and toasties (£3.70-4.45).

OSMOTHERLEY TO CLAY BANK TOP   [MAPS 10-14]

In most people's eyes this **11.1-mile/17.9m stage (3hrs 40mins to 4hrs 40 mins)** is the most spectacular on the entire trail. Spectacular – but also strenuous. The climbing begins as soon as you leave Osmotherley as you follow the main road out of the village, taking a left at **Rueberry Lane** then crossing field and farm to **Arncliffe Wood**. It is here that you are joined by those trekkers on the Coast to Coast Path, who will have already walked almost 140 miles (225km) to get to this same point. You will share the path with them for the rest of this stage and much of the next too, finally leaving them at Bloworth Crossing – 17.6 miles (28.3km) from Osmotherley.

Climbing through the trees you pass a **telecom booster station** on your left and, in the fields on your right, a **trig point** marking the top of **Beacon Hill**. This trig point also marks the start of another long-distance path, the Lyke Wake Walk, a 40-mile tramp across the moors to Ravenscar (which you'll also be visiting on your trek); this is traditionally attempted in a single 24-hour period. Yours should be a more leisurely, sensible amble, however, as you now descend to **Scarth Nick** (Map 11) – another landmark along the old drover's road from Scotland – and on via woodland to the huddle of houses at **Huthwaite Green** (Map 12).

From here a chain of moors now follows, each separated from the next by often steep-sided valleys into which you must plummet before ascending on the opposite slopes to the next moor. The first encountered is **Live Moor**, reached after a fairly stiff climb but one that is rewarded by sumptuous views of the Cleveland Plain on your left-hand side. The path actually takes you through the site of an **iron-age promontory fort**, though there is little to see today and it's only really visible from aerial photographs.

The descent from Live Moor is, on this occasion, fairly shallow and it's not long before you're bouncing along neighbouring **Carlton Moor**, home to a glider runway and another **trig point** marking the moor's highest point (Map 13); keep to the edge of the escarpment up here and don't be tempted by any of the several paths heading off to the right. Descending from here you'll come to the road at **Carlton Bank** and, after that, the welcome sight of the *café* at **Lord Stones** (**Lordstones**; ☎ 01642-778482, 🖳 lordstones.com). *(cont'd on p102)*

ROUTE GUIDE AND MAPS

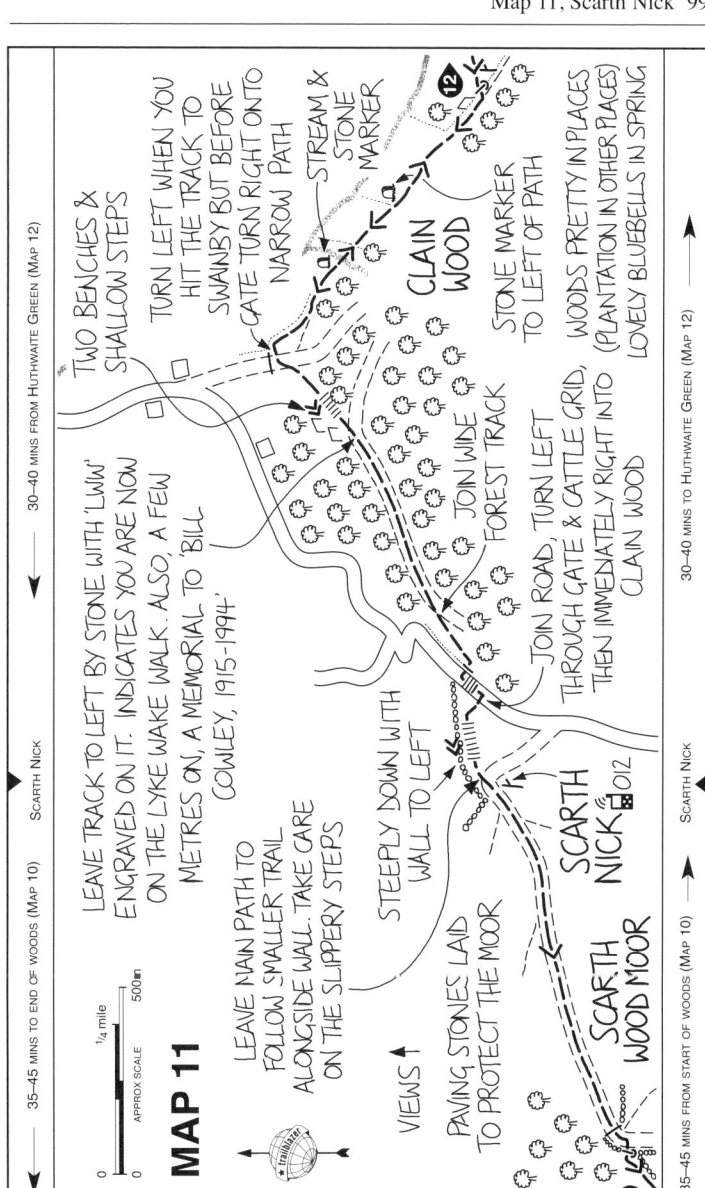

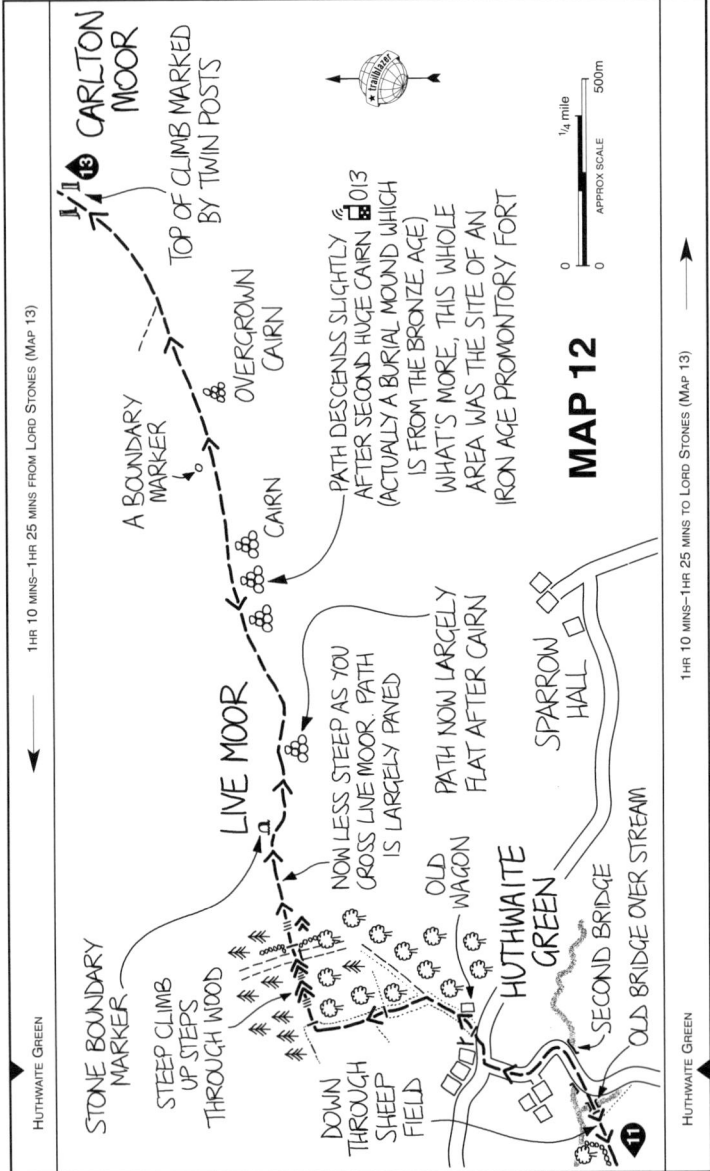

HUTHWAITE GREEN

1HR 10 MINS–1HR 25 MINS FROM LORD STONES (MAP 13)

CARLTON MOOR

13

TOP OF CLIMB MARKED BY TWIN POSTS

trailblazer

¼ mile

500m

0

0

APPROX SCALE

OVERGROWN CAIRN

A BOUNDARY MARKER

CAIRN

PATH DESCENDS SLIGHTLY AFTER SECOND HUGE CAIRN 013 (ACTUALLY A BURIAL MOUND WHICH IS FROM THE BRONZE AGE)

WHAT'S MORE, THIS WHOLE AREA WAS THE SITE OF AN IRON AGE PROMONTORY FORT

MAP 12

STONE BOUNDARY MARKER

STEEP CLIMB UP STEPS THROUGH WOOD

LIVE MOOR

NOW LESS STEEP AS YOU CROSS LIVE MOOR. PATH IS LARGELY PAVED

PATH NOW LARGELY FLAT AFTER CAIRN

OLD WAGON

DOWN THROUGH SHEEP FIELD

HUTHWAITE GREEN

SPARROW HALL

SECOND BRIDGE

OLD BRIDGE OVER STREAM

11

HUTHWAITE GREEN

1HR 10 MINS–1HR 25 MINS TO LORD STONES (MAP 13)

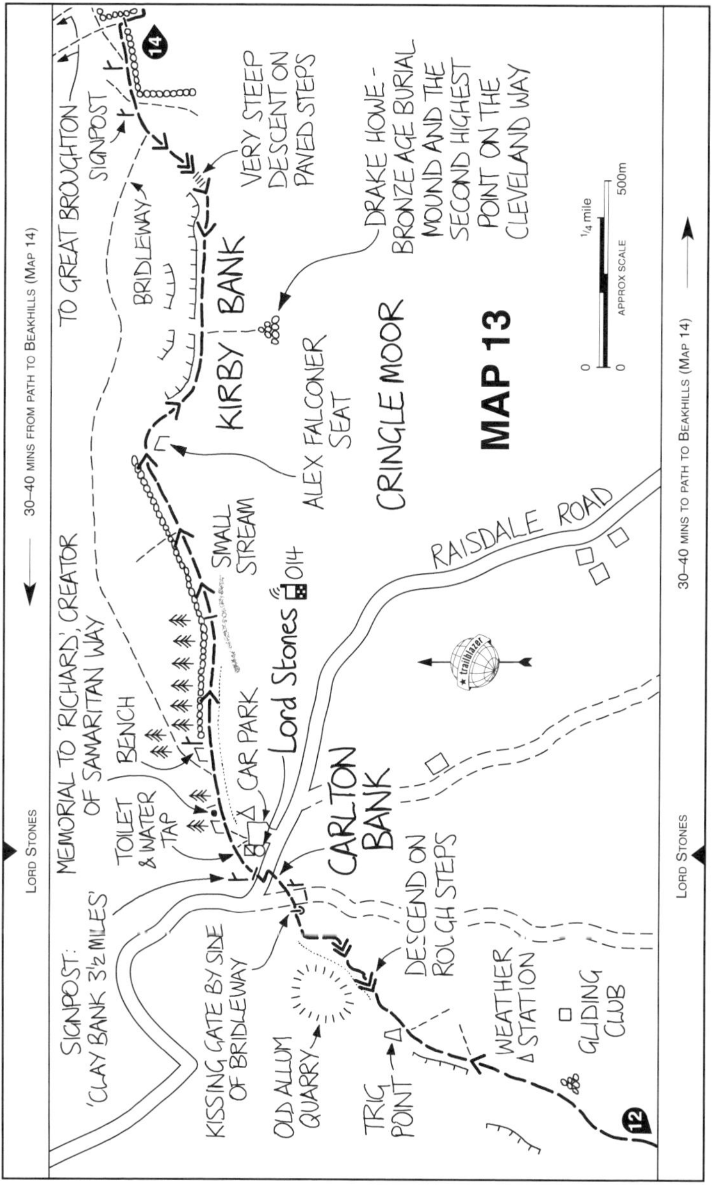

Map 13 (MAP 13) — Kirby Bank / Carlton Bank / Cringle Moor

- 30–40 MINS FROM PATH TO BEAKHILLS (MAP 14)
- TO GREAT BROUGHTON SIGNPOST
- VERY STEEP DESCENT ON PAVED STEPS
- BRIDLEWAY
- DRAKE HOWE – BRONZE AGE BURIAL MOUND AND THE SECOND HIGHEST POINT ON THE CLEVELAND WAY
- KIRBY BANK
- ALEX FALCONER SEAT
- CRINGLE MOOR
- SMALL STREAM
- Lord Stones
- MEMORIAL TO 'RICHARD', CREATOR OF SAMARITAN WAY
- BENCH
- TOILET & WATER TAP
- CAR PARK
- CARLTON BANK
- RAISDALE ROAD
- SIGNPOST: 'CLAY BANK 3½ MILES'
- KISSING GATE BY SIDE OF BRIDLEWAY
- OLD ALUM QUARRY
- TRIG POINT
- DESCEND ON ROUGH STEPS
- WEATHER STATION
- GLIDING CLUB
- LORD STONES
- 30–40 MINS TO PATH TO BEAKHILLS (MAP 14)

Scale: 0 – ¼ mile / 0 – 500m APPROX SCALE

(cont'd from p98) It's surprising to find such a 'complex' so far from any major settlement but they do provide pretty much everything a trekker could want including a **shop and *café*** (both open daily 9am-5pm; WI-FI), where you can get sandwiches (£4.75-9.50) and bigger meals such as steak & ale pie (£9.95). In the evening they open up as the ***Belted Bull*** restaurant (Thur-Sat 6-9pm), with beef from the nearby Belted Galloway herd their speciality (eg 10oz rump for £19). There's also a **campsite** here with ***glamping*** in **pods** which can sleep two adults and two children but would be cosy for four adults (open all year; around £75 per pod per night; 🐾), 4-person **bell tents** (Apr-Oct; £57.50 per tent per night) and 4-person **yurts** (Apr-Oct; £78 per yurt per night) – though note that there's a minimum two-night stay in the high season (May-Sep). Rates are based on two people sharing; each additional person is £7.50pp. There are also shower and toilet facilities. Note that bedding and towels are not provided but the former can be provided for an additional charge.

With even regular **camping** (Apr-Oct) set at £22.50 per tent, most walkers will probably be put off staying here but no matter, for one moor later and you come to a much cheaper option (though it must be said, much more basic too) at Beakhills Farm (see below). Don't be in too much of a hurry to get there, however, for standing between you and your destination is **Cringle Moor**. It's a bit of a tough schlep up to the moor – the hardest of the day, in fact – but once at the top there's the **Alex Falconer Seat** where you can rest your weary limbs and admire the view that takes in such features as Captain Cook's Monument, which is also on the trail, of course, though it's about 15 miles further along. Alex Falconer, incidentally, was a local rambler who campaigned for a long-distance trail to be established across the North York Moors, but sadly he died a year before his dream was realised and the Cleveland Way was opened.

A little further on is the Bronze Age burial mound of **Drake Howe** – at 432m (1427ft) the second highest point on the Cleveland Way.

As for ***Beakhills*** (off Map 14; ☎ 01642-778371, 🖳 cookiesbeakhills@bils dale.org; 1Tr/1Qd, shared facilities; 🐾; WI-FI; ⓛ; 🐾; end Mar-end Oct), this is another great working farm perfectly situated just a few minutes from the Cleveland Way on a part of the trail that isn't exactly over-supplied with accommodation options. They also cater for every sort of trekker, including **campers** (£4pp per night; 🐾; hot showers available) and those who want to stay **B&B**-style in simple but comfy rooms. You're welcomed as part of the family, wet clothes are dried, tea and biscuits proffered and even the wi-fi signal is strong. They also offer an evening meal – pretty much essential in this remote part of the trail – at just £10 for two courses; campers can have breakfast (£6) if requested in advance but not an evening meal. Given that B&B costs just £30pp even if you're staying alone in the room, this is one of the best-value places on the route. One note of warning, however: the farm is also convenient for Coast to Coast walkers so if you know when you want to stay here do book well in advance.

To continue to Clay Bank Top, you'll need to carry on heading east over the next moor in the series – **Cold Moor**. On the way up look to your right and you should be able to make out the entrance to an old **jet mine**, which may provide

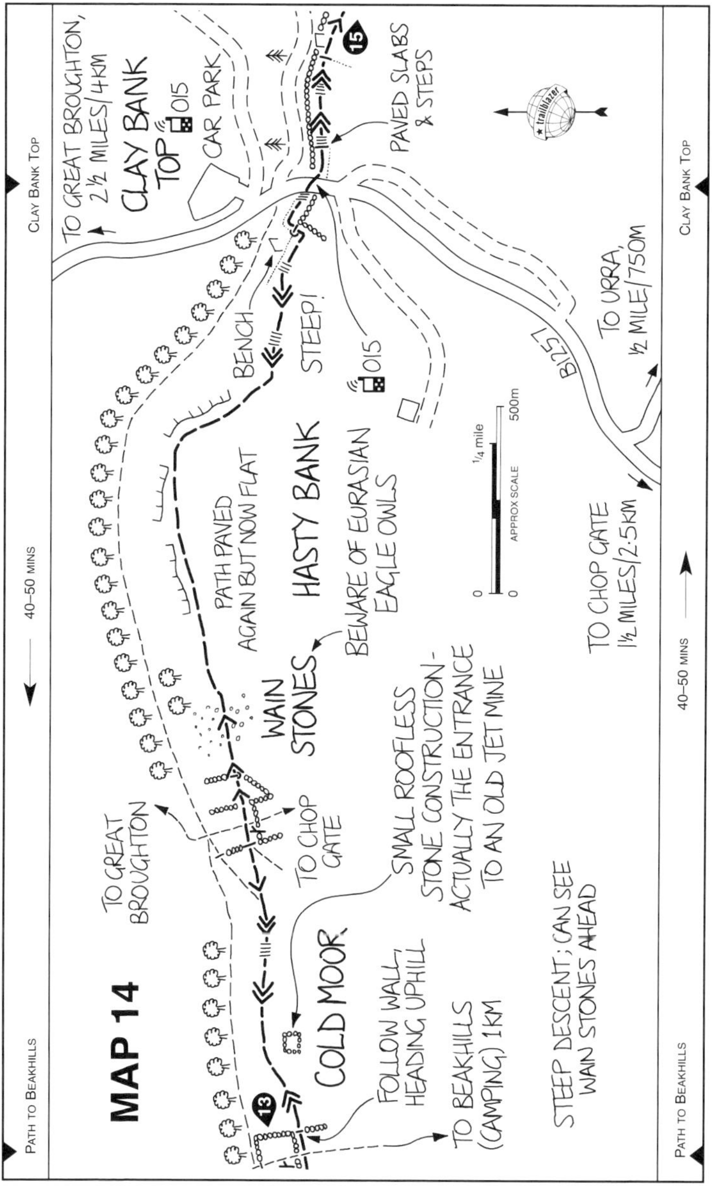

MAP 14

Labels on map:
- PATH TO BEAKHILLS — 40-50 MINS — CLAY BANK TOP
- TO GREAT BROUGHTON, 2½ MILES/4KM
- CLAY BANK TOP ♿ 015
- CAR PARK
- PAVED SLABS & STEPS
- trailblazer (compass)
- BENCH
- STEEP!
- 015
- PATH PAVED AGAIN BUT NOW FLAT
- HASTY BANK
- BEWARE OF EURASIAN EAGLE OWLS
- WAIN STONES
- SMALL ROOFLESS STONE CONSTRUCTION - ACTUALLY THE ENTRANCE TO AN OLD JET MINE
- TO CHOP GATE
- COLD MOOR
- FOLLOW WALL HEADING UPHILL
- TO GREAT BROUGHTON
- TO BEAKHILLS (CAMPING) 1KM
- STEEP DESCENT; CAN SEE WAIN STONES AHEAD
- TO CHOP GATE 1½ MILES/2.5KM
- TO URRA, ½ MILE/750M
- B1257
- APPROX SCALE — ¼ mile — 500m — 0

ROUTE GUIDE AND MAPS

limited shelter if the weather is appalling. Those yearning for a return to civilisation can take the left-hand path that follows the steep descent from Cold Moor, a trail that will take them to **Great Broughton** (see opposite).

Back on the trail, further adventures await as the rocky outcrops and boulders known as **Wain Stones** beckon you ever onwards. For the past year or so the Stones have become best known as a possible nesting site of a rare visitor to these shores: the Eurasian eagle-owl . Though it may have moved on by the time you read this, should it still be in the vicinity, walkers – particularly those with dogs – are advised to leave it well alone and move on as swiftly as possible. The owl is very territorial and not afraid to attack those who get too close – and remember, these birds have a wingspan of approximately two metres and prey on mammals the size of hares and even young deer!

Successfully negotiate this most surprising of hazards and it won't be long before you're dropping off the plateau of **Hasty Bank** and down to the road at **Clay Bank Top**, and, hopefully, a rendezvous with a lift to one of the nearby villages as there is no accommodation at Clay Bank Top itself. However, the B&Bs in Urra & Chop Gate (see below) and Great Broughton (see opposite) earn a decent living by providing accommodation to the walkers on the Cleveland Way and Coast to Coast. Most offer a lift from Clay Bank Top to their B&B and back again the next morning – which, if not essential, is certainly most welcome given how much walking you've probably already done today.

URRA & CHOP GATE
[off MAP 14, p103]

The nearest place to Clay Bank Top is **Urra**, a mile to the south. David, from Australia, and Claire have taken over the long-standing *Maltkiln House* (☎ 01642-778216, 🖥 maltkilnhouse.co.uk; 1D/2Qd, all en suite; ☛; WI-FI; Ⓛ; 🐾) and upgraded the large bedrooms. Charging from £35pp (sgl occ from £60), they also provide dinner at £15pp for two courses and a drink, and offer complimentary lifts from and to Clay Bank. One of the quad rooms is in a self-contained annex and has a kitchen.

They also have a barn which they are converting to a *bunk barn*; it will sleep up to 20 (£20pp) and has shower/toilet facilities and a rustic kitchen. Sheets can be provided but a sleeping bag will be necessary. There is also space for people to *camp* (£5 per pitch for up to two people). If arranged in advance meals are available in the house (and packed lunches to take away).

A mile and a half or so further south is **Chop Gate**. The local pub, *The Buck Inn* (☎ 01642-778334, 🖥 the-buck-inn.co.uk; 5D or T/1Qd, all en suite, 'garden houses'

2T shared facilities; WI-FI main building; Ⓛ; 🐾) hoovers up much of the available custom thanks to some decent rooms and a reputation for good – and fairly imaginative – **food** (Mon-Thur 5-9pm, Wed-Sun noon-9pm, winter hours more limited) including a large selection of German dishes (the landlord is from Heidelberg). Rates are £32.50-43pp (sgl occ £45-70). They also have **camping** at £8.50 per tent (up to three people) and a **pick-up service** from Clay Bank Top (between 3.30pm and 5.30pm), taking everyone back the next morning.

Near the pub is the very hospitable *Forge House* (☎ 01642-778166, 🖥 coast2 coast.co.uk/forgehouse; 2S/1T/1D, shared bathroom; ☛; WI-FI; Ⓛ; 🐾; Apr-Oct).

> ❏ **Be prepared**
> The B&Bs at Urra, Chop Gate and Great Broughton offer a **packed lunch** if arranged in advance – this is a vital service as you have a fair way to go before Kildale (see p109).

B&B costs from £35pp (sgl/sgl occ from £40). Their sandwiches were voted by one of the blogs as the best on the path and indeed a couple of readers have written in to praise the helpfulness of the owners. Chop Gate is a stop on Moorsbus limited M4 **bus** service (see box pp52-3).

GREAT BROUGHTON
[off MAP 14, p103]

Great Broughton lies in the other direction, 2½ miles to the north of Clay Bank Top. It is also a stop on the M4 **bus** (see above).

For **campers** *Jet Miners Inn Caravan and Camping* (☎ 07810-118590; 🐾 on lead) has a few pitches for £5pp; it is adjacent to – but run independently from – the inn of the same name (**food** daily noon-2pm & 5.30-9pm; mains from £10.50).

The walker-friendly *Bay Horse* (☎ 01642-712319, 🖳 thebayhorse-greatbroughton.co.uk; WI-FI; **food** Mon-Fri noon-2pm & 6-9.30pm, Sat noon-9.30pm, Sun noon-4.30pm & 5-9pm) offers sandwiches and snacks as well as a full evening menu and Sunday roasts (£14.95/17.95 for two/three courses).

Most **B&Bs** here also offer lifts from/ to Clay Bank Top including *Newlands House* (☎ 01642-712619, 🖳 newlands house.co.uk; 1D/2T, all en suite; 🐾; WI-FI; Ⓛ) at 7 Ingleby Rd. B&B starts at £40pp (sgl occ from £55).

The Wainstones Hotel (☎ 01642-712268, 🖳 wainstoneshotel.co.uk; 3S/14D/7T, all en suite; 🐾; WI-FI; Ⓛ) is more upmarket: **B&B** rates vary from day to day but are about £39.50-44.50pp (sgl/sgl occ from £59/79). **Food** is served daily in both their *Pembroke* bar (Mon-Sat noon-2pm & 5-10pm, Sun noon-9pm) and *Endeavours* restaurant (Mon-Sat 7-9.30pm, Sun noon-2.30pm), the two sharing the same menu (mains £10.50-17.95 but from £7.95 between 5pm and 7pm).

CLAY BANK TOP TO KILDALE
[MAPS 14-19]

This **9.1-mile/14.6km stage (2hrs 35mins to 3hrs 20 mins)** is one of the shortest and easiest on the trail, a mostly level tramp that comes as something of a relief after the rigours of yesterday. Be warned, however, that there is no place to get anything to eat on the way to Kildale. Once there you can get food at Glebe Cottage Café (see p109) if it is open, but the only place after that is either off the trail at Newton-under-Roseberry, or on the trail at Slapewath – just under 20 miles away. There is little in the way of shelter, too, should the weather on these heights suddenly turn wet and wuthering, as Emily Brontë might say; just come prepared with a packed lunch and waterproofs and you should be OK.

The trail begins, however, in a similar vein to much of the previous stage's, with a breathless climb, this time up the slopes to **Carr Ridge** (Map 15). Look back on your way up and you'll see all the moors of yesterday – Cold, Cringle, Carlton and Live – lined up as if forming a guard of honour for your ascent. At the top is **Urra Moor**. The walking is flat for the next few miles and it's possible to build up quite a speed. Don't be in too much of a hurry, however, or you'll miss some of this stage's most important features, including, perhaps most significantly, a **trig point** on Round Hill that stands on another Bronze Age burial mound and which marks not only the highest point of the moor but also, at 454m/1489ft, the **highest point on the Cleveland Way**. Nearby is one of several stone boundary markers, this one known as the **Hand Stone** for, carved upon it, you may just be able to distinguish two palms and the words Stoxla (for Stokesley) and Kirby (for Kirbymoorside).

More impressive, perhaps, is the carving on the next stone which bears a human face on its eastern side (Map 16).

A little more easy walking will bring you to the former railway junction known as **Bloworth Crossing**, where the old Rosedale Ironstone Railway meets the Rudland Rigg Road. It is also here that you bid a fond farewell to those Coast to Coast Path interlopers with whom you've been sharing the trail; they'll be taking a much more direct route eastwards to the coast while you'll be meandering northwards now, sharing a path instead with cyclists, horse-riders and dirt bikes who are all allowed to use this sandy track.

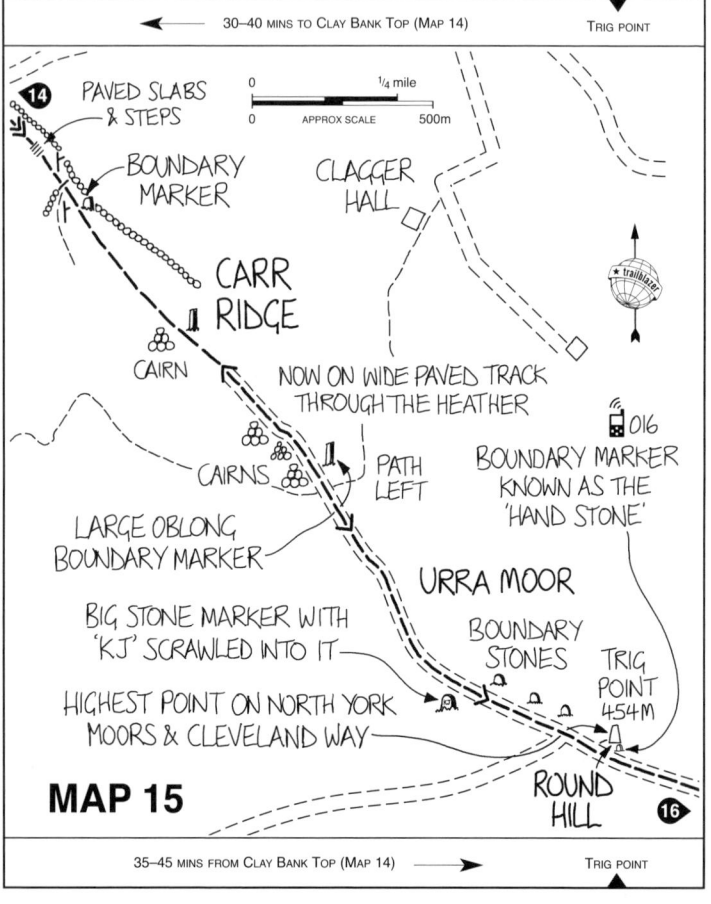

- 30–40 MINS TO CLAY BANK TOP (MAP 14)
- TRIG POINT
- 14 PAVED SLABS & STEPS
- ¼ mile
- APPROX SCALE 500m
- BOUNDARY MARKER
- CLAGGER HALL
- trailblazer
- CARR RIDGE
- CAIRN
- NOW ON WIDE PAVED TRACK THROUGH THE HEATHER
- 016
- CAIRNS
- PATH LEFT
- BOUNDARY MARKER KNOWN AS THE 'HAND STONE'
- LARGE OBLONG BOUNDARY MARKER
- URRA MOOR
- BIG STONE MARKER WITH 'KJ' SCRAWLED INTO IT
- BOUNDARY STONES
- TRIG POINT 454M
- HIGHEST POINT ON NORTH YORK MOORS & CLEVELAND WAY
- **MAP 15**
- ROUND HILL
- 16
- 35–45 MINS FROM CLAY BANK TOP (MAP 14)
- TRIG POINT

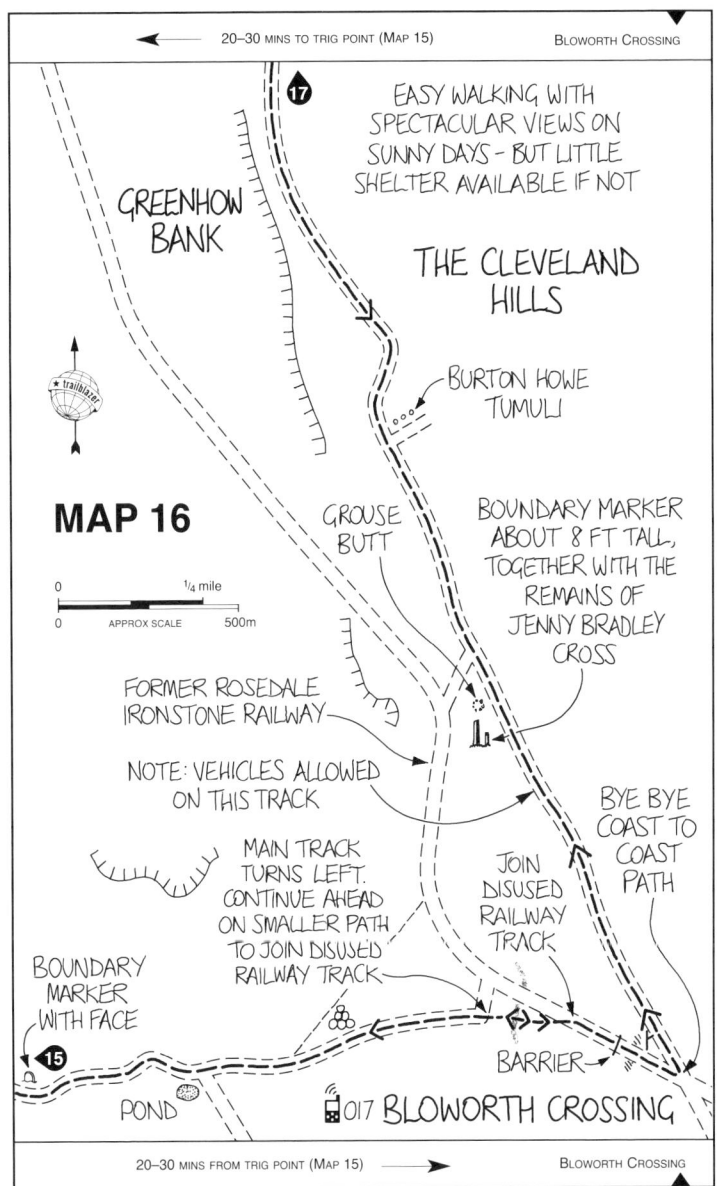

17

EASY WALKING WITH
SPECTACULAR VIEWS ON
SUNNY DAYS – BUT LITTLE
SHELTER AVAILABLE IF NOT

GREENHOW
BANK

THE CLEVELAND
HILLS

★ trailblazer

BURTON HOWE
TUMULI

MAP 16

GROUSE
BUTT

BOUNDARY MARKER
ABOUT 8 FT TALL,
TOGETHER WITH THE
REMAINS OF
JENNY BRADLEY
CROSS

0   ¼ mile

0   APPROX SCALE   500m

FORMER ROSEDALE
IRONSTONE RAILWAY

NOTE: VEHICLES ALLOWED
ON THIS TRACK

BYE BYE
COAST TO
COAST
PATH

MAIN TRACK
TURNS LEFT.
CONTINUE AHEAD
ON SMALLER PATH
TO JOIN DISUSED
RAILWAY TRACK

JOIN
DISUSED
RAILWAY
TRACK

BOUNDARY
MARKER
WITH FACE

15

BARRIER

POND

📱017 BLOWORTH CROSSING

ROUTE GUIDE AND MAPS

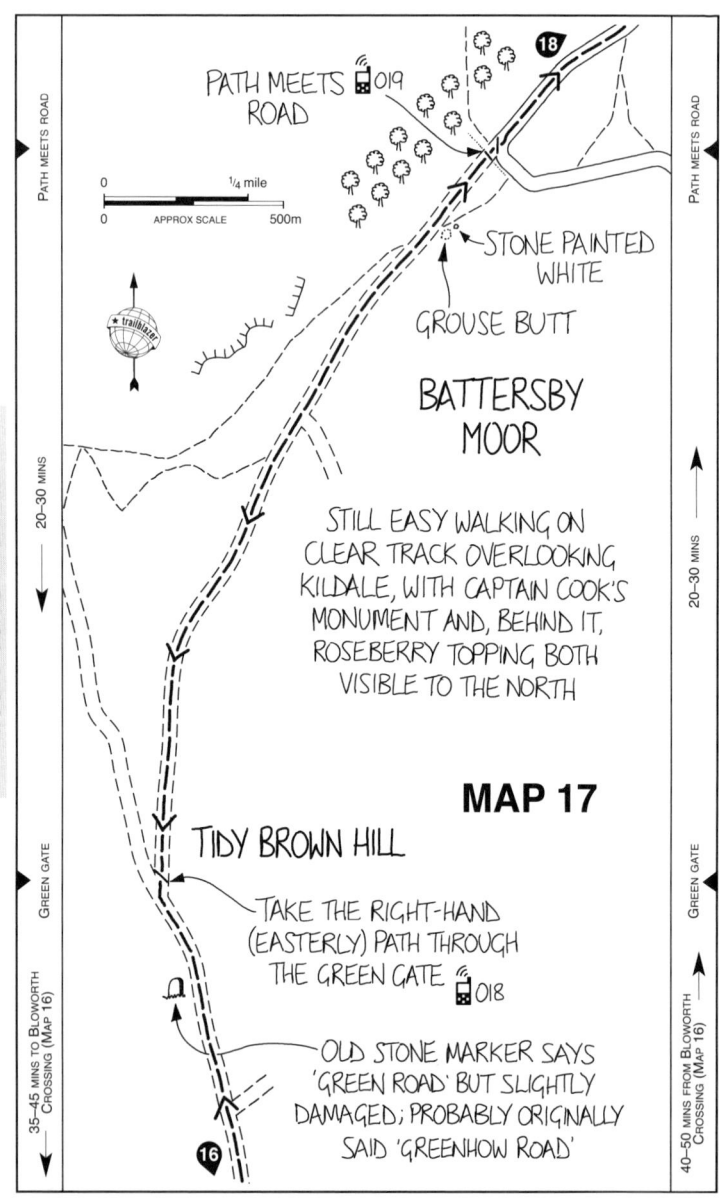

PATH MEETS ROAD

PATH MEETS 📱019 ROAD

18

STONE PAINTED WHITE

GROUSE BUTT

BATTERSBY MOOR

0   ¼ mile
0   APPROX SCALE   500m

★ trailblazer

PATH MEETS ROAD

20–30 MINS

STILL EASY WALKING ON CLEAR TRACK OVERLOOKING KILDALE, WITH CAPTAIN COOK'S MONUMENT AND, BEHIND IT, ROSEBERRY TOPPING BOTH VISIBLE TO THE NORTH

MAP 17

20–30 MINS

TIDY BROWN HILL

TAKE THE RIGHT-HAND (EASTERLY) PATH THROUGH THE GREEN GATE 📱018

OLD STONE MARKER SAYS 'GREEN ROAD' BUT SLIGHTLY DAMAGED; PROBABLY ORIGINALLY SAID 'GREENHOW ROAD'

16

GREEN GATE

35–45 MINS TO BLOWORTH CROSSING (MAP 16)

GREEN GATE

40–50 MINS FROM BLOWORTH CROSSING (MAP 16)

ROUTE GUIDE AND MAPS

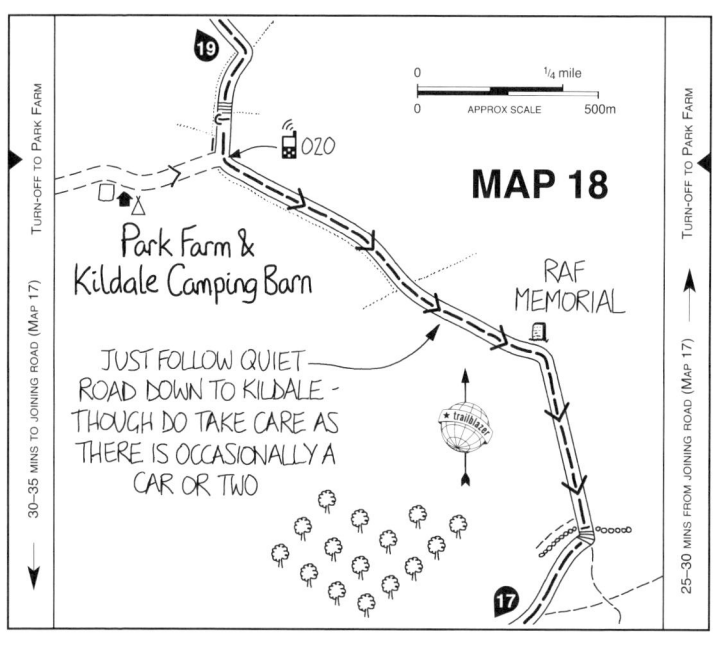

MAP 18

Park Farm &
Kildale Camping Barn

JUST FOLLOW QUIET
ROAD DOWN TO KILDALE -
THOUGH DO TAKE CARE AS
THERE IS OCCASIONALLY A
CAR OR TWO

RAF
MEMORIAL

O2O

30-35 MINS TO JOINING ROAD (MAP 17)

25-30 MINS FROM JOINING ROAD (MAP 17)

ROUTE GUIDE AND MAPS

Along the way you'll pass a tall **stone boundary marker** with the dates 1838 and 1768 etched upon it together with the initials of the landowners who agreed to the position of the boundary; and, next to it, the shaft of a small way-marker that once stood here, known as **Jenny Bradley Cross**. Further along are the Bronze Age Burton Howe burial sites.

Veering right at **Tidy Brown Hill** (Map 17; the name is believed to be a corruption of 'tiddy' meaning small or tiddly), the path soon joins a quiet, steep road that leads you down off the moors, past the turning to Park Farm (see p110), and into the tranquil village of **Kildale**.

KILDALE   [MAP 19, p111]

Kildale is a small but lovely little village. It plays host to the only eatery between the café at Lord Stones (Carlton Bank) and the Fox & Hounds at Slapewath – a distance of almost 23 miles. As such, it performs an absolutely essential role on the Cleveland Way, particularly as the stage to Slapewath is steep and exposed in places and not one to be tackled on an empty stomach.

At the time of writing **_Glebe Cottage Café Tearoom_** (☎ 01642-722774, ▱ face book.com/glebecottagecafe;   Fri-Wed

9.30am-4.30pm, winter hours may vary; WI-FI; 🐾) had just been taken over by the son of the previous owners. The menu includes scones (£2.50 for one with fruit jam & clotted cream, £2.10 for a cheese scone) and big buns 'fadgie style' (£4.50-5.50 depending on the filling; a fadgie is a type of bread roll that is traditional in Teeside. The café is licensed and serves a variety of alcoholic drinks but, if you prefer, a Yorkshire tea costs £1.80. If, incidentally, you do arrive hungry at the village on a day when Glebe

Cottage is closed, the nearest refreshments to be had near the route will be at Newton-under-Roseberry (see opposite).

You can also stay in Kildale – one field away from the trail, *Park Farm and Kildale Camping Barn* (Map 18; ☎ 01642-722847, 🖳 kildalebarn.co.uk; 🐾 on leads) is a convenient and lovely little **campsite** (£8pp) with both a **camping barn** (£10pp; sleeps up to 12), with mod cons including fridge/freezer, hot-water heater, pots and pans, and a more comfortable 'camping byre' (£12pp) with proper beds sleeping up to five people and equipped with oven, microwave, fridge, toaster and kettle. Just remember to bring something to cook!

Booking is preferred. Park Farm is about a mile from Kildale station either across the fields or along the road.

As for **B&Bs**, *The Old Rectory* (☎ 01642-723993, 🖳 theoldrectorykildale.co .uk; 1D/1T, both en suite; WI-FI; Apr-end Oct) is many people's favourite place on the trail. Dating back to the 17th century, the house nevertheless has all the modern facilities with flat-screen TVs in every room. The rate (from £40pp, sgl occ from £60) includes a lift down to the pub for dinner.

The **railway station** at Kildale lies on the Esk Valley Railway (🖳 eskvalleyrail way.co.uk) line, though services are operated by Northern; see box p49 for details.

KILDALE TO SALTBURN-BY-THE-SEA   [MAPS 19-25]

This **14.9-mile/24km trek** (**5hrs 25mins to 6hrs 50mins**) is something of a 'transition stage' as you say a final goodbye to the heather-and-bilberry-covered moors. From now on it's the North Sea which will be providing the backdrop to your walk. However, the moors don't leave you without first providing a couple of memorable landmarks as a parting gift. The first is the 18m (60ft) **Monument to Captain Cook** (Map 20; see also box p130) atop **Easby Moor**, reached about three-quarters of an hour after leaving Kildale on a stiff climb. The monument was erected in 1827 by a banker, Robert Campion, from Whitby and paid for out of his own pocket. The inscription on it has largely worn away but should read as follows:

In memory of the celebrated circumnavigator Captain James Cook F.R.S. A man of nautical knowledge inferior to none, in zeal prudence and energy, superior to most. Regardless of danger he opened an intercourse with the Friendly Isles and other parts of the Southern Hemisphere. He was born at Marton Oct. 27th 1728 and massacred at Owythee Feb. 14th 1779 to the inexpressible grief of his countrymen. While the art of navigation shall be cultivated among men, whilst the spirit of enterprise, commerce and philanthropy shall animate the sons of Britain, while it shall be deemed the honour of a Christian Nation to spread civilisation and the blessings of the Christian faith among pagan and savage tribes, so long will the name of Captain Cook stand out amongst the most celebrated and most admired benefactors of the human race.

Make sure you choose the right path from the Monument (there are many to choose from though the correct one is signposted). Having dipped down to the car park at **Gribdale Gate**, you'll soon find yourself heading upwards again over **Ayton Moor** towards **Roseberry Topping**, which is reached via another rather forbidding descent followed, in short order, by an equally severe climb. Take your time at the summit – you've expended a lot of energy to get here, after all – and appreciate the views west over the Cleveland Plain and east to the sea, which, weather willing, is now clearly visible beyond the town of

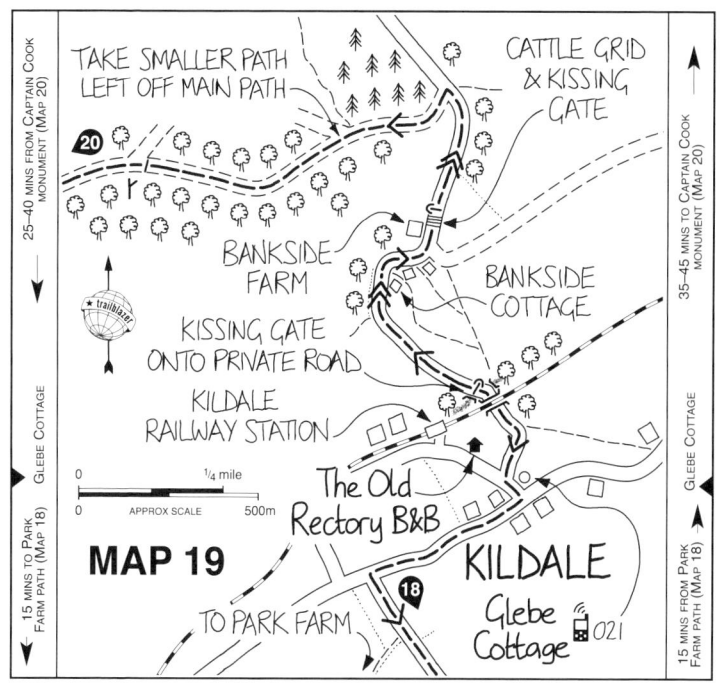

TAKE SMALLER PATH LEFT OFF MAIN PATH

CATTLE GRID & KISSING GATE

25-40 MINS FROM CAPTAIN COOK MONUMENT (MAP 20)

20

BANKSIDE FARM

BANKSIDE COTTAGE

35-45 MINS TO CAPTAIN COOK MONUMENT (MAP 20)

trailblazer

KISSING GATE ONTO PRIVATE ROAD

KILDALE RAILWAY STATION

GLEBE COTTAGE

15 MINS TO PARK FARM PATH (MAP 18)

0 ¼ mile
0 APPROX SCALE 500m

MAP 19

The Old Rectory B&B

KILDALE

Glebe Cottage 021

TO PARK FARM

18

GLEBE COTTAGE

15 MINS FROM PARK FARM PATH (MAP 18)

ROUTE GUIDE AND MAPS

Guisborough. If you're feeling peckish and forgot to pack a picnic, there's a decent pub at the foot of the hill...

NEWTON-UNDER-ROSEBERRY
[off MAP 20, p112]

As tempting as it may be, when you're sitting exhausted at the top of the Topping, to roll down the hill for a pint and something to eat, do remember that you've got to climb back up again afterwards! If you're determined to treat yourself, however, the quickest way to the pub is to follow the stone steps that head off from the northern side of the Topping (ie with your back to the sea, they'll be on your right-hand side). It takes about 20 minutes to reach the A173, with the pub a few metres to your right.

A popular stop amongst 'outdoorsy' types, *The Kings Head Inn* (☎ 01642-722318, 🖳 kingsheadinn.co.uk; 10D/2D or T, all en suite; �; WI-FI; Ⓛ; 🐾) is a dog-

and family-friendly place (one room could sleep two adults with children). The inn is actually a couple of 17th-century cottages that have been knocked together. Rates for their **accommodation** are £57.50-60pp (sgl occ £78-89) including dinner – which is pretty much essential, as there's nowhere else to eat in the vicinity. **Food** is served daily noon-9pm; the mains are imaginative and start from £10.95 for the vegetarian tagine rising to £16.95 for the smoked haddock rarebit; pizzas and burgers are also available.

Newton-under-Roseberry is served by Arriva's No 81 **bus** service and the much more limited Moorsbus M4 service; see box pp52-3 for details.

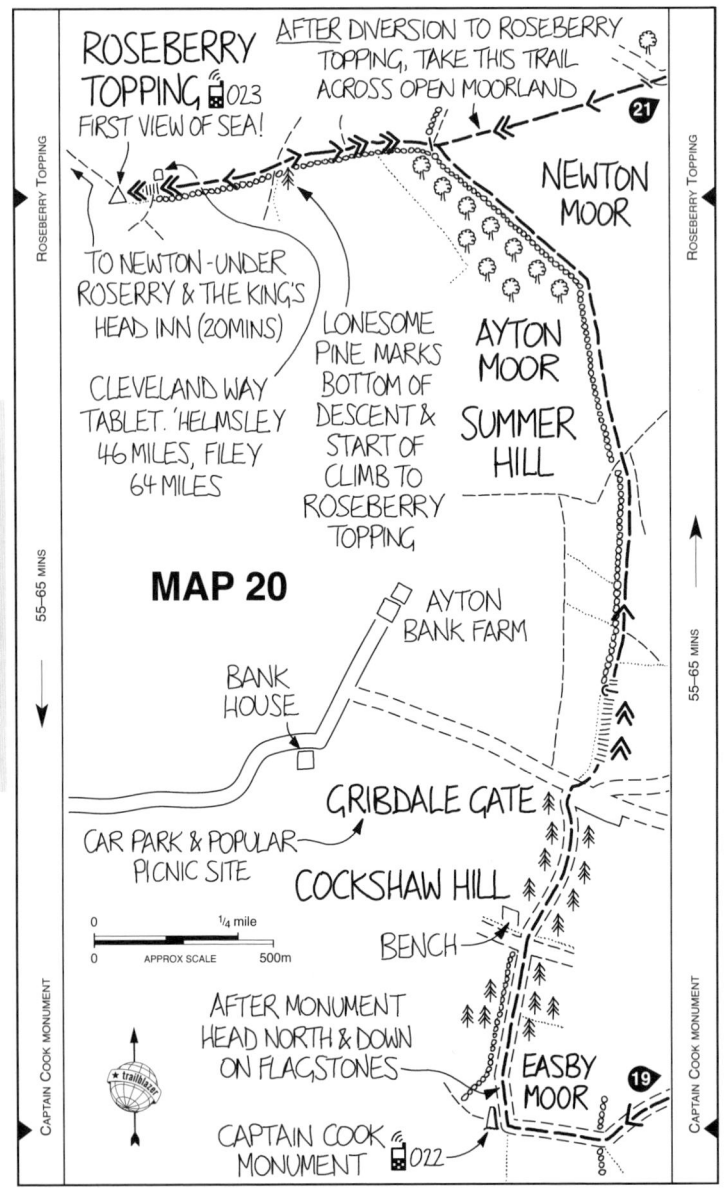

ROSEBERRY TOPPING 023
FIRST VIEW OF SEA!

AFTER DIVERSION TO ROSEBERRY TOPPING, TAKE THIS TRAIL ACROSS OPEN MOORLAND

21

NEWTON MOOR

TO NEWTON-UNDER ROSERRY & THE KING'S HEAD INN (20MINS)

CLEVELAND WAY TABLET. 'HELMSLEY 46 MILES, FILEY 64 MILES

LONESOME PINE MARKS BOTTOM OF DESCENT & START OF CLIMB TO ROSEBERRY TOPPING

AYTON MOOR

SUMMER HILL

MAP 20

AYTON BANK FARM

BANK HOUSE

CAR PARK & POPULAR PICNIC SITE

GRIBDALE GATE

COCKSHAW HILL

BENCH

0   1/4 mile
0   APPROX SCALE   500m

★ trailblazer

AFTER MONUMENT HEAD NORTH & DOWN ON FLAGSTONES

CAPTAIN COOK MONUMENT 022

EASBY MOOR

19

ROSEBERRY TOPPING

ROSEBERRY TOPPING

55-65 MINS

55-65 MINS

ROUTE GUIDE AND MAPS

CAPTAIN COOK MONUMENT

CAPTAIN COOK MONUMENT

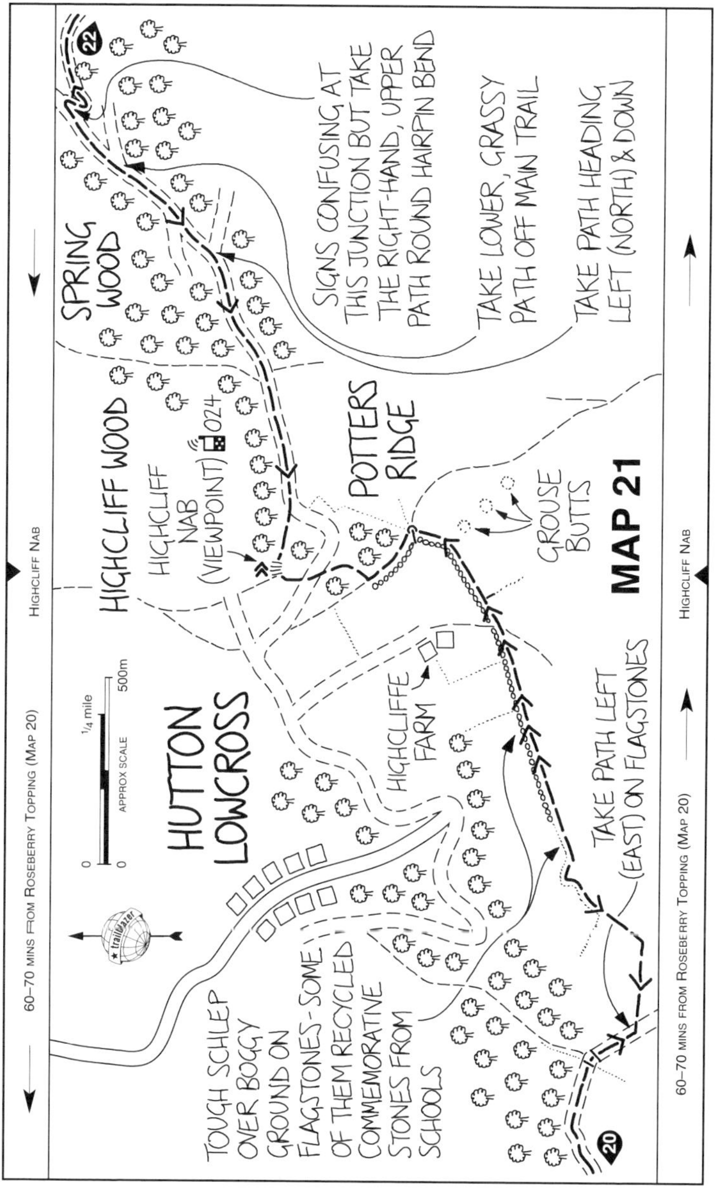
60–70 MINS FROM ROSEBERRY TOPPING (MAP 20)
HIGHCLIFF NAB
22
SPRING WOOD
HIGHCLIFF WOOD
HIGHCLIFF NAB (VIEWPOINT) 024
POTTERS RIDGE
SIGNS CONFUSING AT THIS JUNCTION BUT TAKE THE RIGHT-HAND, UPPER PATH ROUND HAIRPIN BEND
TAKE LOWER, GRASSY PATH OFF MAIN TRAIL
TAKE PATH HEADING LEFT (NORTH) & DOWN
GROUSE BUTTS
MAP 21
HIGHCLIFFE FARM
HUTTON LOWCROSS
APPROX SCALE
0
1/4 mile
0
500m
TAKE PATH LEFT (EAST) ON FLAGSTONES
TOUGH SCHLEP OVER BOGGY GROUND ON FLAGSTONES - SOME OF THEM RECYCLED COMMEMORATIVE STONES FROM SCHOOLS
HIGHCLIFF NAB
60–70 MINS FROM ROSEBERRY TOPPING (MAP 20)
20

Not for the first time, the Cleveland Way asks its followers to retrace their steps, this time back to **Newton Moor** and a major path junction, where you head in a more easterly direction this time.

A final bit of moorland meandering ensues, followed by a fairly dispiriting trudge alongside the walls of **Highcliffe Farm** (Map 21) before the viewpoint at **Highcliff Nab** is gained. From here you have to tackle the woodland trails of Highcliff, Spring and Guisborough woods, but while the trails themselves may be easy to find, route finding here is the hardest of any section on the Way, the signage simply inadequate when it comes to showing walkers which trail to take. Just follow our maps closely and, all being well, you'll soon be walking along the edge of **Guisborough Woods** (Map 22) with the ruins of Guisborough Priory in the distance to your right. Negotiate the motorcycle tracks of the local dirt-bike club, cross the road and you'll come to the Fox and Hounds at Slapewath – probably a most welcome sight after this slightly wearying stretch of fairly unrewarding walking since Roseberry Topping.

SLAPEWATH   [MAP 22]

Translating either as 'Slippery Crossing' or 'Border Place', in recent times the name Slapewath has proved to be rather apt as this little hamlet has regularly 'slipped' between various borders and has been part of three counties – Cleveland, Teeside and North Yorkshire – as the boundaries have changed. It should also be noted that once you reach Slapewath you are no longer in North York Moors National Park, and you won't actually enter back into the park until after Skinningrove, almost 10 miles further along the trail.

Something of an institution on the Cleveland Way, *Fox & Hounds Hotel* (☎ 01287-635280, 🖳 foxandhoundhotel.com; 9D/2T/2Qd, all en suite; 🍽; WI-FI; ⓛ; 🐾) is one of the few bar/restaurants on the first half of the trail that's situated right on the trail. With **rooms** from £25pp (sgl occ from £40) it's better value than you have any right to expect; however, note that breakfast costs £7.50pp extra. **Food** is served daily noon-8pm and includes such simple fare as mince & dumplings (£7.99) up to a very good Sunday carvery (£8.99). They also

own the nearby café *The Chase* (☎ 01287-632964; daily 8am-5pm) with a standard menu of sarnies, breakfasts, jacket potatoes (£5) and warm baguettes (£5).

The nearest **campsite** is *Margrove Park* (☎ 01287-653616, 🖳 margrovepark holidays.co.uk; WI-FI; 🐾 on lead; Apr-end Oct), off Margrove Rd about 0.6 mile (1km) from the trail. (Instead of taking a sharp left turn at the bottom of the woods, continue straight ahead on the minor road parallel to the A171 until you see the turn-off for Margrove Rd on the opposite side.) More of a caravan park than a campsite, they nevertheless allow tents for just £5pp per night.

As for **public transport**, Slapewath's location on the side of a fairly major road does mean that it's blessed with more **bus** services than a settlement of this size would perhaps normally expect, though note that the stop is often called Charltons rather than Slapewath. Services include Arriva's X93 as well as R&C's No 707; see box pp52-3 for details.

From Slapewath the path takes a more agricultural turn as you leave the moors behind in favour of cultivated fields on the way to **Skelton Green** (Map 24), and from there it's just a hop and a skip to **Skelton**.

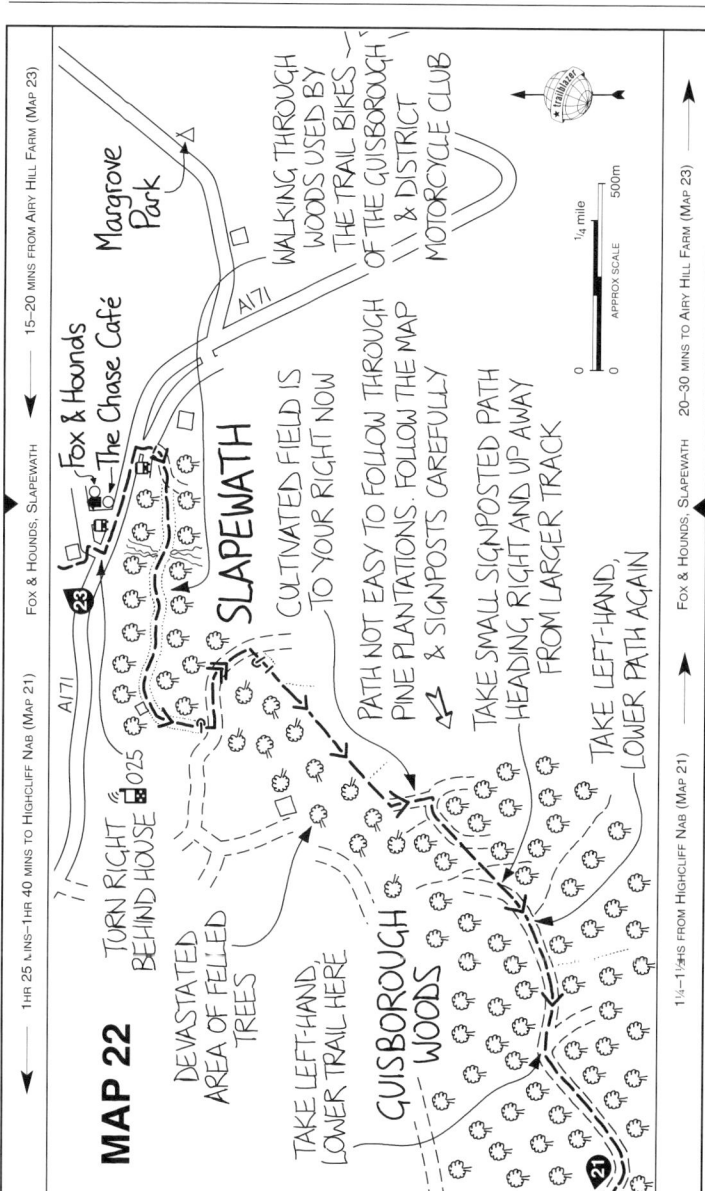

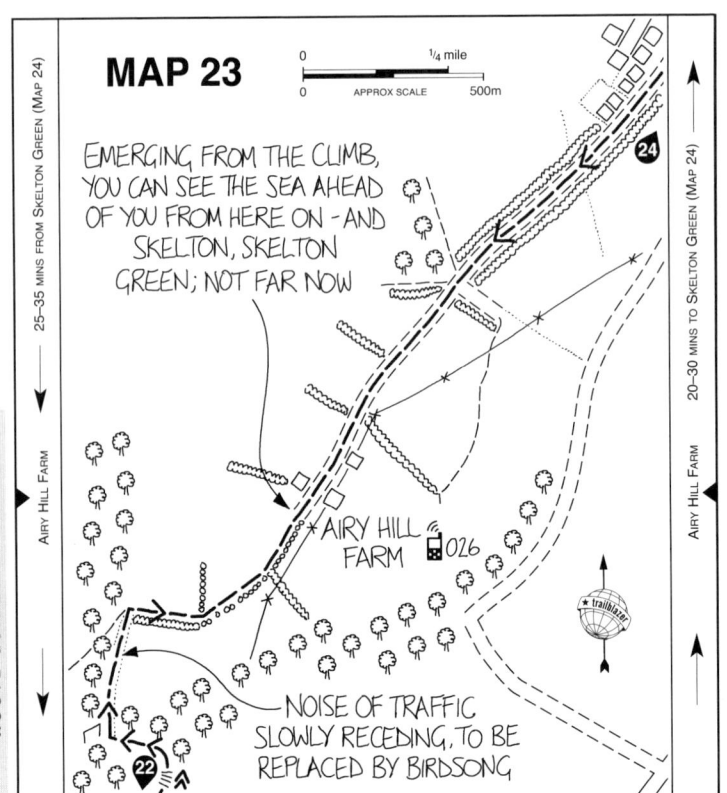

MAP 23

0   ¼ mile
0   APPROX SCALE   500m

EMERGING FROM THE CLIMB,
YOU CAN SEE THE SEA AHEAD
OF YOU FROM HERE ON – AND
SKELTON, SKELTON
GREEN; NOT FAR NOW

25-35 MINS FROM SKELTON GREEN (MAP 24)

AIRY HILL FARM

20-30 MINS TO SKELTON GREEN (MAP 24)

AIRY HILL FARM

24

AIRY HILL
FARM   026

★trailblazer

NOISE OF TRAFFIC
SLOWLY RECEDING, TO BE
REPLACED BY BIRDSONG

22

SKELTON GREEN   [MAP 24]

There's little to delay you in Skelton Green, though if you're ravenous there are two pubs, namely *Green Inn* and the *Miners' Arms*, offering bar snacks (available in both from approximately noon to 10pm). Opposite the latter and near neighbours to the former, *London* (☎ 01287-659079; daily 4.30-11pm) is a fast-food outlet serving pizzas (from £4), kebabs (£4 for a medium doner) and so on. But if you can hang on you'll find more choice (and quality) in Skelton.

On the way out of the village there's the plain-speaking and wonderfully friendly **B&B** at 27 East Parade: *Westerlands*

Guest House (☎ 01287-650690; 2S/2D, private bathroom; ⬤; (Ⓛ); 🐾). Rates are £25pp (sgl/sgl occ from £30) and if requested in advance the proprietor is happy to provide an evening meal (£7). Note there is no wi-fi here. To reach it, where you come to a path junction after leaving Skelton Green, turn left: the house is the first on your right.

There are **bus** stops right where you hit the main road. Arriva's X3 and No 3 services call in hourly; R & C's No 707 (evening-only) also stops here. See box pp52-3 for details.

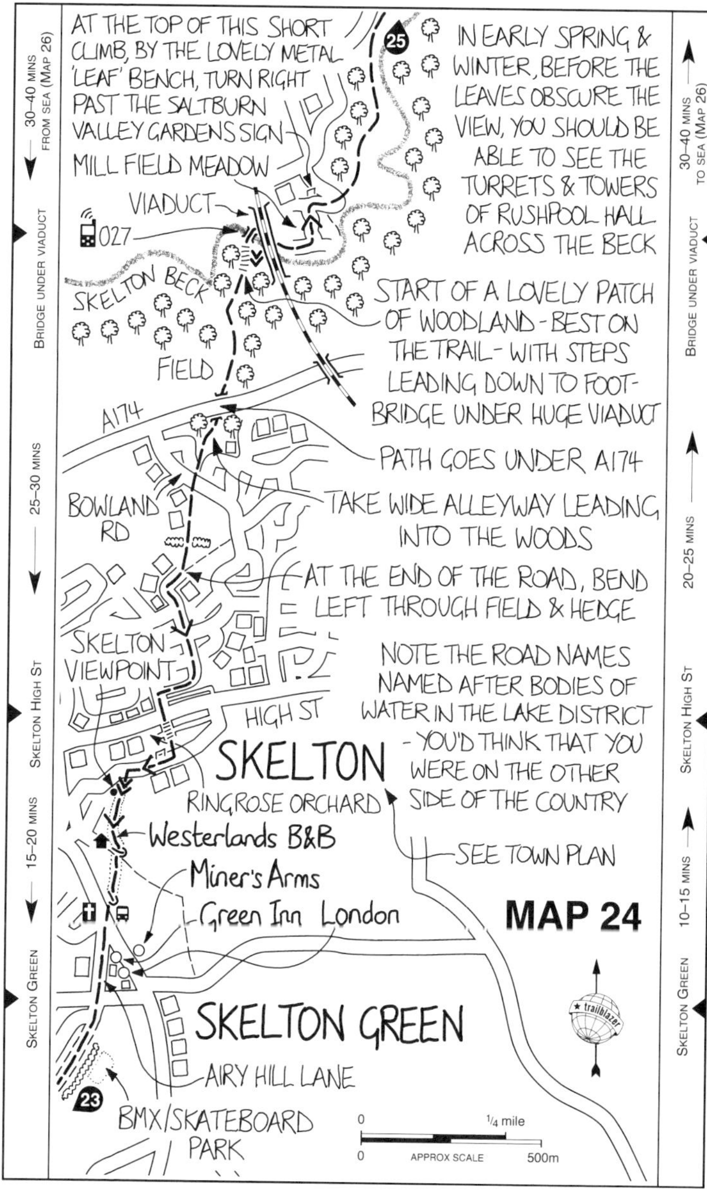

AT THE TOP OF THIS SHORT CLIMB, BY THE LOVELY METAL 'LEAF' BENCH, TURN RIGHT PAST THE SALTBURN VALLEY GARDENS SIGN

MILL FIELD MEADOW

VIADUCT

📱027

SKELTON BECK

FIELD

A174

BOWLAND RD

SKELTON VIEWPOINT

HIGH ST

SKELTON

RINGROSE ORCHARD

Westerlands B&B

Miner's Arms

Green Inn London

SKELTON GREEN

AIRY HILL LANE

BMX/SKATEBOARD PARK

25

IN EARLY SPRING & WINTER, BEFORE THE LEAVES OBSCURE THE VIEW, YOU SHOULD BE ABLE TO SEE THE TURRETS & TOWERS OF RUSHPOOL HALL ACROSS THE BECK

START OF A LOVELY PATCH OF WOODLAND - BEST ON THE TRAIL - WITH STEPS LEADING DOWN TO FOOT-BRIDGE UNDER HUGE VIADUCT

PATH GOES UNDER A174

TAKE WIDE ALLEYWAY LEADING INTO THE WOODS

AT THE END OF THE ROAD, BEND LEFT THROUGH FIELD & HEDGE

NOTE THE ROAD NAMES NAMED AFTER BODIES OF WATER IN THE LAKE DISTRICT - YOU'D THINK THAT YOU WERE ON THE OTHER SIDE OF THE COUNTRY

SEE TOWN PLAN

MAP 24

23

30-40 MINS FROM SEA (MAP 26)

BRIDGE UNDER VIADUCT

25-30 MINS

SKELTON HIGH ST

15-20 MINS

SKELTON GREEN

30-40 MINS TO SEA (MAP 26)

BRIDGE UNDER VIADUCT

20-25 MINS

SKELTON HIGH ST

10-15 MINS

SKELTON GREEN

ROUTE GUIDE AND MAPS

0   1/4 mile

0   APPROX SCALE   500m

★ trailblazer

SKELTON

To avoid confusion with the Skelton near York this Skelton is sometimes referred to as '**Skelton-in-Cleveland**'.

Skelton is a perfectly pleasant little place but there's little reason to stop here unless you're particularly hungry or knackered. But if you do need to stop, don't panic – it's a friendly place with some good cafés.

Services and transport

There's no tourist office but you'll find other amenities here on the High St including a **post office** (Mon-Fri 9am-5.30pm, Sat to 12.30pm), at Nos 129-131, and a **supermarket**, Co-op (daily 6am-10pm), with its own **ATM**, at No 80. There is also a **chemist**, Skelton Pharmacy (Mon-Fri 9am-6pm). just a short hop from the path.

Most of the same **bus** services (see box pp52-3) that serve Skelton Green (ie Arriva's No X3/3 and R & C's evening-only No 707) also serve Skelton. Arriva's 5 & 5A service also stop on the High St, as does R & C's evening-only 708.

Where to stay, eat and drink

At the time of writing **Wharton Arms** (☎ 01287-650618, 🖳 p.cummings4@ntlworld .com; 1Tr/2D/1T, all en suite ☞; Ⓛ; WI-FI; 🐾) was on the market but it was also still open and providing **B&B**; they charge from £27.50pp (sgl occ from £35). Note that: one of the doubles is very small; the bath is in the laundry room, though this can be locked; and they accept cash or cheques only, not cards. The bar is open daily (Mon-Fri noon-11.30pm, Sat & Sun from 11am) but they don't serve food.

There are a few places where you can get takeaway snacks including a branch of the good-value **Cooplands** (🖳 cooplands-bakery.co.uk; Mon-Sat 8am-4.45pm).

If you're walking with your pooch you'll find a disappointing lack of anywhere

Skelton
(Skelton-in-
Cleveland)

serving food that accepts 'man's best friend' on their premises – so be prepared for some al fresco dining if you've brought your bitch. However, if you're dog-free you'll find a fair choice of eateries on the High St. Pick of the bunch is probably *Deli at No 85* (Tue-Fri 9am-4.30pm, Sat to 4pm), where they bake their own bread and make a mighty fine eggs Benedict (£5.95) – just one of many items on their breakfast menu.

We are also fans of *Ha' Penny Vintage Tearooms* (🖥 hapennyvintagetearoom .weebly.com; Mon-Fri 10am-4pm), though this is further from the path at 117 High St. The name, incidentally, refers to the old bridge that used to span the valley from Saltburn – you'll walk past the remnants of it later in the stage; the bridge used to

charge a toll and the board with the list of prices now graces the wall of the café. Food-wise they specialise in cakes though there's also more substantial fare such as jacket potatoes (£5.95) and sandwiches (£4.50).

Cheaper fare can be found on the other side of the path at *Skelton Pantry* (Mon-Fri 9am-2.30pm, Sat 9am-1pm), 73 High St, where a breakfast wrap costs just £3.75 or the Full English is £5.95.

If you're staying in Skelton overnight your choice of dining in the evening is even more limited though there are a couple of fast-food takeaways: *Mamma-mia* (☎ 01287-650055; daily 4-10pm), at 87 High St, and *Peppino's* (☎ 01287-659161; Mon-Sat 4-11pm, Sun to 10pm) at No 68.

From Skelton the path passes through the suburbs and into the pretty wood enveloping the impressive **Saltburn Viaduct**, under which you pass on a bridge over **Skelton Beck**. There then follows an extremely pleasant meander through Saltburn Woods climbing up at the end to reach the town itself.

SALTBURN-BY-THE-SEA [map p122]
Saltburn has a long and interesting history. The original settlement of Saltburn, established by the Anglo-Saxons and called 'Sealt-Burna' (Salt Stream), used to lie down near where The Ship Inn now sits. The resort town you see today, however, started much later, in the Victorian era, and was largely the brainchild of one man. Henry Pease wanted to develop this corner of Yorkshire to rival those of Scarborough and Whitby and the pier, cliff lift and Valley Gardens were all part of Pease's legacy, and today still stand as a testimony to the man's drive and zeal. The roads abutting the cliffs at the top of town, each of which has been named after a precious stone – Garnett St, Ruby St, Emerald St, Diamond St, etc – are also the product of his ambition.

Today, Saltburn remains divided into two halves. Down at the foot of the cliffs lies the 'resort' part of Saltburn, which features on most of the postcards of the place. You'll find few amenities here save for several cafés but you will find **Saltburn Pier**, the last one left in Yorkshire. You'll also

find the ticket office for the tiny **15-inch gauge railway** (Sat & Sun 1-5pm; tickets £1 each way), which runs for a kilometre inland to the **Italian Gardens**.

Connected to this seafront area by a wriggly road, a series of steps and the old **Victorian cliff lift** (the oldest operating water-balance cliff lift in the country, having begun operations in 1884; daily 10am-4pm; £1) is the main town of Saltburn up on the clifftops, where you'll find most of the eateries, accommodation and other amenities. However, at the time of writing, the lift was closed for refurbishment and repair work.

Services
This town centre is itself divided; this time by the train line to Middlesbrough. Most of the tourist facilities lie to the south of the tracks. There is a **tourist office** in Saltburn Library (Mon & Wed-Fri 10am-5pm, Sat 9.30am-12.30pm) but the only people manning it are the librarians; they are fairly knowledgeable about the area but it's not

really their main job. The website 🖳 salt
burnbysea.com is a pretty good substitute.

On Station St, which runs south from
the station, there's a Barclays Bank with an
ATM at No 12, a Boots the **chemist** (Mon-
Fri 8.30am-6pm, Sat to 5pm) at Nos 9-11,
and, virtually opposite – and useful if you
need a chemist on a Sunday – Saltburn
Pharmacy (Mon-Fri 8.30am-6pm, Sat 9am-
5pm, Sun noon-6pm) at No 6. The **post
office** (daily 6am-9.30pm) lies about 300m
to the west of Station St in the Spar (daily
6am-10pm) on Windsor Rd, which also has
its own ATM.

At the northern end of Station St is the
station itself, beyond which is the **supermarket,** Sainsbury's (Mon-Fri 7am-10pm,
Sat to 9pm, Sun 10am-4pm) – again, with its
own ATM. For even longer opening hours
there's also a Spar (daily 5.30am-11pm) to
the north on Milton St, while nearby is the
Stay Smart **Launderette** (daily 8.30am-
5pm; £3 a load).

Transport
The first place on the Cleveland Way to
have a working **railway** station; services to
Saltburn are operated by Northern (see box
p49).

The town is also reasonably served by
buses – by the standards of the Cleveland
Way, at least – including Arriva's X3/X3A/3
& X4, R & C's evening-only 708 and the
limited seasonal Moorsbus M1. See box
pp52-3 for details.

Where to stay
Accommodation in Saltburn is in fairly
short supply. However, *The Victoria* (☎
01287-626131; 3D/1T/1Qd, all en suite;
➼; WI-FI; 🐾) has just converted the previous manager's flat into a variety of rooms
and charges £29.50-39.50pp (sgl occ room
rate). For more details see their Facebook
page: The Victoria Pub, Saltburn.

The other three options for visitors are:
the slightly run-down but friendly *Saltburn
House* (☎ 01287-622008, 🖳 saltburnhouse
.co.uk; 6S/7D/13T/1Qd, all en suite; WI-
FI in bar area but not everywhere) on Marine
Parade, which charges from £27.50pp
(sgl/sgl occ from £30/40) for B&B;

Victorian Guest House (☎ 01287-625237,
🖳 susanandstewart@saltburn-accommo
dation.co.uk; 1D/1Tr in house plus studio
apartment 1D, all en suite; WI-FI; from
£40pp, sgl occ from £60); and the much
smarter *Spa Hotel* (☎ 01287-622544, 🖳
thespahotelsalt burn.co.uk; 16D/5T/3Tr/
2Qd, all en suite; ➼; WI-FI; Ⓛ; 🐾), a welcoming place that's refreshingly free of the
airs and graces you may expect such a
swanky establishment to adopt. Lovely
rooms and a great location make this a top
spot, though such comfort doesn't come
particularly cheaply; rates are £49.50-
62.50pp (sgl occ £79-115).

Where to eat and drink
For food-on-the-go, two **bakeries** vie for
your custom: **Stonehouse Bakery** (Mon-
Fri 8am-4.30pm, Sat to 4pm) on Dundas St
East and, on Station St, the budget chain
Cooplands (🖳 cooplands-bakery.co.uk;
Mon-Sat 8am-4.45pm).

Our favourite place to visit, at least in
terms of atmosphere, décor and the quality
of its coffee, is *The Sitting Room* (☎ 01287-
626150; Mon-Thur 10am-5pm, Fri-Sat
10am-11.45pm, Sun 10am-9.30pm; WI-FI;
🐾). In addition to the huge variety of teas,
coffees and cocktails, the menu is inventive
and varied and the food is delicious (eg
sumac chicken and Moroccan kofta). The
only problem is that the grazing menu is
small and while it's fair value (£4 per dish,
or £10 for three), the owners clearly obey
the edict of leaving the customers wanting
more – about 50% more in our opinion.

If you want something both heartier
and more familiar, *Signals* (daily 8am-
4pm) has a good value if unsurprising
menu. Decent for breakfast (eg bacon &
egg bun £3.30) and great for lunch (with
small hot meals such as a roast dinner just
4.75, or £6 for a regular size), it's probably
the best-value daytime eatery in Saltburn.

There's one other excellent place in
Saltburn, particularly for lunch: *Real Meals*
(Mon-Fri 8.30am-5.30pm, Sat to 5pm, Sun
10am-3pm) is a café-cum-deli on Milton
St. Most meals are in the £7-10 range and
they often have some great specials such as
haddock rarebit with roast tomatoes &

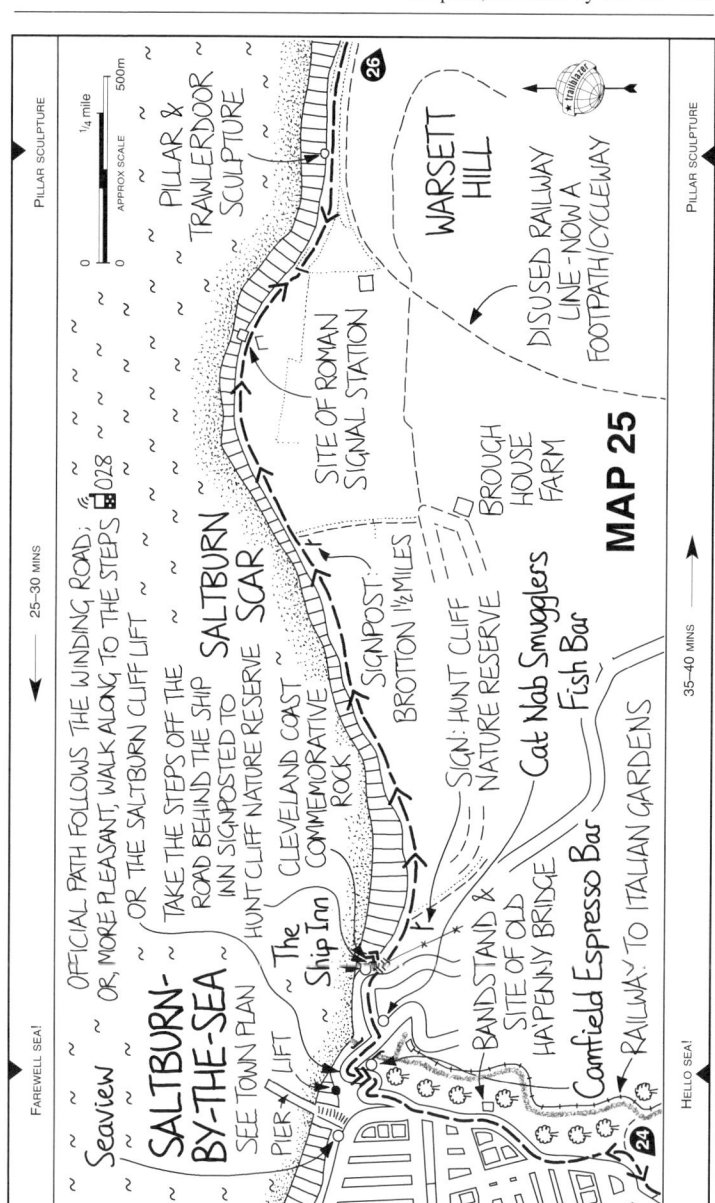

MAP 25

sauté potatoes (£8.45). Great service and delicious food made with fine ingredients – there's much to love about this place.

The most convenient eatery for Cleveland Way walkers in this upper part of town is *Taste* (Mon-Sat 9am-4.30pm, Sun 10am-3.30pm; 🐾). A new place that's very dog friendly and quite amenable towards humans too, we couldn't find fault with this place save that the menu was rather limited, with paninis (£4.25) the most prominent.

If you prefer a seaview with your latte, down on the seafront *Camfields* (Map 25; ☎ 01287-626070, 🖳 camfields.co.uk; school summer holidays daily 9am-6pm, rest of year 9am-4/5pm but 10am-2pm in winter though all weather dependent; WI-FI) describes itself as an 'espresso bar', with blankets folded on the chairs like an après-ski café to help ward off the sometimes bitter wind blowing in off the coast. It's a chic, smart and slightly incongruous place but a decent change from the traditional English 'caff', with *croissants* and *pain au chocolat* replacing the full English; that said, on the menu you can find the odd crispy bacon sandwich (£3.50) among the breakfast smoothies (£3.25-3.50).

For **pub food**, the only option in the upper part of town is *The Victoria* (see Where to stay; Mon-Sat noon-8pm, Sun noon-4pm) which does no-nonsense pub grub starting at £6.95 for a vegetable lasagne, and advertises specials throughout the week (eg Curry Tuesdays, where a curry is just £5.95) and a good roast for Sunday lunch (£5.95-8.95 depending on size). Nothing wrong with this place – indeed, it's very good value – but better quality and more character can be found

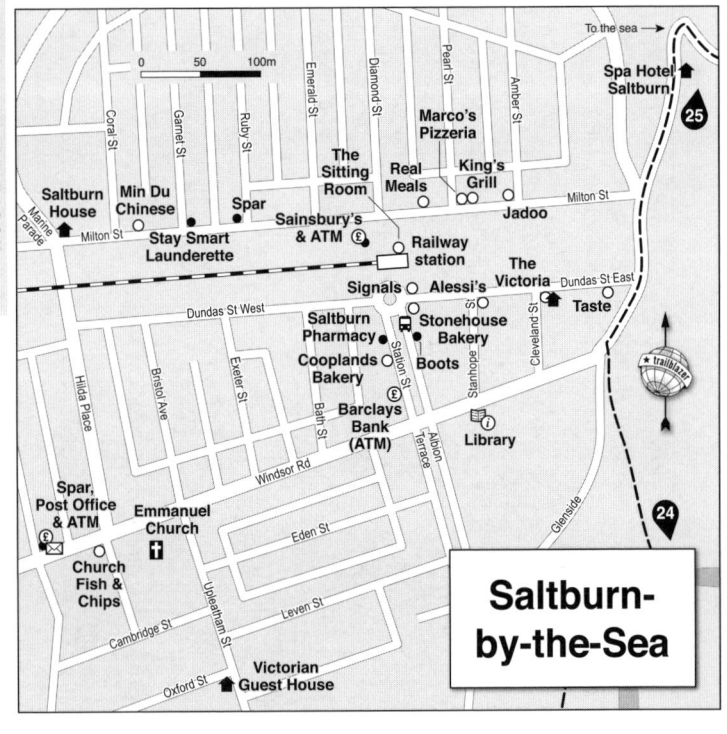

ROUTE GUIDE AND MAPS

Saltburn-by-the-Sea

down on the seafront at the 16th-century *Ship Inn* (Map 25; Mon-Sat noon-9pm, Sun to 8.30pm) where on the menu the pub standards are supplemented by dishes such as the pork loin & black pudding stack with mash and veg (£14.95).

Other evening options include *King's Grill* (☎ 01287-625354, 🖳 thekingsgrill .uk; food Thur-Sat 6-9pm) on Milton St, selling pizzas, burgers and grilled meat; mains start at £14, rising to £29 for the beef fillet with winter greens, creamed potato & horseradish. Just along the road is the upmarket *Jadoo* (Mon-Sat 5.30-11pm, Sun to 10.30pm) at 9 Milton St, serving Nouveau Indian cuisine with mains starting at £8.90 for the vegetarian options, or £9.40 for the chicken korma; while over on Dundas St is the Italian *Alessi's* (☎ 01287-625033, 🖳 alessissaltburn.com; Mon-Sat 3.30-9.30pm, Sun 4-9pm), at 9-10 Dundas St, with all pizzas and pasta dishes a very fair £8.95.

Fast-food outlets include *Marco's Pizzeria* (☎ 01287-623623, 🖳 marcos squarepizzeria.co.uk; daily 5-11pm), at 17a Milton St, with (square) pizzas starting at £4 for a small margherita; and *Min Du* (☎ 01287-624699; Sun-Thur 5-11pm, Fri & Sat to midnight), at No 47, the local Chinese with mains from £5.70.

If you've been dreaming about **fish & chips** since Helmsley but decided to wait until you saw the sea before having any, there are three choices here: we preferred *Church Fish & Chips* (Mon-Sat 11.30am-8.30pm, Sun noon-8.30pm), 1 Macnay St, where a large cod costs £4.50 and chips are £1.90. The only problem is that it's about as far away from the sea as you can get in Saltburn; luckily, there are a couple of places down on the seafront at either end of the price spectrum, including upmarket *Seaview* (Map 25; ☎ 01287-626585, 🖳 the seaviewrestaurant.co.uk; food Mon-Thur 11.30am-7.30pm, Fri & Sat to 8.30pm, Sun to 6.30pm) where mains start at £15 and can rise to £21 for the roast halibut with potato terrine; next door is their chippy, with cod for £6.70. Or there's the more traditional *Cat Nab Smugglers Fish Bar* (Map 25; daily 9am-5pm), with haddock & chips for £7.70.

SALTBURN-BY-THE-SEA TO RUNSWICK BAY [MAPS 25-30]

This **11.8-mile/19km stage (3hrs 55mins to 4¾hrs)** stage is many trekkers' favourite, a lovely jaunt along the clifftops with plenty of interest along the way, including a Roman ruin, an abandoned port, seabird colonies galore and several intriguing sculptures and other works of art. It's also a relief, after the remote and lonely trail you've walked along thus far, to trek along a path with so many places where you can stop and pick up a bite to eat and find a bed for the night. It will be like this for the rest of the trail too.

Beginning from the beach at Saltburn, the path bends behind The Ship Inn to climb **Hunt Cliff**, where the remains of a **Roman signal station** have been found. The station would presumably have been situated there to keep a look-out for Anglo-Saxon ships from Germany and Denmark, and to warn the locals (presumably by lighting a fire) of any approaching danger. Abandoned when the Romans left in the 5th century, it was left to the local Romanised Britons to man.

❏ **Important note – walking times**
Unless otherwise specified, **all times in this book refer only to the time spent walking**. You will need to add 20-30% to allow for rests, photography, checking the map, drinking water etc. When planning the day's hike count on 5-7 hours' actual walking.

The discovery in 1923 of several skeletons from this period dumped at the bottom of a well provides evidence of their fate after the Saxons over-ran the station.

A little further along the cliff is the first – Richard Farrington's '*Pillar*' – of the many artworks (see box below) that decorate the seaside stretch of the Cleveland Way. Just before it, though invisible from the path, is *Trawlerdoor*, another of Farrington's creations. Further on (Map 26) is the most prominent of his works, '*Circle*'. From here, on your right you get the best view of the

❏ Art and sculptures along the Cleveland Way

It's one of the most unexpected pleasures of the latter half of the Cleveland Way: dotted along the trail are several works of art that have been commissioned by the local authorities (and, in one or two cases, probably weren't commissioned at all but just 'appeared' overnight). You may not like all the works displayed – though most people, in our experience, tend to view them quite favourably – but you can't deny that they add interest to the Way and those responsible are to be applauded for their efforts.

The first works you see occur soon after leaving Saltburn (Map 25), with a trio of sculptures created in 1990 by local artist Richard Farrington. Each has been rendered in steel that was produced by the local Skinningrove plant. The first lies to the left of the path near where you are joined on the trail by the old railway line that sweeps in on your right. Called *Pillar*, it represents a ridged marker post with abstract representations of the artist's version of the four natural elements – sky, earth, sea and air in this case – hanging from it by a chain. Nearby, and hidden from the trail, is *Trawlerdoor*, a miniature rendition of the doors of an open trawl net complete with its catch, including a large fish and plankton.

However, it is the third of Richard's sculptures that is the most visible and celebrated. Titled *Circle*, it lies a few hundred yards along from the other two and is impossible to miss, standing on a small hillock right on the trail (Map 26). The work resembles a giant charm bracelet with each of the 10 'charms' representing something of significance to the local area. This is actually the second '*Circle*' created by Farrington — the first was removed from its base by vandals using special tools, who then rolled it over the cliff edge and into the sea. Luckily, most locals have a greater appreciation of the piece and it has actually been the location of at least one wedding! The charms dangling from the *Circle* include: a horse to represent the Cleveland Bay horse, a local breed; Thor's hammer to represent the Viking conquest of the area; a mermaid; a mermaid's purse (the egg case of the dog fish); a starfish to represent the nearby sea and the local legends that have grown up around it; a cat, which either refers to Cat Nab (the hill at Saltburn), or possibly refers to the story that locals used to hunt cats on High Cliff back in the 1300s; and a pigeon, which represents the local pastime of pigeon racing.

There's a second artwork dedicated to pigeon-fancying further down the coast in Skinningrove where outside the local homing society's hut stands a near life-size chain-saw sculpture of one of their members releasing a bird into the air. The work was completed in 2011 by artist Steve Iredale from Staithes; he also had a hand in the nearby *Repus* sculpture on the other side of the bridge, which celebrates another local tradition, that of fishing. Steve provided the two figures that man the traditional local fishing boat called a *coble*; this one was actually found in bad repair at nearby South Gare and was discovered to have belonged to a Skinningrove fisherman who had died in the 1980s.

The boat was restored by the locals in 2008 before being placed on the seafront and 'manned' by Iredale's sculptures to provide a memorial to all the fishermen who railway tracks running from Boulby potash mine. These pass by the remains of the old **Guibal Fanhouse**, which used to provide fresh air to the miners working in the nearby ironstone mine. You can visit the ruins of the fanhouse today by taking the path by the information board.

From here the path hugs the coastline closely, eventually dropping down to the beach to what looks like a harbour arm, though in fact is a dilapidated jetty built in 1886 for loading ironstone, that precedes the settlement of **Skinningrove**.

have lost their lives just doing their job. The name, incidentally, spells 'Super' backwards.

Just before you get to *Repus* there's a rather splendid bit of graffiti of a man in a spacesuit breathing sea air (*Sea Air*; Map 26). Though very reminiscent of the work of Banksy, the spray-painted stencil is actually by 'Karl Striker' (though, like Banksy, this is just a pseudonym to keep his real identity secret). The work used to reside on the jetty before being moved ashore for reasons of preservation.

Towards the end of the walk there are two huge figures that are clearly the work of the same person. The first, *Freddie Gilroy and the Belsen Stragglers*, stands – or, rather, sits, in Scarborough's North Bay (Map 43) and is the work of Durham artist Ray Lonsdale. The work depicts a figure seated on a bench, dressed in cloth cap and overcoat and holding a walking stick, all rendered in rusting steel. As the title suggests, the work commemorates all those who left their day-to-day lives to fight for their country during World War II. The sculpture is actually based on a real person, the Freddie Gilroy of the title, a Durham miner who survived the war but who, just shy of his 24th birthday, became one of the first Allied troops to enter Bergen-Belsen concentration camp and thus witnessed the immediate aftermath of one of the most despicable horrors of the entire conflict. The piece was originally just loaned to Scarborough for a month, but locals campaigned to keep it there and raised money to try to buy it. With the deadline fast approaching and the funds amassed insufficient for the purchase, one local pensioner stumped up £50,000 – and thus Freddie remained in the town.

At the very end of the trail, at the northern end of Filey Bay on the seafront (see map p179), at a place called Coble Landing, is the second of Ray Lonsdale's works: *A High Tide in Short Wellies* is another greater-than-life-size figure, this time a 12ft tall fisherman wearing, as the title suggests, short boots. The man stands as a silent witness to the decline of the local fishing industry and the need to preserve local fish stocks, a sentiment reinforced by the following poem that can be found at the fisherman's feet:

> *That's it for me I'll see you later,*
> *Gonna wrap this catch in protective paper,*
> *Gonna face the sea with a thousand mile stare,*
> *And wish that I was floating there.*
>
> *In its summertime.*
>
> *Down on the pier I saw a man with a board,*
> *It read 'the end is near accept your lord',*
> *Then underneath this some fisherman wrote*
> *'I can see the end from the back of my boat'*
>
> *This is wintertime.*

ROUTE GUIDE AND MAPS

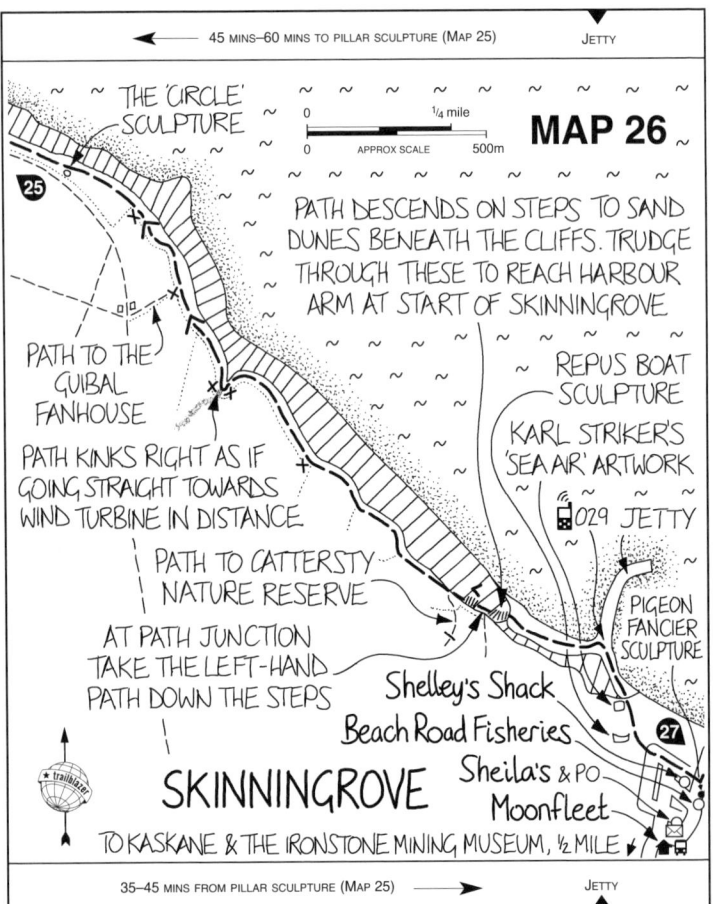

45 MINS–60 MINS TO PILLAR SCULPTURE (MAP 25)

JETTY

THE 'CIRCLE' SCULPTURE

MAP 26

0 ¼ mile

0 APPROX SCALE 500m

25

PATH DESCENDS ON STEPS TO SAND DUNES BENEATH THE CLIFFS. TRUDGE THROUGH THESE TO REACH HARBOUR ARM AT START OF SKINNINGROVE

PATH TO THE GUIBAL FANHOUSE

REPUS BOAT SCULPTURE

KARL STRIKER'S 'SEA AIR' ARTWORK

PATH KINKS RIGHT AS IF GOING STRAIGHT TOWARDS WIND TURBINE IN DISTANCE

029 JETTY

PATH TO CATTERSTY NATURE RESERVE

PIGEON FANCIER SCULPTURE

AT PATH JUNCTION TAKE THE LEFT-HAND PATH DOWN THE STEPS

Shelley's Shack

Beach Road Fisheries

27

SKINNINGROVE

Sheila's & PO

Moonfleet

trailblazer

TO KASKANE & THE IRONSTONE MINING MUSEUM, ½ MILE

35–45 MINS FROM PILLAR SCULPTURE (MAP 25)

JETTY

SKINNINGROVE [MAP 26]

Scruffy, hard-bitten and a bit run down, Skinningrove tends to be a place that Cleveland Way walkers hurry through. This could possibly be because the neighbouring settlements – Saltburn and Staithes – are blessed with more facilities (and, it must be said, are better looking too). But if you can afford to give some time to Skinningrove, it does reward those willing to give it more than just a cursory glance.

On the trail itself are some **artworks** (see box pp124-5) that merit your attention.

The village's main attraction is **Ironstone Mining Museum** (off Map 26; ☎ 01287-642877, 🖥 ironstonemuseum.co .uk), on the site of old Loftus Mine, once the third-biggest in the country; between 1865 and 1958, over 500 men and boys were employed here, making this, Loftus Mine, the third largest mine in Cleveland.

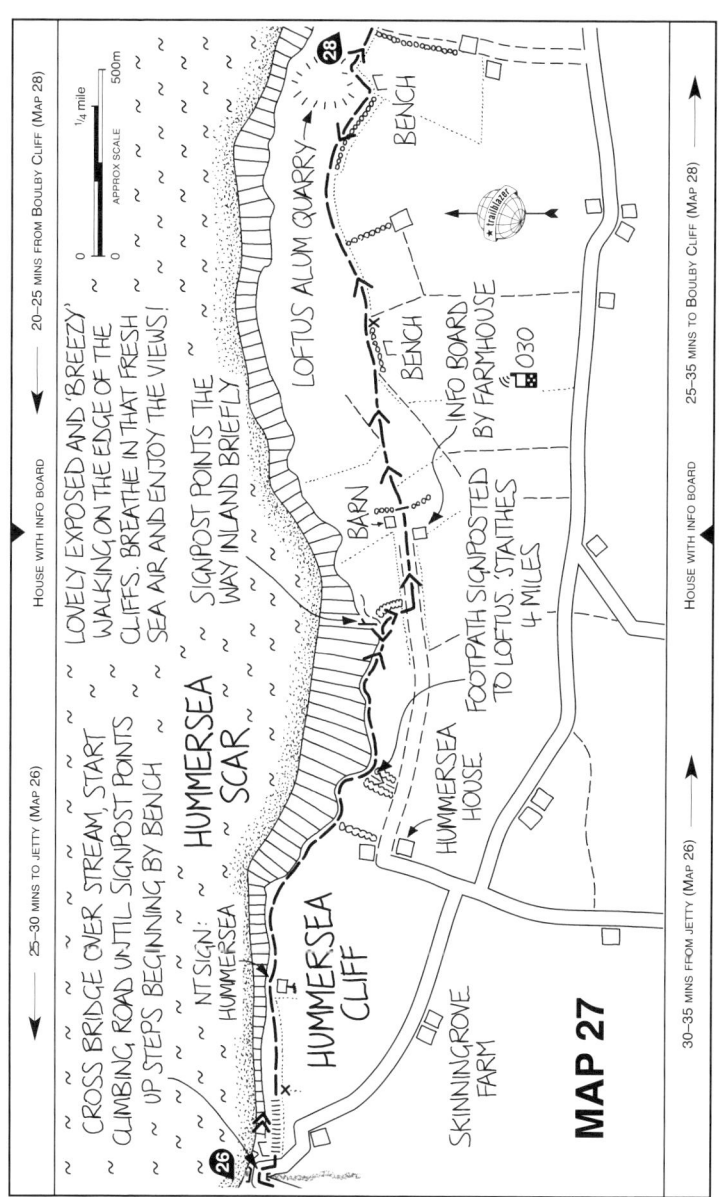

The museum is neatly laid out, allowing you to explore the history of ironstone mining in the area just as you explore the tunnels and buildings of the mine itself. However, it does lie half a mile (0.8km) from the trail and at the time of writing it was scheduled to close so that a new exhibition centre can be built. It is not expected to reopen till late 2019; check the website for details.

Facility-wise, Skinningrove has a local **store**, Sheila's General Dealers (Mon-Fri 7.30am-1pm & 2-5pm, Sat 8am-2pm, Sun 10am-noon), which also houses the **post office** (Mon & Wed-Fri 9am-1pm & 2-5.30pm, Tue & Sat 9am-noon). On the way you'll pass a **burger van**, *Shelley's Shack*, right on the trail (variable opening times; burgers from £2.50) and the local **chippy**, *Beach Road Fisheries* (Mon-Thur 11.30am-1.30pm, Fri 11.30am-1.30pm & 4.30-6.30pm, Sat 11.30am-2pm).

For a greater choice of dishes, you'll have to head about half a mile (0.8km) from the trail (and on the same site as the museum) to *Kaskane* (off Map 26; ☎ 01287-644203, ⌨ www.kaskane.co.uk; Mon-Sat 11am-8.30pm; WI-FI; 🐾 bar area and conservatory only), the centre of the community and the only place to sit down in and eat of an evening; the food is great value, too, with lamb shank for £8.25 and even the most expensive item on the menu, the 8oz sirloin steak, only £12.95. Booking is recommended.

Near Sheila's is the smart and chic *Moonfleet* (☎ 07572-743951, ⌨ moonfleet guesthouse.co.uk; 6D, all en suite; ✉; WI-FI; Ⓛ; 🐾), housed in a listed former manor house. It's a fascinating place with a breakfast that regularly receives rave reviews, and prices are fair at £40-55pp (sgl occ £60-80) for **B&B**.

There are a few **buses** serving Skinningrove: Arriva's No 5, R & C's evening only No 708 and their No 752. See box pp52-3 for details.

There now follows one of the larger climbs on the whole of the Cleveland Way – from near enough sea level at **Skinningrove** to Boulby Cliff, the highest point on England's east coast. It's a fairly tough climb particularly at the start as you leave Skinningrove to climb up **Hummersea Cliff** (Map 27). The route takes you via an isolated farmhouse where you can read about the exploits of Lewis Hunton, who lived at nearby Hummersea House. Though he died of tuberculosis aged just 23, in his short life Lewis managed to invent a whole new scientific discipline, called 'biostratigraphy', where ammonites help to date rocks in which they're found. His work had important ramifications for the neighbouring alum industry, enabling them to identify shale deposits that would be suitable for investigating and processing; see also box p158.

Climbing still further, the path passes above the **alum quarries** of **Loftus** and **Boulby** (Map 28); above the latter there's a useful information board telling you more about the industry that thrived here for over 200 years; but of more interest, perhaps, is the **trig point** that lies on the other side of the path. It is this place that, at 203m (666ft) is the highest point on England's east coast. Having posed for the obligatory photo, you then plod down the slopes along the coast to the next settlements on the trail, namely **Cowbar** (Map 29) and, more significantly, the lovely seaside village of **Staithes**.

STAITHES [map p133]

This lovely little fishing village that spills down steeply from the top of the surrounding cliffs to its picturesque harbour has a couple of claims to fame. The first is its association with explorer Captain James Cook (see box p130), who was apprenticed to a grocer in the village as a young lad. The second claim to fame is more modern:

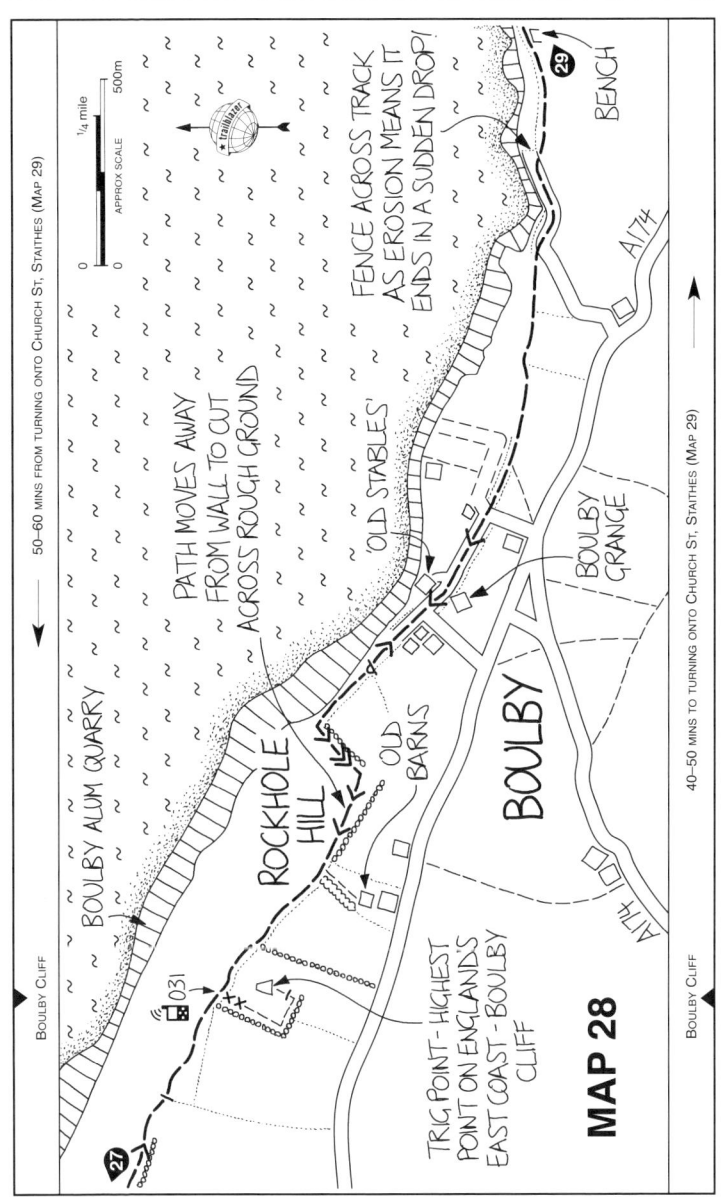

BOULBY CLIFF

BOULBY ALUM QUARRY

PATH MOVES AWAY FROM WALL TO CUT ACROSS ROUGH GROUND

FENCE ACROSS TRACK AS EROSION MEANS IT ENDS IN A SUDDEN DROP!

'OLD STABLES'

BENCH

A174

BOULBY GRANGE

ROCKHOLE HILL

OLD BARNS

BOULBY

A174

031

TRIG POINT – HIGHEST POINT ON ENGLAND'S EAST COAST – BOULBY CLIFF

MAP 28

BOULBY CLIFF

50–60 MINS FROM TURNING ONTO CHURCH ST, STAITHES (MAP 29)

40–50 MINS TO TURNING ONTO CHURCH ST, STAITHES (MAP 29)

APPROX SCALE

0   500m

0   ¼ mile

ROUTE GUIDE AND MAPS

❏ Captain Cook, worldwide celebrity – and local hero

Though universally famous for his worldwide explorations in the 18th century, particularly in the Pacific and Australia, many of Captain James Cook's formative years were spent in rather less exotic places on and around the Cleveland Way. Born in 1728 in the Yorkshire village of Marton, near Middlesbrough, James moved with his family to Great Ayton at the age of eight and attended the local school there. On reaching his teenage years he began to work for his father, a farm manager, often climbing Roseberry Topping during his days off to enjoy the peace and solitude there. Those climbing the summit today will soon realise that they can see the sea very clearly from here – leading us to ask whether it was at Roseberry Topping that James first developed his yearning for the sea.

Three years later, aged just 16, he moved across the moors to Staithes, working as an apprentice to the local grocer and haberdasher, William Sanderson. His talents as a shopkeeper appear to have been pretty dismal, however, and it wasn't long before Cook was on the move again, this time, like many Cleveland Way trekkers after him, down the coast to Whitby, where he met some friends of the Sandersons, John and Henry Walker, who happened to be prominent local ship owners. Swapping his shopkeeper's apron for a sturdy pair of sea legs, Cook became an apprentice on one of the Walkers' boats that ferried coal between Newcastle and London. Menial though many of his tasks undoubtedly would have been, it was during his apprenticeship on the coal boats that Cook studied navigation, astronomy and the other skills that would all help shape his future.

But it was after he left North Yorkshire to join the Royal Navy, that his career really took off. Sent to fight against the French in Canada, whilst there Cook successfully surveyed and mapped the coast of Newfoundland (maps that would still be used over 200 years later, such were their accuracy). His abilities did not go unnoticed by his superiors and in 1766 the Admiralty engaged Cook to command a scientific voyage to the Pacific Ocean.

Setting sail from England on 26 August, 1768, Cook's craft, *HMS Endeavour*, headed south-west to round Cape Horn, the southernmost point of South America, before arriving at Tahiti almost eight months later. The primary purpose of the trip was to record the transit of Venus across the sun in order to accurately determine the distance from the Earth to its nearest star. It was also around this time that Cook wrote that his ambition was to go not only 'farther than any man has been before me, but as far as I think it is possible for a man to go'; and it's fair to say that in that endeavour (and, indeed, in that *Endeavour*), Cook enjoyed almost complete fulfilment. Sailing on from Tahiti, Cook then completed a survey of the entire coast of New Zealand before becoming the first European to see Australia's eastern coastline in 1770 – and the first to make landfall on the continent, at a place that he christened Botany Bay.

In all, Captain James Cook undertook three voyages to the Pacific, dying on his last adventure in Hawaii on Valentine's Day, 1779, having been stabbed by local villagers. A 27ft obelisk still stands on the beach near the spot where he fell. In addition there are also statues of him (or monuments to him) overlooking Botany Bay in Cooktown, Sydney; close to Admiralty Arch in London; plus, of course, atop Easby Moor (see p110), and by the Whalebone Arch in Whitby(see map p145) – both, of course, on the Cleveland Way. There are also no fewer than *four* museums dedicated to him in the local area, each celebrating a different stage of his life: Captain Cook Birthplace Museum in Marton, Captain Cook Schoolroom Museum in Great Ayton, Captain Cook and Staithes Heritage Centre (see opposite), and Captain Cook Memorial Museum in Whitby (see p144 & p146) – with both the last two, once again, lying very near the Cleveland Way.

if you live in the UK and have a young child, you may have watched the Cbeebies programme *Jack's Old Boat* – in which case, the idyllic seaside village in which it is set will be familiar to you. Tranquil and timeless though it may appear today, records of Staithes date back 'only' to 1415 – making it a veritable youngster for these parts, where archaeological projects regularly dig up villages six thousand years old. It has also changed frequently over the centuries, with stormy seas often claiming the seafront cottages, including an entire row of 13 of them in 1745. Nevertheless, it remains one of the most picturesque places on the trail and even though there's not much to do here – save, perhaps, for a quick scoot around **Captain Cook and Staithes Heritage Centre** (school summer hols daily 10am-4pm, winter weekends only) to see the recreation of the shop where Captain Cook was employed before starting his naval career – a day spent in Staithes is never a day wasted.

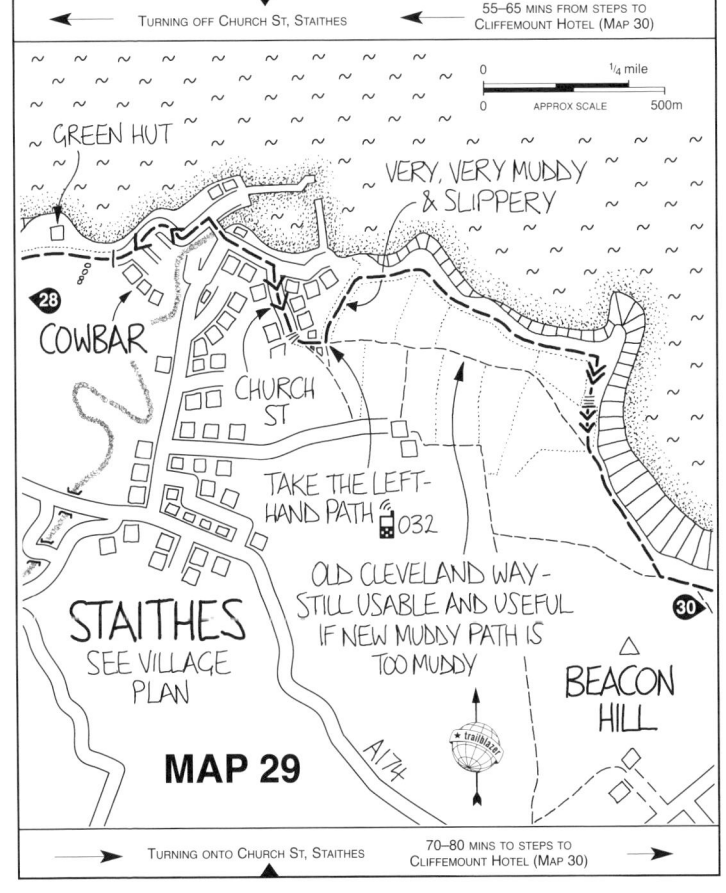

TURNING OFF CHURCH ST, STAITHES

55–65 MINS FROM STEPS TO CLIFFEMOUNT HOTEL (MAP 30)

0   ¼ mile

0   APPROX SCALE   500m

GREEN HUT

VERY, VERY MUDDY & SLIPPERY

28

COWBAR

CHURCH ST

TAKE THE LEFT-HAND PATH 032

OLD CLEVELAND WAY - STILL USABLE AND USEFUL IF NEW MUDDY PATH IS TOO MUDDY

30

STAITHES
SEE VILLAGE PLAN

BEACON HILL

MAP 29

A174

★ trailblazer

ROUTE GUIDE AND MAPS

TURNING ONTO CHURCH ST, STAITHES

70–80 MINS TO STEPS TO CLIFFEMOUNT HOTEL (MAP 30)

Services and transport
Given the number of tourists who make a pilgrimage to Staithes every day in the summer, it's a little surprising that there aren't more facilities for them. There's no post office, or chemist, for example, and the nearest **supermarket**, Co-op (daily 6am-10pm), is on the A174, well away from both the trail and the old heart of Staithes; you'll also find the nearest **ATM** here.

There *is* a **tourist office**, in Gateway Centre at the top of the old town, but it's staffed by volunteers and as a result the opening times vary from day to day, though you can usually rely on it being open daily from 11am to 4pm or thereabouts. The website 💻 visitstaithesandrunswick.com is also pretty good.

For public transport, Arriva's **bus** No X4 lands by the top, newer part of town; see box pp52-3 for details.

Where to stay
Unlike other places around here (Saltburn, Skinningrove) Staithes is actually blessed with quite a few accommodation options. Some of the B&Bs are very smart, too, especially down in the older part of town on the way to the harbour including **Dotty's** (☎ 01947-841096, 💻 trudiemward@hotmail .co.uk; 2D, both en suite; WI-FI; ①) in the attic above the delightful café of the same name. Spotless and serene, it's a lovely place and guests also share a lounge and the rooms are decorated in the same quirky vintage style as the café (though mercifully a little less cluttered). B&B costs from £42.50pp (sgl occ from £85).

Next door, **The Endeavour** (☎ 01947-841029, 💻 www.endeavour-restaurant.co .uk) used to be the village's finest restaurant, though now it operates on a pop-up only basis about a dozen times a year; not a problem, however, for you can still get the full **Endeavour** experience by staying in their lovely **B&B** (2D/1D or T/1Tr, all en suite; 🛏; WI-FI; ①; 🐾). The only disadvantage with this place is their reluctance to take advance bookings for a one-night stay over a Saturday night, however, if they have availability nearer the time they will; that and the fact that it's often filled already

with guests who booked with the walking companies. Otherwise, this place is lovely and good value starting at £50pp (sgl occ from £85).

A third smart option, **Staithes Retreat** (☎ 07557-873033, 💻 www.staithesretreats .co.uk; 1Tr, private facilities; 🛏; WI-FI; 🐾) lies in the heart of the old town and comprises two rooms; a double and a small double suitable for one person which can only be booked in addition to the main double. B&B costs from £42.50pp (sgl occ £70-80). It's a pleasant place with an equally amiable owner who offers acupuncture, reflexology and Indian head massage. The B&B sits opposite the Heritage Centre but the house is called Westgate and has the name written in glass above the blue front door.

Opposite Dotty's, the rooms at **The Royal George** (☎ 01947-841432, 💻 the royalgeorgestaithes.co.uk; 2D, both en suite 1D private facilities; ①; WI-FI; 🐾 bar only), on the High St, are smart and comfy and we also liked the fact that, if you prefer, they'll include dinner, or a packed lunch, rather than breakfast in the rates, which are from £42.50pp (sgl occ from £65).

Moving to the top of town, now under new ownership, **Roraima House** (☎ 01947-841423, 💻 bedandbreakfast-staithes.co.uk; 2D, plus apartment with 1D/1T, all en suite; 🛏; WI-FI) is a long established and highly regarded B&B boasting an upper floor apartment with two rooms plus its own kitchen. Rates start at £42.50pp (sgl occ from £75) but see their website for details of rates in the apartment; take off £10pp if you don't require breakfast.

Finally, up at the top of the old town by the car park is **Captain Cook Inn** (☎ 01947-840200, 💻 captaincookinn.co.uk; 5D/4Qd, all en suite; 🛏; WI-FI; ①; 🐾), 60 Staithes Lane, which charges from £40pp (sgl occ from £50).

Where to eat and drink
As pretty as Staithes undoubtedly is, there is a limit of what you can do other than take lots of photos and browse the half-dozen shops. Which is just fine, as it leaves you plenty of time to go and stuff your face somewhere. The first place to head to is

Dotty's (see Where to stay; WI-FI; 🐾; daily 10.30am-4.30pm), which is very friendly to both humans and dogs (we were presented with a small bag of dog treats before we'd even sat down). Boasting wi-fi, tea served in (mismatched) China crockery, Nina Simone on the playlist and a 'retro-chic' décor that manages to be both fascinating and cosy, it's safe to say that this is our favourite place in Staithes by quite a distance. Our only gripe is that their menu at the moment is limited to hot drinks and cakes, with the only savoury option being their delicious cheese scones with a chunk of cheddar cheese & chutney (£3.75).

Rival cafés include *Sea Drift* (Sat-Thur 10am-4pm) which describes itself as the home of the 'coble cake' (a mélange of apricots, walnuts and cinnamon filled with apple, then served warm with cream; £3.45). If the sun is shining it's a lovely place to sit outside and watch the comings and goings of the harbour.

There are other options. *The Tea Shop* (daily 10am-4pm), at the top of the hill, is fine but not really worth the hard schlep up from the seafront and the Cleveland Way, and they accept neither dogs nor debit/credit cards. The simple menu of sandwiches and breakfasts is fine and fairly priced but we think there are better places back down the hill.

There are also three **pubs** in the town that serve food. What many walkers want from a pub when it comes to food, *The Royal George* (see Where to stay; food Mon-Fri noon-2.30pm & 5.30-8.30pm, Sat & Sun noon-3pm & 5.30-8.30pm) serves up simple, honest, well-priced grub (nearly all dishes are just £7.50 at lunch, £9/10 in the evening), the menu is familiar rather than fancy but the dishes are all very hearty. Further down the lane, right on the harbour, *Cod & Lobster* (☎ 01947-840330, 🖳 codandlobster.co.uk; WI-FI; 🐾; food Mon-Thur noon-3pm & 5.30-8.30pm, Fri noon-3pm & 5.30-9pm, Sat noon-9pm, Sun noon-8.30pm; also breakfasts Fri, Sat & Sun & daily in school summer hols 9.30-11.30am) has a large menu in which fish, as you'd expect, features prominently. Most dishes are under a tenner but it's

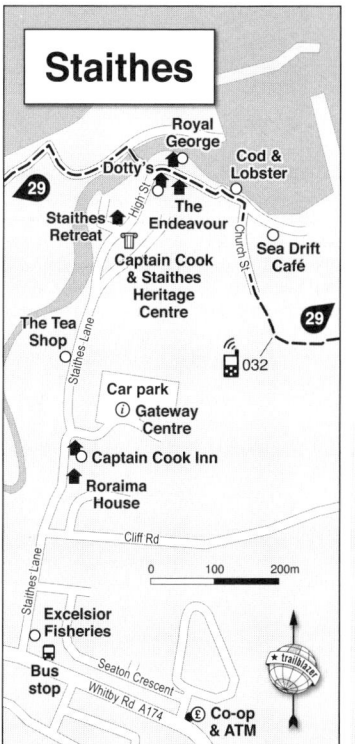

worth paying more to sample the more interesting items such as the seafood kebab (£12.95), or the monkfish wrapped in parma ham (£14.95).

Up the hill by the car park, *Captain Cook Inn* (see Where to stay; food served Mon-Fri noon-3pm & 5-8.30pm, Sat & Sun noon-9pm) is a very friendly place and the food is pretty good value with the most expensive item the full side of ribs (£13.50).

Finally, if you can't do without your **fish-and-chip** fix there's *Excelsior Fisheries* (Tue & Wed 11.30am-1.30pm & 4-7pm, Fri & Sat 4-8pm) on the way out of town near the A174.

ROUTE GUIDE AND MAPS

Soon after leaving Staithes the Cleveland Way follows the newly established England Coast Path rather than its original, more direct course through the horse fields. It's not long before you find yourself walking past the ironmongery on the outskirts of Port Mulgrave, all of which hint at this sleepy hamlet's former importance.

PORT MULGRAVE [MAP 30]

It may come as something of a surprise to find that the only place on the Cleveland Way that has the word 'port' in its title actually stands on the cliffs well above the sea. But there's a reason for this. The port actually does still exist, or at least the remnants of it, at the foot of the cliffs immediately below the Cleveland Way. But the ironstone mine that was the reason for Port Mulgrave's existence was abandoned when the mine was exhausted; and though the port that served the mine was still used to ship ironstone from nearby Grinkle Mine up until 1917, it too was abandoned when Grinkle was connected to the Middlesbrough to Whitby rail line (a section of which you've already seen on this walk). Today, only a few old bits of ironmongery provide any clue as to the port's former importance.

The path down to the port is officially closed and, though there's nothing to stop you taking it, you will have to scramble using ropes that have been attached to the steep bank in order to get to the bottom. Do so and you'll find that several locals have built beach shacks (one of them even has two storeys!) down near the shore. This is also one of the best beaches to look for fossils – largely, perhaps, because of the lack of competitors here.

Whether you choose to risk your neck on the path down to the port is your business but one place we do urge you to visit is *The Ship* (☎ 01947-840303; 1D/1D or T, all en suite; WI-FI; 🐾 tearoom only). You can imagine Sunday supplements would work themselves up into a right lather over this place and justifiably so. Once a pub, at the time of writing it had just been taken over by a new proprietor and in addition to the simple but exquisite little tearoom it also offers B&B.

B&B costs from £42.50pp (sgl occ from £45); a single room is also available as long as one of the other rooms has been booked, so this would be a good place for three people walking together.

The **tea room** is open at weekends (Sat & Sun noon-6pm) but the new owner hopes to open daily in the peak season; the details will be put on signs on the trail so keep an eye open. The menu includes traybake cakes (£2.45-3.75), toasted tea cake (£2.90-3.75), soups and sandwiches (from £3.95). They are licensed so can sell alcohol, but only serve bottled drinks. However, they also have homemade lemonade (£1.75); if it is anything like as good as that made by the previous owners it will be worth coming here for.

If I have a complaint to make it's that it's just too close to Staithes and thus many people will decide against visiting or staying here.

HINDERWELL [off MAP 30]

Though there's nothing wrong with this simple settlement stretched out along the A174, there would be little reason to visit Hinderwell if it wasn't for *Serenity Camping* (☎ 01947-841122, 🖥 serenity camping.co.uk; WI-FI; 🐾; Mar-Oct), the nearest **campsite** to Staithes. The site boasts a 'Wi-Fi & Information Cabin' (open 24hrs) and you can charge your phone at reception. Backpackers are charged £10pp, though there may be a 2-night minimum stay in July and August and at weekends at other times. **Glamping** in a shepherd's hut (£60-70 sleeping up to two), bell tent (£60-90 sleeping up to two) and even a 'potting shed' (described as a 'boutique two-room

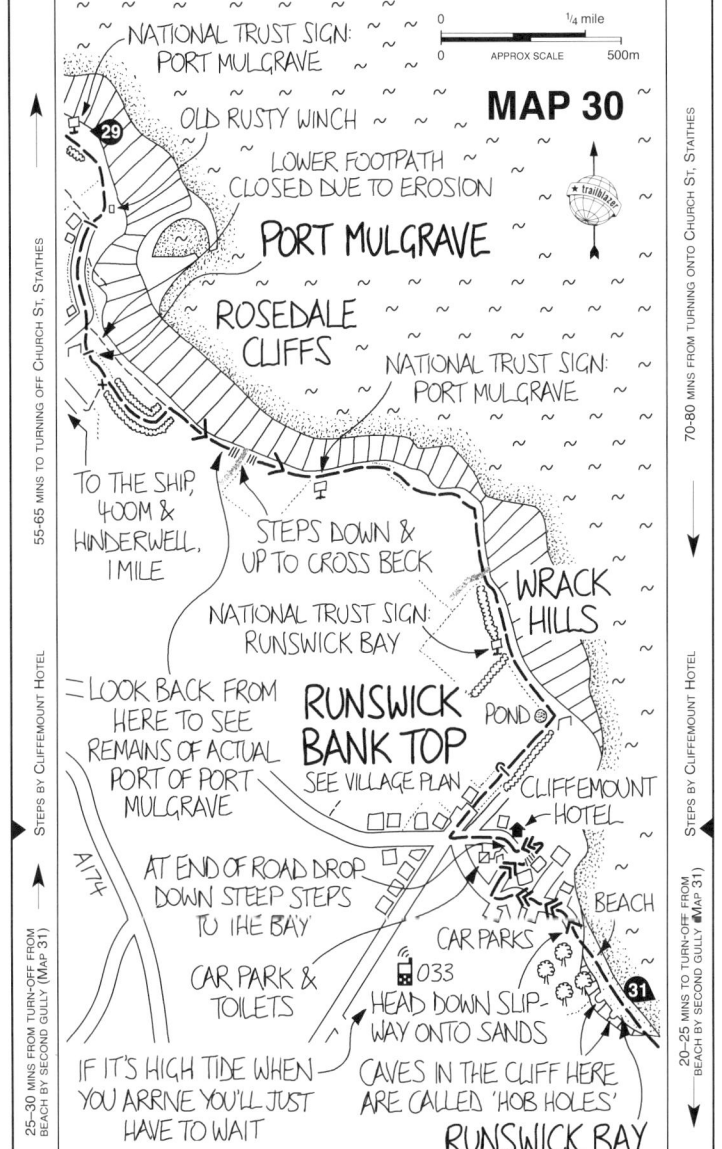

NATIONAL TRUST SIGN: PORT MULGRAVE

OLD RUSTY WINCH

LOWER FOOTPATH CLOSED DUE TO EROSION

MAP 30

PORT MULGRAVE

ROSEDALE CLIFFS

NATIONAL TRUST SIGN: PORT MULGRAVE

TO THE SHIP, 400M & HINDERWELL, I MILE

STEPS DOWN & UP TO CROSS BECK

NATIONAL TRUST SIGN: RUNSWICK BAY

WRACK HILLS

LOOK BACK FROM HERE TO SEE REMAINS OF ACTUAL PORT OF PORT MULGRAVE

RUNSWICK BANK TOP
SEE VILLAGE PLAN

POND

CLIFFEMOUNT HOTEL

A174

AT END OF ROAD DROP DOWN STEEP STEPS TO THE BAY

BEACH

CAR PARKS

CAR PARK & TOILETS

☎ 033

HEAD DOWN SLIP-WAY ONTO SANDS

IF IT'S HIGH TIDE WHEN YOU ARRIVE YOU'LL JUST HAVE TO WAIT

CAVES IN THE CLIFF HERE ARE CALLED 'HOB HOLES'

RUNSWICK BAY

0 ... 1/4 mile
0 ... 500m
APPROX SCALE

55-65 MINS TO TURNING OFF CHURCH ST, STAITHES

STEPS BY CLIFFEMOUNT HOTEL

25-30 MINS FROM TURN-OFF FROM BEACH BY SECOND GULLY (MAP 31)

70-80 MINS FROM TURNING ONTO CHURCH ST, STAITHES

STEPS BY CLIFFEMOUNT HOTEL

20-25 MINS TO TURN-OFF FROM BEACH BY SECOND GULLY (MAP 31)

ROUTE GUIDE AND MAPS

cabin suitable for two to share'; £70-80) is also available; add a £30 'bed linen bundle' to these glamping prices and note that there's a minimum two-night stay in the shepherd's hut and potting shed.

Before you even get to Hinderwell you stumble across **St Hilda's Boutique** (☎ 01947-841935, 🖳 rlsenterprises.co.uk; 6D in house, all en suite; ➤; WI-FI), though by the time you get here it may be called *St Hilda's Court*. Describing itself as a 'Boutique B&B', St Hilda's boasts six 'suites', each inspired by an international city from Cairo to Los Angeles via Venice, Paris, London and Cape Town. Eccentric it may be, but you can't help but admire the effort (and investment) that has gone into each room, and the facilities – spa bath with Jacuzzi jets, plasma TVs, four-poster beds etc – with which each has been fitted. Rates start at around £45pp in the Los Angeles room, though the other rooms are nearer the £75pp mark (sgl occ room rate).

For **food**, campers and B&Bers may want to visit the **Runcible Spoon** (summer school holidays Mon & Wed-Sun 10am-4pm, also Thur-Sat 7-9pm, rest of year Wed-Sun 10am-4pm), a friendly place with a large menu including several breakfast options from the Full English (£6.95) down to a simple breakfast roll (£3), as well as a

decent line in lunchtime wraps (£6.95). They also offer **B&B** (☎ 01947-840700; 1S/3D, all en suite; also one apartment (1D) with kitchenette; ➤; WI-FI; 🐾) charges £37.50-42.50pp (sgl/sgl occ £70-75). They don't have email so, apart from calling, the best way for people to contact them is through their Facebook page.

Shuffle a few metres along the way and you reach the only pub in the village that's currently trading. However, at the time of writing it was due to be taken over by new owners and it wasn't certain the details would stay the same; hopefully the phone number at least won't change. *The Brown Cow* (☎ 01947-840694; 3D shared bathroom, 1D en suite; ➤; WI-FI; Ⓛ; 🐾) offers basic and very cheap accommodation. Rooms are from £22.50pp even for single occupancy, with breakfast £5pp extra. They also do **food** (daily noon-7.45pm) including a selection of curries (from £9.15) and a fair-sized fish menu, with fish dishes from £8.65 up to £9.75 for the salmon, lemon & dill fishcakes.

The only other eating option is the local chippy, **Robinson Fish & Chips** (Tue & Thur 5-8pm, Fri & Sat 11.45am-1.30pm & 5-8pm).

Arriva's **bus** No X4 serves the village; see box pp52-3 for details.

From Port Mulgrave the path continues along the coast to **Runswick Bay**, emerging in the car park of Runswick Bay Hotel.

RUNSWICK BANK TOP

Often described as one of Yorkshire's best-kept secrets, the settlement of **Runswick Bay** is divided into two parts: a more modern part atop of the cliffs (properly called **Runswick Bank Top**) and a far more charming old town down at the foot of the cliffs near the beach, which pedestrians reach via the vertiginous set of steps that form part of the Cleveland Way, and drivers reach by shutting their eyes, clenching their buttocks, and edging their vehicles down what must be the steepest road on the Yorkshire coast – and possibly on the planet.

Make it to the bottom in one piece and you'll find a lovely, cosy, rabbit-warren of

a village, and a gorgeous arc of golden sand stretching away to the south. The thatched cottage at the end of the village here, overlooking the sea, is said to be the only thatched house on the North Yorkshire coast and was a holiday home used by James Herriot, who accurately described Runswick Bay as 'so picturesque and scenic that it hardly seems real'.

Most of the accommodation can be found at the top of the village, including the **campsite**, *Runswick Bay Caravan & Camping Park* (☎ 01947-840997, 🖳 runs wickbaycaravanandcampingpark.co.uk; WI-FI; 🐾), where backpackers are charged £10pp to stay.

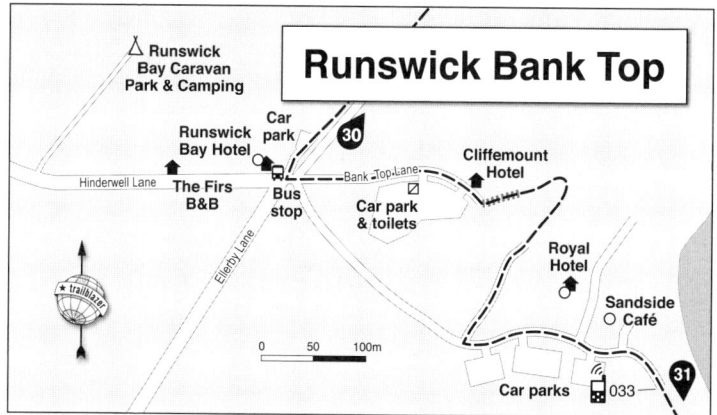

Runswick Bank Top

ROUTE GUIDE AND MAPS

Near to the campsite's entrance at 26 Hinderwell Lane, *The Firs* (☎ 01947-840433, 🖳 the-firs.co.uk; 1S/6D/1T/3Tr, all en suite; 🛏; WI-FI; Ⓛ; 🐾; end Mar-end Nov) charges from £47.50pp (sgl occ from £75).

We like *Runswick Bay Hotel* (☎ 01947-841010, 🖳 therunswickbay.co.uk; 3D/1Tr/1Qd, all en suite; 🛏; WI-FI; Ⓛ; 🐾), whose car park you walk through on the Cleveland Way, very much both as somewhere to eat and somewhere to stay; it is also very dog friendly. Rates for **B&B** are from £47.50pp (sgl occ from £80). **Food** is served daily 6-9pm (from 5pm in summer), and they also open daily at lunchtimes (noon-3pm) during the busy school summer holiday season. Mains are in the £10-15 region, though the rib-eye is £18.50 and the food is very good.

Their main rival is *Cliffemount Hotel* (☎ 01947-840103, 🖳 cliffemounthotel.co .uk; 16D/1T/1Tr, all en suite; 🛏; WI-FI; Ⓛ; 🐾), at the end of Bank Top Lane where the Cleveland Way drops down to the lower part of town. Though it looks more impressive than its competitor, we found it less friendly – though you have to admire the views over the bay from some of its rooms. Rates vary widely (£42.50-82.50pp, sgl occ £70-155).

Facilities are fewer in the lower, older part of town though you will find the convenient *Sandside Café* (daily 10am-5pm, to 5.30pm in summer), where sandwiches start at £4.50. Behind it, within the web of tiny streets, is *Royal Hotel* (☎ 01947-840215, 🖳 theroyal-runswick.com; **food** school holidays daily noon-9pm, rest of year Mon-Fri noon-3pm & 5-9pm, Sat & Sun noon-9pm), owned by Runswick Bay Hotel (see column opposite) and serving jacket potatoes and sandwiches during the day as well as standard pub classics, starting at £9.95 for the ham, tuna and prawn salad.

Public transport, like most of the places along this stretch of coastline, is limited to Arriva's **bus** No X4 which calls in at the top, newer part of town; see box pp52-3 for details.

❏ **Where to stay: the details**
In the descriptions of accommodation in this book: 🛏 means at least one room has a bath; Ⓛ means a packed lunch can be prepared if arranged in advance; 🐾 signifies that dogs are welcome in at least one room but also subject to prior arrangement, an additional charge may also be payable; WI-FI means wi-fi is available. See also p76.

RUNSWICK BAY TO ROBIN HOOD'S BAY [MAPS 30-37]

This **15.2-mile/24.5km stage** (4¾hrs to 5¾hrs) provides some exhilarating clifftop walking. It's not an easy day – there are plenty of ups and downs as you follow the contours of the cliffs which will have your thigh muscles begging for mercy. But there are also plenty of things to see and places to rest too – all of which makes for a wonderful day's walking.

The day begins with a bit of seafront strolling as you cross Runswick's beautiful beach. Note that during certain high tides the path may actually be impassable for a short time. There is the odd sign placed hereabouts that provides walkers with routes you can take to circumvent the beach – but to be honest, we think you may as well just wait until the tide recedes (it shouldn't take long) and then set off.

The path off the sand (Map 31) wasn't signposted at the time of research but you need to aim for the second gully, ie the one *past* the distinctive blue-painted hut, and *not* the one before it. The climb up the appropriately named **High Cliff** and on to **Kettleness** is long and tiring, and the rewards at the top are uncertain (we heard of a café called Kettleness Tea Parlour that was being set up here, and even found a Facebook page dedicated to it, though we failed to find any sign of it when we passed through). But no matter, for at least you can comfort yourself with the fact that, for the next couple of miles at least, the trail is fairly level as it plots a course along the cliffs, with Lythe's church steeple visible ahead on your right.

LYTHE [Map 32, p140]

This small unassuming village lies about a mile from the path and probably wouldn't feature in this book were it not for its campsite, the last until Whitby. *Lythe Caravan & Camping Park* (☎ 01947-893300, 🖳 lythe cc.co.uk; WI-FI pub only; 🐾; mid Feb to early Jan) has a few spaces for small tents for £8-10pp; booking is recommended for peak periods. They also have a few **camping pods** (from £43 per night per pod). They come with heating and lighting but not much else (so you'll still need a sleeping bag and mattress) though they're quite cosy; as they can sleep up to four adults they could also be a very good deal. Note that over weekends and bank holidays there's a minimum 2- to 4-night stay for advance bookings but a single-night stay may be possible near the time.

Like everything else in the village, the campsite lies near to the main road junction, where you'll also find a local **grocery shop**, Lythe Community Shop (☎ 01947-893983; summer Mon-Fri 8am-5.30pm, Sat to 4pm, Sun 10am-4pm) home to the village **post office** (Mon-Fri 8am-5.30pm, Sat to 1pm). They also do a nice line in simple snacks (bacon or sausage buns) in the summer months, which is quite lucky as the local pub, *The Stiddy* (same phone number as for campsite, 🖳 stiddy.net; WI-FI; 🐾; bar summer school holidays daily from 6pm & Sun noon-2pm, rest of year Tue & Thur from 7pm, Fri & Sat from 6pm, Sun noon-2pm & from 6.30pm) only serves **food** on Friday and Saturday 6-8pm (summer Wed-Sat 6-8pm) and Sunday noon-2pm. They offer room only **accommodation** (1D/1Tr, both en suite) from £30pp (sgl occ room rate).

Arriva's X4 **bus** leaves from near The Stiddy on its way up and down the coast; see box pp52-3 for details.

Sticking with the main trail, the path continues to **Deepgrove Wyke** (Map 32), where a steep descent through the trees leads to a pleasantly straightforward

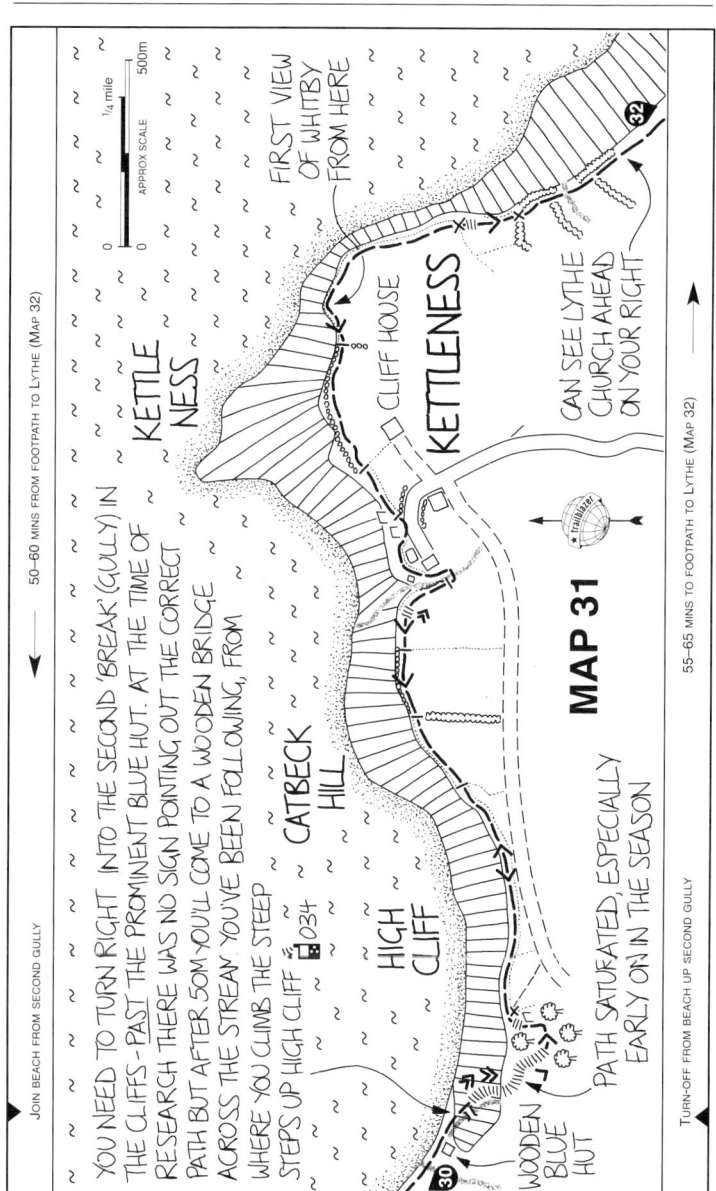

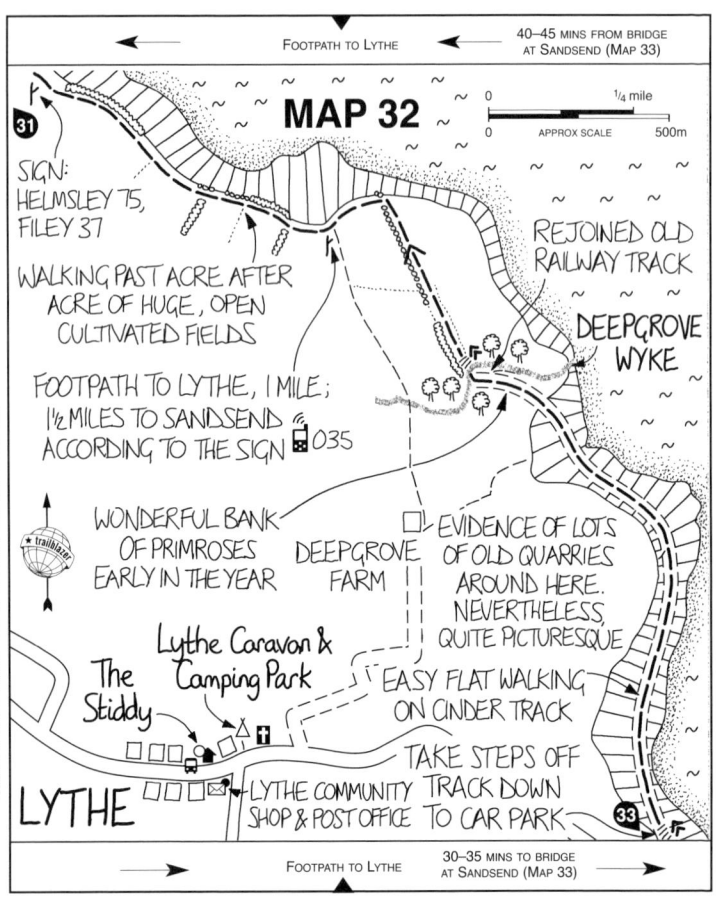

bit of walking along an old railway track; alight at the end of the line down the steps to the car park at **Sandsend**.

SANDSEND [MAP 33]

A row of buildings lining the seafront road, Sandsend dribbles along the coast for half a mile. It's not an unattractive place, there are several very decent eateries and the beach is terrific. But with Whitby just over the next hill, it maybe doesn't get quite the custom it should from Cleveland Way walkers.

The first place you come to is also the best for walkers. ***Wits End and Walled Garden Café*** (☎ 01947-893658, 🖥 witsend cafe.co.uk; WI-FI; 🐾; Easter-Dec daily 9am-5pm, Jan-Easter Wed-Sun 9am-5pm) welcomes walkers and their canine friends and while the menu isn't particularly

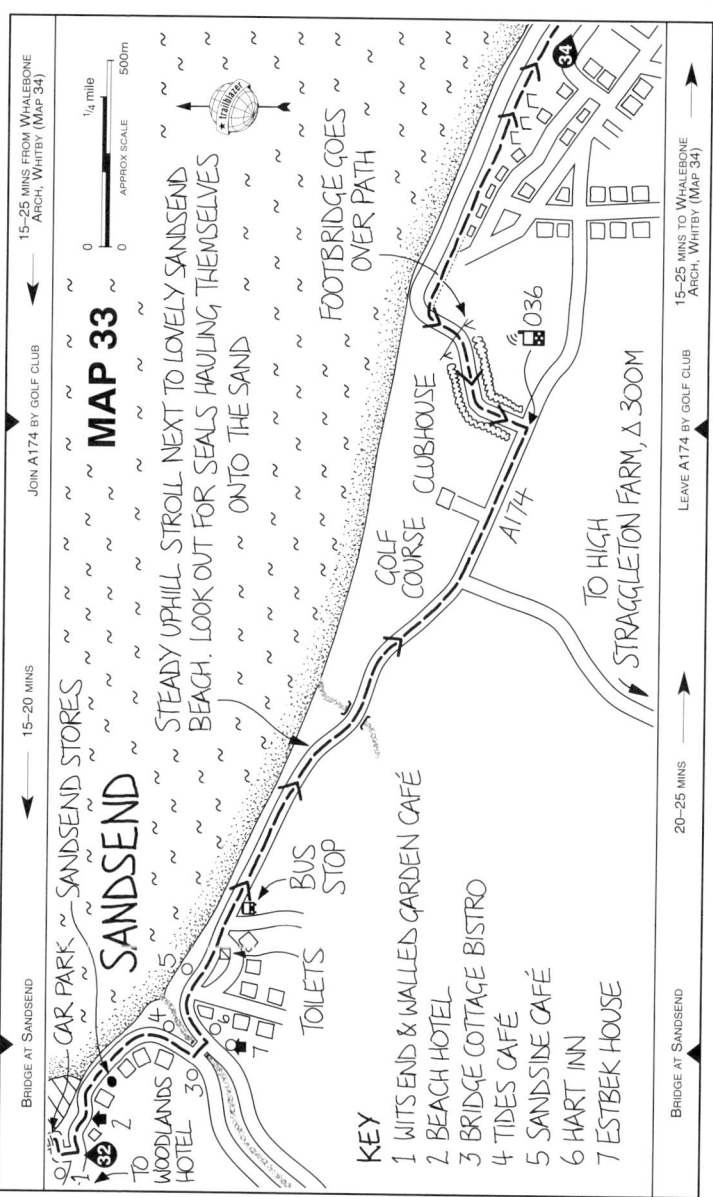

inventive, with jacket potatoes (£6-8), sandwich rolls (£5-7) and toasties (£6-7) to the fore, the food is good and it can all be washed down with a cup or two of their excellent coffee.

Even simpler fare can be found at *Tides* (daily 9am-5pm) which mainly specialises in hot drinks, while further along is *Sandside Café* (☎ 01947-893916, 🖳 sand sidecafe.co.uk; mid Mar-mid Nov daily 9am-4.45pm, rest of year Thur-Mon from 9am but closing hours are weather dependent), whose menu highlights are the crab sandwiches (around £7.95).

Even the local shop, **Sandsend Stores** (☎ 01947-893214; daily 8am-5pm, though closing time is seasonally dependent), gets in on the act by offering simple snacks such as cheese toasties (£3.80).

Smartest of all for lunchtime fare is *Bridge Cottage Bistro* (☎ 01947-893438, 🖳 bridgecottagebistro.com; Tue-Sun 10am-4pm, also Thur-Sat from 7pm; WI-FI; 🐾 small and on lead) with a menu that changes daily but may include slow-cooked belly pork with creamed potatoes and sticky toffee pudding for dessert (£15.80).

Their closest rival in terms of both quality and geographical location is the award-winning *Estbek House* (see column opposite; ☎ 01947-893424, 🖳 estbekhouse .co.uk; daily 6.30-9pm) whose fish-heavy menu rarely dips below the £20-mark for mains but does include such delights as Whitby whole lobster (£39).

Next door, for superior pub food there's *Hart Inn* (☎ 01947-893304; food Mon-Fri 11am-2.30pm & 5-8.30pm, Sat 11am-8.30pm, Sun 11am-2.30pm only; WI-FI; 🐾), with their Sunday roasts (£10) very popular. Note that the pub closes at 6pm on a Sunday.

Given the wonderful opportunities for fine dining, it's not a bad idea to stay the night in Sandsend and there are several **accommodation** options – though it should be noted that for campers the nearest option is High Straggleton Farm (see p147) near Whitby, or back in Lythe (see p140). The smart *Estbek House* (see column opposite; 4D/1D or T, all en suite; WI-FI; Feb-Dec) is as luxurious as the food they serve in their restaurant; rates start from £115pp and it can be an eye-watering £205 for single occupancy, though this includes a three-course dinner as well as B&B.

More affordable, *Woodlands Hotel* (☎ 01947-893899, 🖳 thewoodlandssandsend .co.uk; 5D, all en suite; ▼; WI-FI) is a smart, bijou hotel with rooms starting at around £70pp (sgl occ room rate). One room is suitable for adults with up to two children under 16.

Meanwhile, the rooms at *The Beach Hotel* (☎ 01947-893200, 🖳 beachhotelsand send.co.uk; 2T/5D, all en suite; WI-FI variable; 🐾), though simply furnished, are all en suite, and if you can tear yourself away from the flatscreen TVs they've just had installed you'll notice they all boast sea views too. Rates are from £55pp (sgl occ from £70).

As for public transport, Arriva's **bus X4** drives down the seafront road on its way between Whitby and Middlesbrough; see box pp52-3 for details.

The longest stretch of road walking on the entire Cleveland Way now follows as you stay on the pavement through Sandsend and beyond, only saying ta-ta to the tarmac 1¼ miles later to head off through a golf course and on, eventually, to lovely **Whitby**.

WHITBY   [map p145]

Situated at the mouth of the River Esk that divides the town, Whitby has been welcoming tourists since the Georgian period at the start of the 19th century. And it remains one of Yorkshire's main draws to this day, thanks largely to its maritime connections (the fishing port is one of the busiest on this stretch of coastline, and the town used to be an important port in the coal and alum trades as well as in shipbuilding and whaling) and literary heritage (in addition to Bram Stoker setting his horror novel

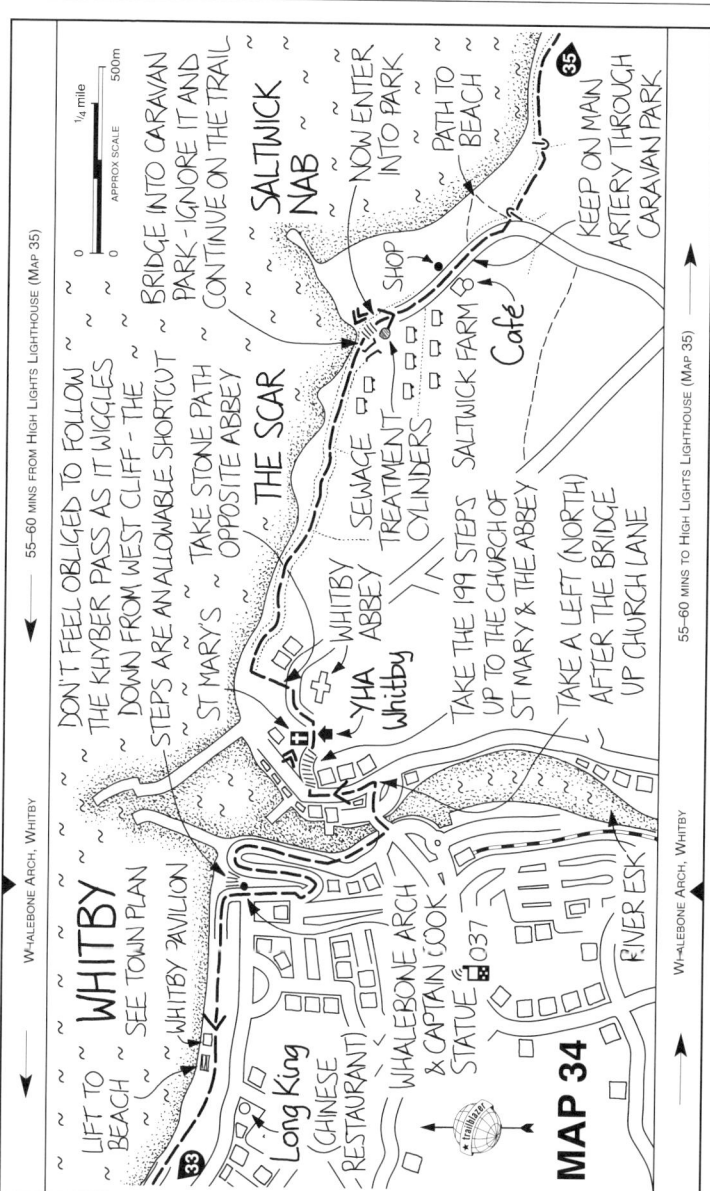

Dracula here, the earliest recognised English poet, Caedmon, also hailed from hereabouts) as well as its association with the black gemstone, jet, which is cut and traded here. A good deal prettier and more charming than Scarborough, the other major settlement on the trail, it's also more quirky and interesting, too, and for this reason we advise that, if you've never been before and have a day to spare on your walk, Whitby would be the most rewarding place on the trail in which to spend it.

What to see and do
As with many places on the Cleveland Way, the town rather rewards those who like to wander aimlessly about the streets. The 'official attractions' are fine but there aren't many.

First and foremost there's **Whitby Abbey** (Map 34; 🖳 english-heritage.org .uk; Apr-end Sep daily 10am-6pm, Oct to 5pm; £7.90), the haunting Gothic ruin that sits above the town and its harbour. The abbey was founded in AD657 by the Anglo-Saxon King Oswy. It was at this abbey that the Synod of Whitby took place in AD664, an important moment in the history of religion in the country where the two strands of English Christianity, Roman and Celtic,

clashed. At the end of the council King Oswy decided that the Northumbrian church should follow the Roman example in matters of how the monks should dress, and how to calculate Easter. Fast forward a few hundred years and in AD1100 a Benedictine monk, Reinfrid, founded a new religious community at the site, which since the 9th century had been abandoned (along with the port and town itself) due to Viking raids. This lasted until the middle of the 16th century when, inevitably, Henry VIII's soldiers came to tear the place apart and steal all its wealth as part of the Dissolution of the Monasteries. The ruins you see today are actually the remains of the abbey's **church**, together with the abbot's lodgings that became a private house, Abbey House, during the 17th century.

The church that you pass by on the way up the steps to the abbey is **St Mary's** (Map 34) and was founded in 1110 by the Normans, and the tower and transepts are from this time. Standing in the graveyard, one of the locations used by Bram Stoker in *Dracula*, is **Caedmon's Cross**, a late Victorian construction that celebrates the 7th-century poet who lived at the abbey.

Another attraction that we think will be of interest to most people is **Captain**

❏ Fishing trips & whale-watching trips
It may come as something of a surprise to find that Whitby is actually one of England's foremost places to go **whale-watching**, but it shouldn't do. After all, the town was founded on the fishing industry, which grew prosperous thanks to the huge shoals of herring that migrate here in late summer and autumn. These herring, in turn, attract larger fish such as sharks, seabirds, plus, of course, cetaceans and other marine mammals. Seals, porpoise and dolphins (white-beaked and bottlenose) are all seen relatively frequently, but it's the minke, humpback, sei and fin whales that arouse the most excitement. And even if you don't see any, the opportunities a trip offers to enjoy some first-rate birdwatching are not to be missed. To book a trip, visit 🖳 whit bywhalewatching.net (note that trips may only be available in September), or 🖳 whit bycoastalcruises.co.uk.

If, instead of marvelling at the wonders of Nature, your first thoughts on seeing one of God's marine creatures is to wonder what it would taste like served in parsley sauce, perhaps a **fishing trip** would be more appropriate for you. Whitby Fishing Trips (🖳 whitbyfishingtrips.co.uk) is just one of several companies operating out of the harbour, providing 3hr 'taster' trips twice daily throughout the week (£20pp) as well as longer trips over the reefs and wrecks nearby. Codlings, halibut, ling, flounder, poutings, whitings and mackerel all frequent these waters and are the most common catch.

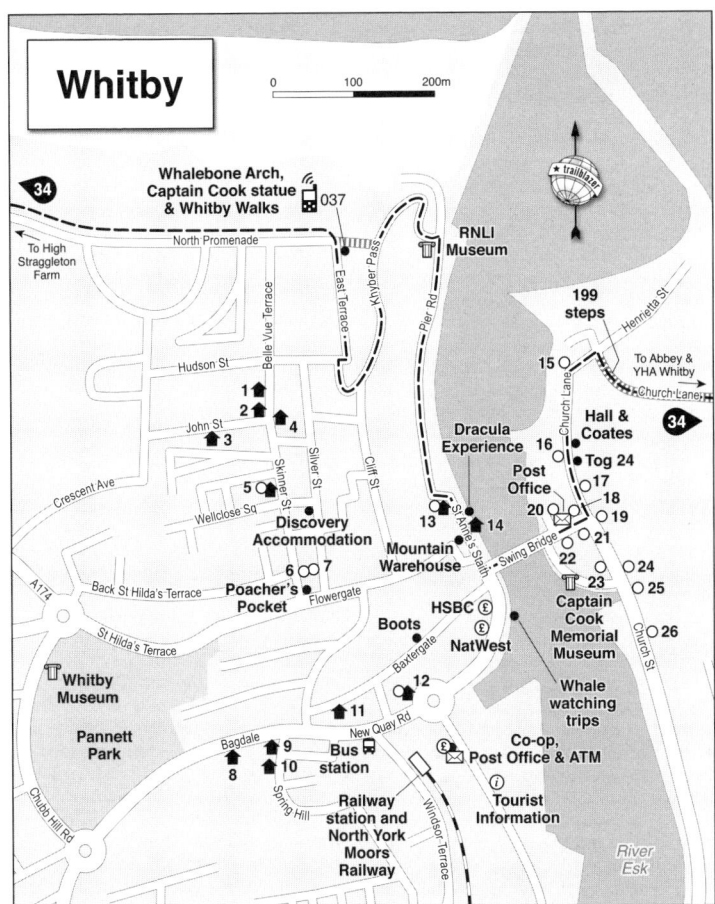

Whitby

0   100   200m

To High Straggleton Farm

Whalebone Arch, Captain Cook statue & Whitby Walks

037

North Promenade

RNLI Museum

199 steps

To Abbey & YHA Whitby

Henrietta St

Church Lane

15

Belle Vue Terrace

East Terrace

Khyber Pass

Pier Rd

Hudson St

John St

1
2
4
3

Church Lane

Hall & Coates

Dracula Experience

16

Tog 24

Post Office

17

Crescent Ave

Skinner St

Silver St

Cliff St

5

18

20

19

Wellclose Sq

Discovery Accommodation

Mountain Warehouse

St Ann's Staith

13   14

Swing Bridge

21

22

24

Back St Hilda's Terrace

6   7

Flowergate

Poacher's Pocket

23

25

St Hilda's Terrace

HSBC

Boots

Baxtergate

NatWest

Captain Cook Memorial Museum

Church St

26

A174

Whitby Museum

12

Whale watching trips

Pannett Park

11

New Quay Rd

Co-op, Post Office & ATM

Bagdale

9

Bus station

8   10

Spring Hill

Railway station and North York Moors Railway

Windsor Terrace

Tourist Information

River Esk

Chubb Hill Rd

trailblazer

ROUTE GUIDE AND MAPS

34

34

Where to stay		
Where to stay	13 The Marine	17 Crumbs 'n' Cobbles
1 No 5	14 Moon & Sixpence	18 Robertson's
2 Bramblewick		19 Carol's Coffee
3 Elizabeth House	**What to eat and drink**	20 Jane's Kitchen
4 Sandpiper House	5 Granby Hotel	21 Hadley's
5 Granby Hotel	6 Beckett's	22 The Edge
8 No 4 Bagdale	7 Rusty Shears	23 Cosa Nostra
9 Bagdale Hall	12 Angel Hotel	24 Mr Chips
10 Bagdale Lodge	13 The Marine	25 Indian Moments
11 George Hotel	15 Duke of York	26 The Endeavour
12 Angel Hotel	16 Monk's Haven Café	

Cook Memorial Museum (💻 cookmuse umwhitby.co.uk; daily mid Feb-Mar 11am-3pm, Apr-Oct 9.45am-5pm; £5.90) housed in the same 17th-century terraced building where the man himself lodged while serving his apprenticeship, in the back alley known as Grape Lane, just down from the bridge. Highlights include the original artworks, letters and documents from many of his voyages, as well as models of Cook's ships. We also liked the museum's idea of comparing maps of the world from both before and after Cook's journeys, thus showing how his work increased our knowledge of our planet in general, and in particular the Pacific region. The museum is fairly small but the uniqueness of the collection goes a long way towards justifying the entrance fee.

There are more Cook-related items at **Whitby Museum** (💻 whitbymuseum.org .uk; Tue-Sun & Bank Hols 9.30am-4.30pm; £5), set in Pannett Park as well as excellent displays on fossils, jet, whaling and maritime heritage and archaeological finds from Whitby Abbey.

Nearer to both harbour and the Cleveland Way, Whitby's **RNLI Museum** (💻 rnli.org; Easter-Oct daily 10am-5pm, Nov-Dec 11am-4pm, Jan-Mar Sat & Sun 11am-4pm; free admission) is housed in the double boathouse as you reach the harbour on the Cleveland Way. It's worth whiling away 10 minutes or so perusing the photographs, medals and mementoes.

If you've decided to spend two nights in Whitby, we recommend you take advantage of the fact that the town lies at one end of the 24-mile **North York Moors Railway** (💻 nymr.co.uk; daily late Mar-early Nov plus in holiday periods such as Christmas/New Year and February half-term, weekends only at other times; 6-8/day depending on the time of year) to Pickering via Grosmont, Goathland, Newtondale & Levisham. Though not cheap (a single is £18.60 during peak season for the 100-minute journey, return £31), it's a beautiful line and it's particularly good at showing you much of the national park that the Cleveland Way doesn't cover.

The town has long exploited its most famous literary association and these days there's even a **Dracula Experience** (💻 draculaexperience.co.uk; daily 9.45am-5pm, Nov-Easter weekends only; £3) at 9 Marine Parade. The rather negligible entrance fee should give you an indication that this isn't the most high-tech of attractions but we do like the use of live actors in some of the scenes (though usually during peak season only). You can also go on a Dracula walk, just one of several offered by **Whitby Walks** (☎ 01947-880485, 💻 whit bywalks.com). Walks start at Whalebone Arch, usually last at least an hour and cost £5; there's no need to book but do check the website for dates as they don't run everyday.

Services

The **tourist information office** (💻 discov eryorkshirecoast.com; Apr-Oct daily 9.30am-5pm, Nov-Mar Thur-Sun 10.30am-4pm but note that the winter hours may change) lies by the River Esk, just to the south of the railway station. It's the only one on the route that is a 'normal', 'traditional' office – that is to say not one that's been stuffed into the corner of a library (see Saltburn), nor staffed entirely by volunteers (Staithes), nor has had its funding cut so drastically that it's little more than a rack of brochures and a telephone (Filey and Scarborough). As such, it's the most useful and best on the trail. It doesn't have a direct phone line, but there is a central contact office in Scarborough (see p167). The websites 💻 thewhitbyguide.co.uk and 💻 visit whitby.com are also useful resources.

Conveniently, just to the north of the tourist office is the town's **post office** (Mon-Fri 8.30am-5.30pm, Sat 9am-5.30pm), which is located in the Co-op **supermarket** (Mon-Sat 6am-11pm, Sun 10am-4pm); you'll also find a **ATM** there, and there are several others nearby close to the bridge.

Not too far away on the major shopping thoroughfare of Baxtergate is a **Boots the Chemist** (Mon-Sat 9am-5.30pm, Sun 11am-4pm). There are a couple of **outdoor shops** nearby, Poacher's Pocket (Mon-Fri noon-5pm, Sat 10am-5pm) and Mountain Warehouse (Mon-Sat 9am-5.30pm, Sun 10.30am-4.30pm), with another two across the river on Church Lane: Hall & Coates (daily 10am-5pm) and Tog 24 (Sun-Thur 10am-5pm, Fri & Sat to 6pm).

Transport

The bus and railway stations are next to each other. Most Cleveland Way walkers will find Northern's **train service** (see box p49) to Middlesbrough of limited use but the most popular Cleveland Way **buses** – Arriva's X4 to Middlesbrough, and their X93 (Scarborough to Middlesbrough) – do call in at the bus station. To get away from the Cleveland Way, take Yorkshire Coastliner's 840 bus to York and Leeds. See box pp52-3 for details.

Where to stay

There are several **campsites** for Whitby, one of which is reasonably close to the path, though note that it is 2 miles (3.2km) from the town centre; the friendly *High Straggleton Farm* (off Map 33, p141; ☎ 01947-602373, 🖳 highstraggleton.co.uk; 🐾 on lead; Mar to end Oct) is ostensibly a caravan site though there's a field set aside for campers too; rates are £8.50/14 for one/two people.

Whitby is blessed with a fine hostel. *YHA Whitby* (Map 34; ☎ 01947-602878, ☎ 0345 371 9049, 🖳 yha.org.uk/hostel/yha-whitby; 2 x 2-, 1 x 3-, 11 x 4-, 1 x 5-, 6 x 6-, 4 x 8-, 1 x 10-bed rooms; some en suite; WI-FI; Mar/Apr-end Oct daily, Nov-Mar weekends only) certainly wins the award for the best location, high on the hill, right by the abbey and very close to the trail. The building, too, is a bit of a stunner, a Grade-1 listed mansion set in award-winning gardens. Two of the 4-bed rooms have a double bed and are en suite. As for the facilities, there is a self-catering kitchen and the hostel even has its own little *café* (Mar/Apr-end Oct daily 9am-8.30pm, Nov-Mar weekends only). There are also laundry facilities; check in is from 3pm and once checked in there is 24hr access.

With a dorm bed starting for as little as £15pp (though £30pp is more normal in

high summer) if there are two of you it's worth enquiring about a private room as they start from £25 for two sharing – it could be exceptional value.

If you're looking for a **B&B**, perhaps the first place to try is the website of **Discovery Accommodation** (☎ 01947-821598, 🖳 discoveryaccommodation .com). They have 14 properties here, mainly around the Silver St/Skinner St area. Rates start at about £25pp for a simple double, rising to £75pp for a one-bedroom seafront apartment; single occupancy is the full room rate. Dogs are welcome in most places and wi-fi is available at all. Breakfast, which is optional and costs £7, is taken in their central office on Silver St, where you can also use their swimming pool (£3pp).

There are several decent B&Bs nearby on Belle Vue Terrace and surrounding streets. They include the trendy and friendly *Sandpiper House* (☎ 01947-600246, 🖳 sandpiperhouse.co.uk; 5D, all en suite; 🐾; WI-FI), at 4 Belle Vue Terrace, where the walls are all painted in fashionable, muted, Farrow & Ball tones and the rates are from £42.50pp (sgl occ £75-80). The owners also run *Elizabeth House* (🖳 elizabethhouse whitby.co.uk; 2D/2Qd, all en suite; 🐾; WI-FI), a series of apartments with kitchen facilities at 12 John St. The room-only price is from £30pp (sgl occ from £50).

Nearby, *Number 5* (☎ 01947-606361, 🖳 number5whitby.co.uk; 2S share facilities, 2D or T/4D, all en suite; 🐾; WI-FI; 🐾), at 5 Havelock Place, charges from £39pp (sgl occ from £58), or from £37 in one of the singles – one of the cheaper rates for a single room we could find.

Just down the road at 3 Havelock Place, flower-festooned *Bramblewick* (☎ 01947-604504, 🖳 bramblewickwhitby .com; 2S private facilities, 5D/1T, all en suite; 🐾; WI-FI) has rooms from as little as £38.50pp (sgl occ £40-45, sgl occ £60-75), and their breakfast menu includes fish smoked at the smokery across the harbour.

Sticking to the western side of the harbour, on your left as you climb up Bagdale from the centre is *Bagdale Hall* (☎ 01947-602958, 🖳 bagdale.co.uk; 6D, all en suite; 🐾; WI-FI), with rooms from £70pp (sgl occ from £140). The same people also own a couple of other places nearby: **No 4 Bagdale** (12D, all en suite; ☛; WI-FI) with rooms, also with four-posters, for the same price as the Hall; and **Bagdale Lodge** (13D, all en suite; WI-FI), with rooms of a slightly lower spec, which is reflected in the lower price of £60pp (sgl occ from £120).

Several pubs also provide accommodation in Whitby. At 34 Skinner St, **Granby Hotel** (☎ 01947-601747, 🖳 thegranbyho tel.co.uk; 3D/1Qd, all with shower; WI-FI; ☕ bar only) offers standard, cheap accommodation with rates starting at £32.50pp (sgl occ room rate), though note that while there's a shower in the bedroom you do share a toilet with other residents. Note, too, that they have live music most weekends so try to get a room as far away from the bar as possible to improve your chances of a good night's sleep.

At 38 Baxtergate, **George Hotel** (☎ 01947-602565, 🖳 georgehotelwhitby.co .uk; 7D/7T/3Tr/4Qd, most en suite, rest shared facilities; WI-FI) is noisy and no-frills – and some of the rooms on the lower floors may be disturbed by the live music that often goes on below – but it's cheap (en suite rooms from £35pp, or £25pp in a room with shared facilities; sgl occ room rate). Note that the rate includes a continental breakfast but a cooked breakfast costs £5 extra.

Nearer the bridge at 1 New Quay Rd is the large, Wetherspoon's-owned **Angel Hotel** (☎ 01947-824730, 🖳 jdwetherspoon .com; 1S/23D/6D or T/4Qd, all en suite; ☛; WI-FI) with room rates that vary according to demand but start at £36.25pp (sgl/sgl occ from £52.50).

More upmarket, **The Marine** (☎ 01947-605022, 🖳 the-marine-hotel.co.uk; 4D, all en suite; ☛; WI-FI) has luxurious rooms starting at £75pp with no discount for single occupancy, though their sister hotel, **The Moon & Sixpence** (☎ 01947-604416, 🖳 moon-and-sixpence.co.uk; 3D, all en suite; ☛; WI-FI), also situated on Marine Parade just 20m away, has cheaper rooms starting from £50pp (sgl occ room rate).

Where to eat and drink

Our favourite place is actually set back from the water on Silver St. **Rusty Shears** (☎ 01947-605383, 🖳 restaurantsnapshot .com/RustyShears; WI-FI; ☕; daily 9.30am-5pm) is a vintage tea-shop-cum-gin-bar (with over 180 gins to choose from) as well as a music venue and even a gift shop! It's also very dog friendly. Food-wise their lunch menu (1-3pm) is heavy with sandwiches (£6.95-7.95), soups (from £4.95) and sharing platters (from £11.95), though they also offer about half-a-dozen more substantial dishes (eg Moroccan lamb parcel, or mushroom & chestnut pasty, both £6.95) for those with bigger appetites.

Nearby is our second-favourite place, **Beckett's** (Thur-Sat 10am-4pm, Sun 11am-4pm; ☕), another top, dog-friendly choice with enormous portions of cake (£3.30) and possibly the best coffee on the entire trail.

More convenient for Cleveland Way walkers, Church Lane is the home of many, many cafés and restaurants – which is lucky, as it's also the road the path takes to head out of town. Recommended eateries include the dog-friendly **Monk's Haven Café** (daily 9am-5pm, later in summer) with a large range of lunchtime options, none of which costs more than the £9.95 for the steak pie; and **Crumbs 'n' Cobbles** (daily 9am-5pm) with a large range of sarnies, paninis and quesadillas (£4.95-5.25).

Down at the bottom of the street, on Swing Bridge, are several other reasonable options including fairly smart **The Edge** (daily 8.30am-9.30pm) with good breakfast options including pancake stack and eggs Benedict (both £4.95).

For more staple, cheaper fare seek out **Jane's Kitchen** (daily 8am-5pm, cash only), on Sandgate, very close to the bridge – with breakfast bagels for £3.95 and breakfast sarnies from just £2.20. Cheaper still, **Carol's Coffee Corner** (daily 10am-5pm; cash only), charges just £1 for a bacon bun.

This area east of the bridge is also the place to come for **fish & chips**, and Whitby is arguably the best place to sample this British delicacy. **Robertson's** (daily 11am-7pm, open to later in summer), **Mr Chips**

(Sun-Thur 11.30am-9.30pm, Fri & Sat to 10pm) and *Hadley's* (daily 11am-7pm, later in summer) are all clustered around here and all operate both a restaurant and a takeaway section. Incidentally, if you're looking for a venue where you can eat them, just down the road is *The Endeavour*, a pub that has no problem with customers bringing their own food.

Other evening options hereabouts include *Indian Moments* (☎ 01947-820871, 💻 indianmomentswhitby.co.uk; Tue-Sun 5-11pm), on Church St, with mains starting at £6.95 for a chicken tandoori; and the Italian *Cosa Nostra* (☎ 01947-602030; food daily 4-9pm but can be later in summer) almost opposite, a two-level smart Italian with some seldom-seen dishes such as 'anatra duck' (roasted duck breast with a cherry dressing; £15.90).

For **pub food**, head over the bridge. For standard, no-nonsense, proper good-value pub food, we liked the *Granby* (see Where to stay; food daily noon-9pm) with most dishes priced at £7.50, the mixed grill at £10.95 being the only outlier. The Wetherspoon's-owned *Angel Hotel* (see Where to stay; food 7am-10pm) serves some lovely grub too – the 14oz rump steak is excellent value at £13.59 including a free drink. Or there's the swanky *Marine* (see Where to stay; food daily 8.30am-10pm), our favourite of several fish specialists in this part of town, with seafood mains starting at £14 for the mussels but rising to £75 for the platter for two, including whole lobster, Whitby crab, oysters, prawns, marine gravadlax & crevettes.

Across the harbour on Church Lane, is the *Duke of York* (☎ 01947-600324, 💻 dukeofyork.co.uk; food daily noon-9pm; WI-FI), the food is nothing special – just standard pub mains (£9.50-15.95) on the whole – but the chance to grab a window seat and gaze over the harbour is not to be missed.

Leaving Whitby via the **199 Church Steps**, the way continues to hug the cliffs on its way to Robin Hood's Bay. This is a tough but beautiful section, the many creeks and gullies that you encounter, though often really pretty, sapping both morale and energy. Keep going, however, and before long you'll be passing **Hornblower Lodge** (Map 35), originally built as a lighthouse in 1858 but converted into a Foghorn Station in 1900. Its neighbour, just a little further along, is the Whitby Lighthouse, also known as **High Lights**, built at the same time and still in use today.

There then follows a very picturesque stretch of coastline. It's exhausting, but the creeks are wonderful, sun-dappled places to recover for a few minutes. Soon after passing through **Northcliffe Holiday Park** (Map 36) you come to a junction and a rendezvous with your old friends on the Coast to Coast Path (or, rather, new friends, for whereas you may have taken three days to travel the 41.9 miles (67.4km) since you last saw them at Bloworth Crossing, they will probably have taken just two days and travelled just 29.6 miles (47.6km) to get here – so in all probability, the Coast-to-Coasters you see on this part of your walk will be different to the ones you met previously).

You may even find yourself in a race with them to reach their ultimate destination, Robin Hood's Bay, for while they may have more miles in their legs – they will have travelled 186.7 miles (300.4km) in total to get to this point, whereas you'll have 'only' completed 80.8 (139.2km) – you'll be more practised in the art of coastal walking. It's a race where everyone's a winner, however, for no matter long you take to get there, Robin Hood's Bay is a wonderful destination.

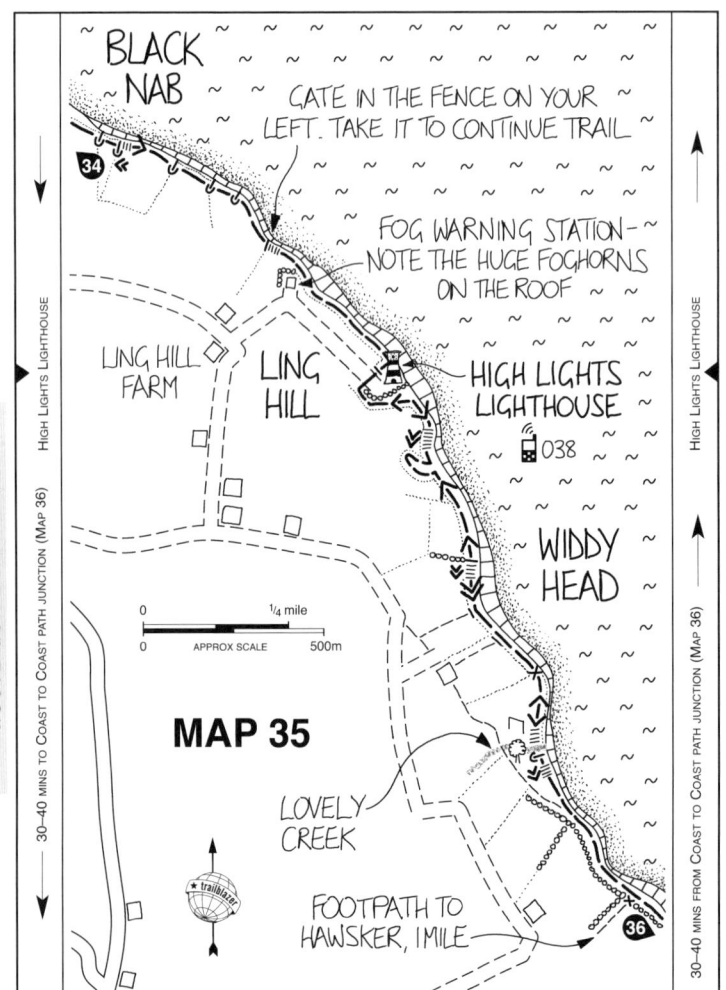

BLACK NAB

GATE IN THE FENCE ON YOUR LEFT. TAKE IT TO CONTINUE TRAIL

34

FOG WARNING STATION – NOTE THE HUGE FOGHORNS ON THE ROOF

LING HILL FARM

LING HILL

HIGH LIGHTS LIGHTHOUSE

038

WIDDY HEAD

0   1/4 mile

0   APPROX SCALE   500m

MAP 35

LOVELY CREEK

trailblazer

FOOTPATH TO HAWSKER, 1 MILE

36

ROUTE GUIDE AND MAPS

30–40 MINS TO COAST TO COAST PATH JUNCTION (MAP 36)

HIGH LIGHTS LIGHTHOUSE

HIGH LIGHTS LIGHTHOUSE

30–40 MINS FROM COAST TO COAST PATH JUNCTION (MAP 36)

ROBIN HOOD'S BAY   [map p155]

Robin Hood's Bay is a quaint, cosy little fishing village that in high summer becomes a busy seaside resort. Though fishing has declined since its heyday in the 19th century, there's been a revival thanks to its crab grounds, said to be amongst the best in the north. The old town huddles around the Dock, row after row of terraced, stone cottages arranged haphazardly uphill with numerous twisting interconnecting alleyways and paths to explore. Within them are a number of pubs and tearooms

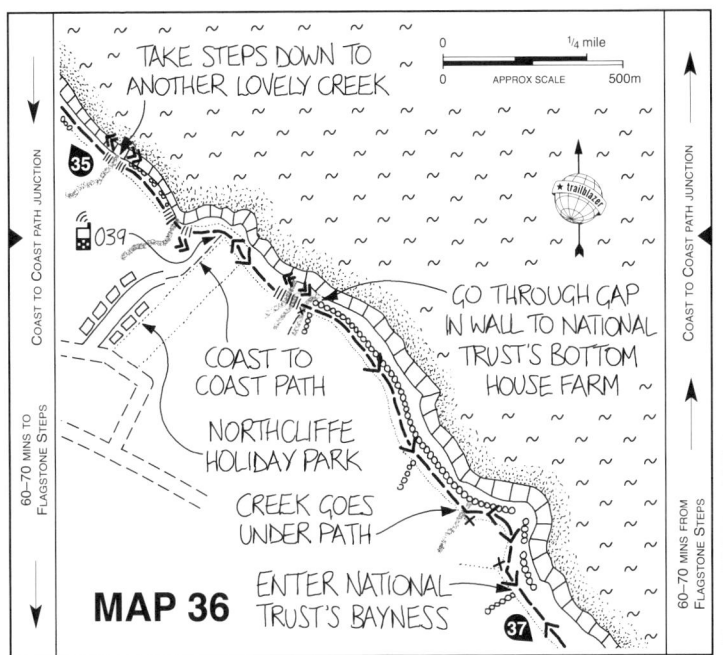

where you can celebrate. There are also gift, souvenir and antique shops aplenty.

The **Old Coastguard Station National Trust Visitor Centre** (☎ 01947-885900; Easter-Sep daily 10am-5pm, Oct-Easter generally weekends only 11am-4pm but check) sits on the slipway and has some great displays including a mini wind machine and an aquarium of marine life. There's also a small **museum** (🖥 museum .rhbay.co.uk; June & Sep Sun only noon-4pm, July-Aug Sun-Fri noon-4pm). Note that the opening times depend to a large degree on the availability of volunteers to man the museum.

Services

The official tourist information **website** (🖥 robin-hoods-bay.co.uk) has plenty of useful information, including a comprehensive list of **accommodation**.

The **general store** (Mon-Sat 8am-5.30pm) near the top of the hill doubles as the **post office** (Mon-Fri 9am-5.30pm, Sat 9am-12.30pm) and triples as an informal tourist office too. They also offer **cashback**, the only place to get money in the village. There's another **grocery shop** (daily, winter 8am-5.30pm, summer up to 8 or 9pm) in the lower part of town.

Transport

Arriva's **bus** X93 (see box pp52-3 for details) runs daily north to Whitby (20 mins) and on to Middlesbrough (90 mins) for train connections to Darlington – or heads south to Scarborough (40 mins), the nearest place to catch a train to York. The bus stop is on Thorpe Lane, just north of the main car park.

For a **taxi**, call Bay Private Hire on ☎ 01947-880603.

Where to stay

Robin Hood's Bay is divided into **Upper Bay**, the development dating from the Victorian era at the top of the hill, and the quainter and more congested 17th-century **Lower Bay** or 'Old Town' down by the sea, where there are fewer accommodation options and rooms are less spacious.

Rooms at weekends and in holiday periods may be hard to come by and many places now insist on a **minimum of two nights stay** for advance bookings.

For **hostel** accommodation you will need to walk on to YHA Boggle Hole (see p156).

There are two **campsites** and both can be pretty crowded in summer with families, dogs and caravans. The first, *Middlewood Farm Holiday Park* (☎ 01947-880414, ☐ middlewoodfarm.com; WI-FI; 🐾) is a smart and efficient operation with a laundry room (coin-operated machines) and, according to some, the finest ablutions block around. **Camping** (Easter-end Oct) costs from £8pp; showers and toilets are free but for £1 you can even take a bath. They are very 'pro' walkers and will always endeavour to accommodate campers arriving on foot even at busy times, but prefer 24 hours' warning of your arrival if possible. They also have their own version of **glamping**, this time in 'gypsy cabins' (sleeping up to 4 people; £42 for up to two plus £10 per additional person), with microwave oven, kettle, fridge and electricity sockets all provided, but not bedding so you need to bring a sleeping bag. Note that a minimum *three-night* stay is required for advance bookings but a one-night stay may be possible if there is availability on or near the required date. To get to the park, from the Bay Hotel head up Albion Rd past the chippy, past the steps where the Cleveland Way turns off, and continue for 10 minutes along the path.

High on a hill above the town, you may want to check into the no less popular *Hooks House Farm* (off Map 37; ☎ 01947-880283, ☐ hookshousefarm.co.uk; 🐾 on a lead; Mar-end Oct) before walking the last mile or two down to the sea as the walk back can be quite an effort. **Camping** here costs £8-10pp including showers and use of kitchen; booking is recommended.

Back in town there are around three dozen hotels, guesthouses and B&Bs to choose from; the official town website mentioned on p151 has a fuller list. Accommodation is most abundant in Upper Bay, the top of the village, where *Thackwood* (☎ 01947-880858, ☐ thackwood.com; 2D/1T, all en suite; 🛏; WI-FI) is the first B&B you spot as the trail comes into town. B&B costs from £42.50pp (sgl occ room rate). On the same street is *Manning Tree* (☎ 01947-881042, ☐ manningtreebnb.co.uk; 2D/1T, all en suite; WI-FI) offering a similar standard of accommodation; B&B costs from £37.50pp (sgl occ from £55).

On Mount Pleasant Rd there's more of the same including *Lee-Side* (☎ 01947-881143, ☐ lee-side.rhbay.co.uk; 1D/1T/1D or T, all en suite, 1D private bathroom; 🛏; WI-FI) with B&B starting at £40-42.50pp (sgl occ from £55), and *Streonshalh* (☎ 01947-881065, ☐ streonshalh.co.uk; 2S/2D/2D or T, all en suite; WI-FI), costing £40-52.50pp for B&B (sgl from £45, sgl occ room rate). The name is the Viking name for Whitby and it is basically pronounced 'Strenshal'.

On Station Rd, at the junction with Whitby Rd, is *The Grosvenor Hotel* (☎ 01947-880320, ☐ thegrosvenor.info; 6D/2Tr/2Qd, all en suite; 🛏; WI-FI) with B&B from £35pp (sgl occ from £50); note that the cheapest rooms are above the bar so may be noisy (see Where to eat). Still on Station Rd, *The Villa* (☎ 01947-881043, ☐ thevillarhb.co.uk; 2D/2D or T, all en suite; WI-FI) is another Victorian property. The friendly owners have retained the period features such as the cast-iron fireplaces and the servant bells. B&B rates are from £40pp (sgl occ from £60).

Take the alleyway next to Victoria Hotel and it leads onto a road with great views down to the old town. This is where you'll find *Raven House* (☎ 01947-880444, ☐ ravenhouse.rhbay.co.uk; 1S/2D/1D or T, all en suite, 1T private bathroom; 🛏; WI-FI), which more than one reader of our *Coast to Coast* guide has recommended. Edwardian rather than Victorian,

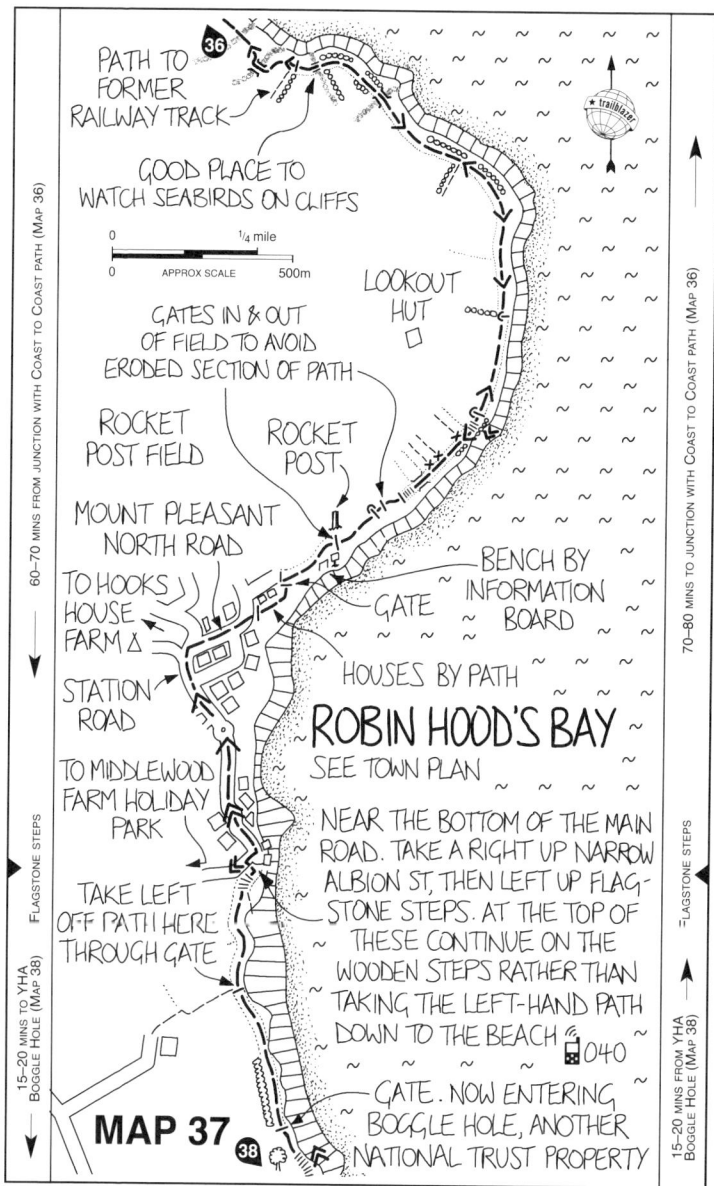

PATH TO FORMER RAILWAY TRACK

GOOD PLACE TO WATCH SEABIRDS ON CLIFFS

0   ¼ mile
0   APPROX SCALE   500m

LOOKOUT HUT

GATES IN & OUT OF FIELD TO AVOID ERODED SECTION OF PATH

ROCKET POST FIELD

ROCKET POST

MOUNT PLEASANT NORTH ROAD

TO HOOKS HOUSE FARM △

STATION ROAD

TO MIDDLEWOOD FARM HOLIDAY PARK

TAKE LEFT OFF PATH HERE THROUGH GATE

BENCH BY INFORMATION BOARD

GATE

HOUSES BY PATH

ROBIN HOOD'S BAY
SEE TOWN PLAN

NEAR THE BOTTOM OF THE MAIN ROAD. TAKE A RIGHT UP NARROW ALBION ST, THEN LEFT UP FLAGSTONE STEPS. AT THE TOP OF THESE CONTINUE ON THE WOODEN STEPS RATHER THAN TAKING THE LEFT-HAND PATH DOWN TO THE BEACH 📱040

GATE. NOW ENTERING BOGGLE HOLE, ANOTHER NATIONAL TRUST PROPERTY

MAP 37   38

60–70 MINS FROM JUNCTION WITH COAST TO COAST PATH (MAP 36)

FLAGSTONE STEPS

15–20 MINS TO YHA BOGGLE HOLE (MAP 38)

70–80 MINS TO JUNCTION WITH COAST TO COAST PATH (MAP 36)

ROUTE GUIDE AND MAPS

FLAGSTONE STEPS

15–20 MINS FROM YHA BOGGLE HOLE (MAP 38)

the two double rooms and the single (which the proprietor admits is small) enjoy great panoramas. B&B costs £40-45pp (sgl/sgl occ from £45/60).

In the **old town**, most of the accommodation has been given over to self-catering holiday apartments for those intending to stay for a week or more. You may get a one-night stay at *Ingleby House* (☎ 01947-880887, 💻 inglebyhouseinrobinhoods bay.com; 1D en suite, three apartments sleeping up to two people; 🛏; WI-FI; 🐾 in one apartment only) if you contact them on the day you want to stay, but advance bookings are for a minimum of two nights and in July and August a longer stay may be required. The apartments come with cooking facilities and cost from £80pp (sgl occ full rate) for two nights; the double room costs from £27.50pp (sgl occ room rate) and includes a light continental breakfast.

Of the B&Bs, many request a minimum stay of two nights. If you can't stay that long, try *The Boathouse* (☎ 01947-880099, 💻 boathouserhb.co.uk; 2D/1D or T with kitchenettes; WI-FI). Right in the centre of the action, the rates are £45-50pp (sgl occ from £65) though this is for room only; breakfast is not provided. Most rooms can be booked for a single-night stay other than over bank holiday weekends.

Close to the Dock, *Bramblewick* (☎ 01947-880187, 💻 bramblewick.co.uk; 4D, all en suite; WI-FI), 2 King St, retains the feel of its 17th-century origins with B&B for £45-55pp (sgl occ room rate); and finally, *Bay Hotel* (☎ 01947-880278, 💻 bay hotel.info; 2D en suite, 1D private bathroom; 🛏; WI-FI) where B&B costs £40-47.50pp (sgl occ room rate).

Where to eat and drink

The cuisine here is largely seaside traditional – pubs, takeaways and bucket 'n' spade snackeries – though there are a few notable exceptions, and in particular there are several good tea rooms. *Secret Seaview* (☎ 01947-880180, 💻 secretseaview.co.uk; summer daily 10am-5pm, winter to 3.30pm or 4pm), in the heart of the old-town alleyways, is the smartest place. Formerly a Wesleyan chapel, it's now part gallery, part

café and has lovely views over the sea from its veranda. The menu is simple (sarnies from £4.50/5.50 takeaway/eat in, jacket potatoes from £5.95) though the food is fine and we also think they do the best coffee in town.

On the way you'll pass *Old Bakery Tearoom* (daily 10am-4pm), a more traditional place with doorstop bacon sandwiches (£4.50) as tall as the bay's surrounding cliffs.

Down on the High St, *Elle Estelle's* (daily 9.30am-5pm) offers simple café fare at reasonable prices, with all sandwiches and toasted sarnies priced at £4.95. Nearby, *Coffee Shack* serves up huge slices of cake for £2.40. But the most charming café in town is the dog-friendly *Tea, Toast & Post* (daily 9am-3pm; 🐾), just above the Bay Hotel. Run by the amiable Luke, the cakes here are fantastic and they do a delicious 'Yorkshire rarebit' too (£4).

Up near the top of the hill, *Fish Box* (Mon-Sat 11am-7pm, Sun to 6pm) has a flagstone terrace where you can devour a decent serving of haddock & chips for £4.80 whilst admiring the great sea view.

The *Bay Hotel* (see Where to stay; 🐾; food served daily noon-9pm) serves standard pub food but it's reasonable value with most mains costing no more than the £12.95 for the gammon steak; it can sometimes get very busy, however, with Coast-to-Coasters celebrating the end of their trek.

In the old town there are two smart options facing each other. *Smugglers Bistro* (see The Boathouse in Where to stay; food daily noon-4pm & 6-9pm; booking essential for evenings) seems to cover almost every base with their pizza/grill/bar-snack menu, though the *moules frites* (£11.95) is always a favourite here. Its rival opposite is *Bramblewick* (see Where to stay; WI-FI; food Wed-Fri noon-3pm & 5-9pm, Sat noon-3pm & 5-9pm, Sun noon-2pm), the swishest option in the old part of the village with some wonderful fish dishes including roasted sea bream fillets with shrimp butter, king prawn & fries (£22). It is also open for breakfast (Sat & Sun 8.30-11am) for non residents.

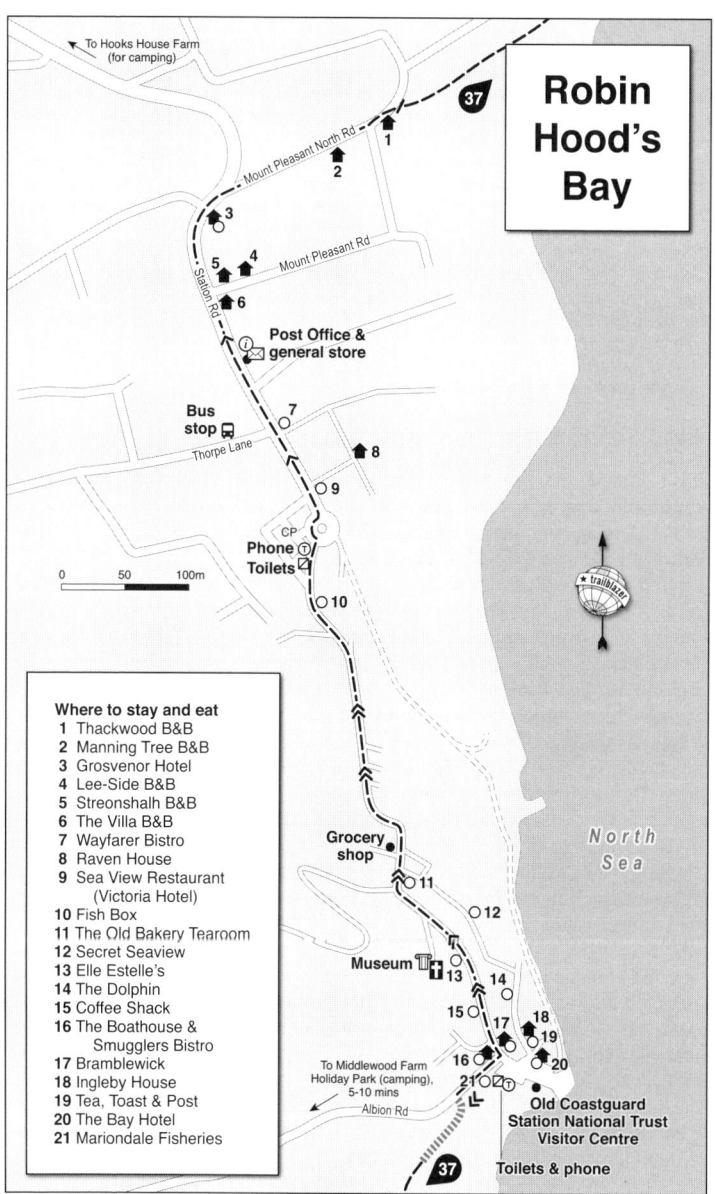

Robin Hood's Bay

To Hooks House Farm
(for camping)

37

1

Mount Pleasant North Rd

2

3

4

5

Mount Pleasant Rd

6

Station Rd

Post Office &
general store

Bus
stop

Thorpe Lane

7

8

9

CP

Phone
Toilets

10

0   50   100m

Where to stay and eat
1 Thackwood B&B
2 Manning Tree B&B
3 Grosvenor Hotel
4 Lee-Side B&B
5 Streonshalh B&B
6 The Villa B&B
7 Wayfarer Bistro
8 Raven House
9 Sea View Restaurant
   (Victoria Hotel)
10 Fish Box
11 The Old Bakery Tearoom
12 Secret Seaview
13 Elle Estelle's
14 The Dolphin
15 Coffee Shack
16 The Boathouse &
   Smugglers Bistro
17 Bramblewick
18 Ingleby House
19 Tea, Toast & Post
20 The Bay Hotel
21 Mariondale Fisheries

Grocery
shop

11

12

Museum

13

14

15

16

17

18

19

20

21

To Middlewood Farm
Holiday Park (camping),
5-10 mins

Albion Rd

North
Sea

Old Coastguard
Station National Trust
Visitor Centre

37

Toilets & phone

Sticking with the old part of town, on King St *The Dolphin* (food served daily noon-2pm & 6.30-8.30pm) serves some local fish dishes – though pride of place goes to their 'dirty chilli' (chips covered with chilli and topped with cheese and sour cream; £8.95) as well as boasting a good range of real ales and occasional live music sessions.

People queue expectantly at *Mariondale Fisheries'* **chippy** (Sun-Wed noon-7pm, Thur to 7.30pm, Fri & Sat to 8pm) up an alleyway by the Smuggler's and thus right on the Cleveland Way; skate wing & chips costs £7.70.

The best place to eat at the top of town is the contemporary *Wayfarer Bistro*; Feb-Oct Tue-Sun from 6pm; Nov-Dec Thur-Sun from 6pm). The menu features grills and seafood; booking advised. Main courses cost £12-18.

Also in the higher part of town, the *Sea View Restaurant* (☎ 01947-880205, ⌨ vic toriarhb.com; WI-FI; 🍴 bar; food daily noon-8.30pm), in Victoria Hotel, is popular, as is *The Grosvenor Hotel* (see Where to stay; 🍴 bar; food served Apr-Oct daily noon-9pm, Nov-Mar Mon-Fri 6-9pm, Sat & Sun noon-9pm) which serves curries, steaks and burgers for £8.95-16.95. There's live music on Tue and most Sat nights.

ROBIN HOOD'S BAY TO SCARBOROUGH [MAPS 37-44]

This is another pretty tough stage, this time **13.9-mile/22.4km (4½hrs to 5hrs 40mins)** in length. By now, however, you'll be used to the rigours of coastal walking and are familiar with the fact that, while there may be difficulties along the way, the rewards are often manifold too.

Before we begin our description of the stage it should be pointed out that at the time of research a **long-term detour route** here was in place following a dangerous landslip between Ravenscar and Hayburn Wyke. While this does add about 600m (0.4-mile) to the overall distance covered on this trail (making the stage **14.3-mile/23km** in total and adding about 10 minutes to the total time taken, **ie 4hrs 40mins to 5hrs 50mins**) we have to say that we are rather fond of this diversion. After a couple of days' walking along the coast this inland route really is a welcome change; what's more the woods that you walk through on the way are just delightful. So don't despair if the diversion is still in place when you visit – you may end up enjoying it more.

But you've got a lot of ground to cover before then. The stage begins by climbing out of Robin Hood's Bay on a steep flight of steps. At the top, a rather precarious path that flirts with some extensive cliff erosion leads the way to *YHA Boggle Hole* (Map 38; ☎ 0845-371 9504, ⌨ yha.org.uk/hostel/boggle-hole; 1 x single, 1 x 2-, 6 x 3-, 5 x 4-, 6 x 5-, 2 x 6-, 1 x 9-bed rooms, some en suite; WI-FI communal areas; Ⓛ; Mar-end Oct daily, Nov-Feb weekends only) housed in a former corn mill. Some of the rooms, including strangely the 9-bed room, have a double bed. Dorm beds cost from £21pp (though from £35pp in summer) and a private room is from £25 for two sharing (around £39.50 in summer). Check in is from 3pm; there is a drying room and self-catering facilities. The hostel is also popular with non-residents thanks to its *Quarterdeck Café* (☎ 01947-880352; mid Feb to end Oct daily 7.30am-10.30pm, rest of year Fri-Sun 7.30am-3pm though sometimes open later; food generally served noon-8pm, tea

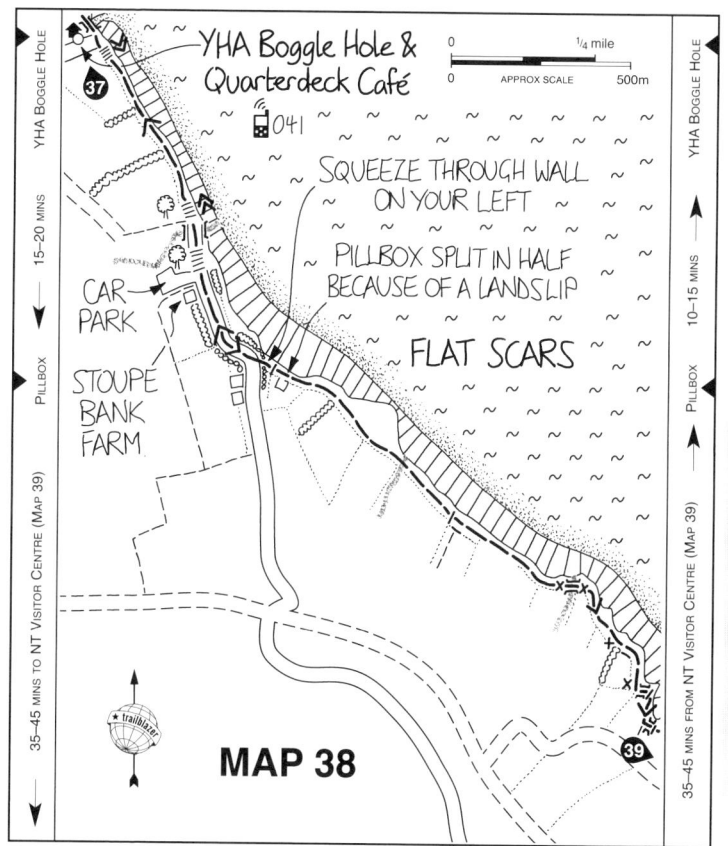

YHA Boggle Hole & Quarterdeck Café

SQUEEZE THROUGH WALL ON YOUR LEFT

PILLBOX SPLIT IN HALF BECAUSE OF A LANDSLIP

FLAT SCARS

CAR PARK

STOUPE BANK FARM

MAP 38

ROUTE GUIDE AND MAPS

and cakes at other times; WI-FI; 🐾) where a cuppa and a cake will set you back no more than £3.50; it is also licensed. It's a lovely place, hampered only by its proximity to Robin Hood's Bay – anywhere else and this place would, we feel, be at least three times as popular.

Boggle Hole is just the first of several short but steep-sided little creeks on the way to Ravenscar that will wear down your knee ligaments faster than the North Sea erodes the cliffs round these parts. But all being well it won't be long before you're tripping down the slopes to the ruins of **Peak Alum Works** (Map 39; see also box p158) – the most extensive on the trail, and the most accessible too – then clambering up the slopes to the **National Trust Visitor Centre**, just off the main road in **Ravenscar**.

RAVENSCAR [MAP 39]

Undoubtedly one of the most curious 'attractions' along the Cleveland Way, Ravenscar has received a certain degree of fame as 'the town that never was'. Christened 'Peak', this unfinished settlement was the brainchild of Victorian entrepreneurs, the Peak Estate Company, who invested many millions in trying to build a seaside resort to rival those of Scarborough and Whitby. Unfortunately, despite constructing an extensive sewer system, laying out a road network (you can still find evidence of this on the ground today) and building a few smart houses, the resort never really got off the ground – perhaps because the climb down to the beach was simply too steep and long – and the company went bankrupt.

What is left today is a smattering of houses scattered along the cliffs in an apparently random fashion, a defunct railway station and a huge, oversized hotel that pre-dates the Peak resort and was, apparently, once the home of the physician to George III (he of madness, porphyry and purple urine fame).

Ironically, probably because it does have such an unusual history, Ravenscar today receives a visiting population that never came when the town was trying to become a holiday resort, whether they're walkers (as well as lying on the Cleveland Way the place also serves as the terminus of the Lyke Wake Walk), cyclists (the defunct railway station used to lie on the Scarborough to Whitby line that's now

❑ The Alum industry

Since Boulby Cliff you will have noticed that vast swathes of the North Yorkshire coast were, at one time, devoted to the production of alum. This chemical compound of potassium, aluminium and sulphur, that in its natural state is a beautiful, translucent crystal, was essential in the 16th century as a fixative for dyes. For centuries, Britain's supply of alum came from Italy, where the industry was largely under the control of the Vatican. Unfortunately, when Henry VIII broke with Rome during the Reformation, the supply of alum was cut off and Britain was forced to look for a supply within its own borders.

The first alum works in Britain was set up in Guisborough by Thomas Challoner, who recognised that the fossils from the nearby Yorkshire coast were similar to those found in the alum mines of Italy and deduced that this meant that the rocks could be similar too. The coastal location also meant that access to the shale from which alum can be extracted was easier – and the transportation of the finished product by ship to London and elsewhere was more straightforward too.

Extracting alum, however, was a messy and protracted business. Once the shale had been collected from places such as Loftus Quarry, north of Staithes, it was then transferred to the processing works at Ravenscar where it was burned for up to nine months. Leaching pits were then used to extract a liquor of aluminium sulphate, which was then mixed with human urine to extract the alum crystals. Vast quantities of human urine were required for this process, more than could be supplied by the workers at the quarry, so urine was imported from the big population centres of London, Newcastle and Hull where it was often left in buckets on street corners to be collected.

The industry thrived in Yorkshire until the middle of the 19th century and the arrival of a synthetic substitute. The last Alum works closed on the North Yorkshire coast in 1871. Nevertheless, the impact the industry had on the local area is still with us today. The cliffs at Loftus are much changed due to the industrial quarrying that took place for more than a century here. Vast swathes of forest were chopped down, too, in order to provide fuel for the fires and furnaces that were used in the production – forests that have never recovered to this day.

been repurposed as the 21½-mile/34.4km Cinder Track bicycle route), wedding guests (Raven Hall Country House Hotel survives largely on their custom), or simply those intrigued to see what this curious, aborted town looks like. The place also gets its fair share of fossil hunters, the beach being one of the best places to find them.

Serving these visitors is a simple tourist infrastructure including a **National Trust Visitor Centre** (Easter-Oct daily 10am-5pm, Nov-Dec Sat & Sun 10am-4pm) and *café*, with a second eatery near the old railway station platform, *Ravenscar*

Tearoom (🖥 ravenscartearooms.co.uk; mid Feb to end Oct daily 10am-5pm), which also doubles as a B&B, *Ravenscar House* (☎ 01723-870444, 🖥 ravenscarhouse.co .uk; 1D/1D or T, both en suite; ●; WI-FI; Ⓛ ; mid Feb to end Oct), which has rooms with expansive sea views for £47.50pp (no discount for sgl occ). Guests of the **B&B** can choose something from the tearoom menu for their evening meal, but while they do a mighty fine fried egg sandwich (£3.75) and a good selection of cakes, there's not too much hot food available. For this reason, guests may prefer to walk along to the

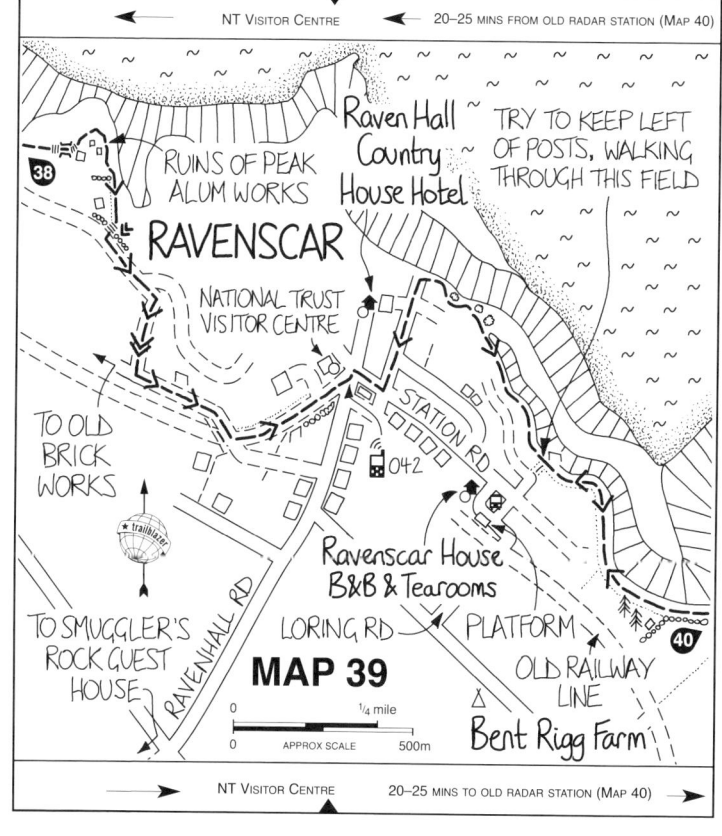

ROUTE GUIDE AND MAPS

rather grand clifftop **Raven Hall Country House Hotel** (☎ 01723-870353, 🖳 raven-hall.co.uk; **food** daily noon-9pm). The menu changes daily and while it's not especially cheap – £24.50 for two courses, £29.50 for three courses plus coffee – there's usually a good choice on the menu and the food can be great. You can of course stay at the hotel too (6S/21D/20T/4D or T, all en suite; 🛏; WI-FI; ⒧; 🐾), though it's fair to say that it's not your usual trekkers' accommodation, for it's grand enough to have its own golf course, tennis courts and croquet lawn. Rates in the high season are about the £67.50pp mark, with singles about £77.50 (sgl occ rates on request).

There is a third B&B option, **Smuggler's Rock Guest House** (☎ 01723-870044, 🖳 smugglersrock.co.uk; 1S/4D/1T/1Tr, all en suite; WI-FI; ⒧; Easter-end Sep) though it's just under a mile from the trail along the main road into Ravenscar and they operate a two-night minimum stay policy (though they will take last-minute one-night bookings on the door for a per room supplement of about £5). As such, it's very much the third choice, to be considered only if the others are full. Rates are £38-52.50pp (sgl from £60, sgl occ £66-95), the price being highest at weekends in summer.

There is also the option to **camp** near Ravenscar. **Bent Rigg Farm** (☎ 01723-870475; 🐾) is open Easter to November and while they don't have showers, just a sink and toilet, at £3pp per night who's complaining? Booking is recommended for peak periods. To reach the farm from Ravenscar, take the track running parallel to the old rail line from the south-eastern corner of the square (ie the opposite corner to the tearoom); this bends round to become Loring Rd, at the end of which you should take a left.

Ravenscar does have a skeletal **bus service** with EYMS's No 115 (see box pp52-3 for details) running between Ravenscar's Station Square and Scarborough.

Leaving Ravenscar, within quarter of an hour you come across the remains of the disused radar station that's worth a few minutes of your time. Officially known as **Ravenscar Chain Home Low Radar Station** (Map 40), the site dates back to WWII and is now owned, like much of the land around here, by the National Trust. There are four brick buildings that remain standing: the communications hut, with its distinctive barrel-shaped corrugated roof, where both enemy aircraft and our own were tracked; a transmitter/receiver block, a fuel store and engine house. In addition, you can also make out the foundations of about a dozen barrack blocks. Though you can't enter any of the buildings today, you are welcome to peer inside them though they're all pretty empty and there's little to see; the information boards, however, do help you to imagine what they would have been like in their heyday.

A few fields further on and you reach the point where the path has fallen into the sea and the **detour route** has been put into place (see p156). If the coastal route has reopened you'll find it straightforward enough to negotiate the undulations down to lovely Hayburn Wyke. If you do have to take the diversion, **follow the instructions on Maps 40 and 41** rather than the signposts on the trail which are, on occasion, a little misleading. The diversion will take you past several large farms on its way to the wood-cosseted stream leading to **Hayburn Wyke** (Map 41).

Note that the two paths reunite after the stream, but it is worth dropping down to the point where the stream meets the beach and the **small waterfall**

(cont'd on p164)

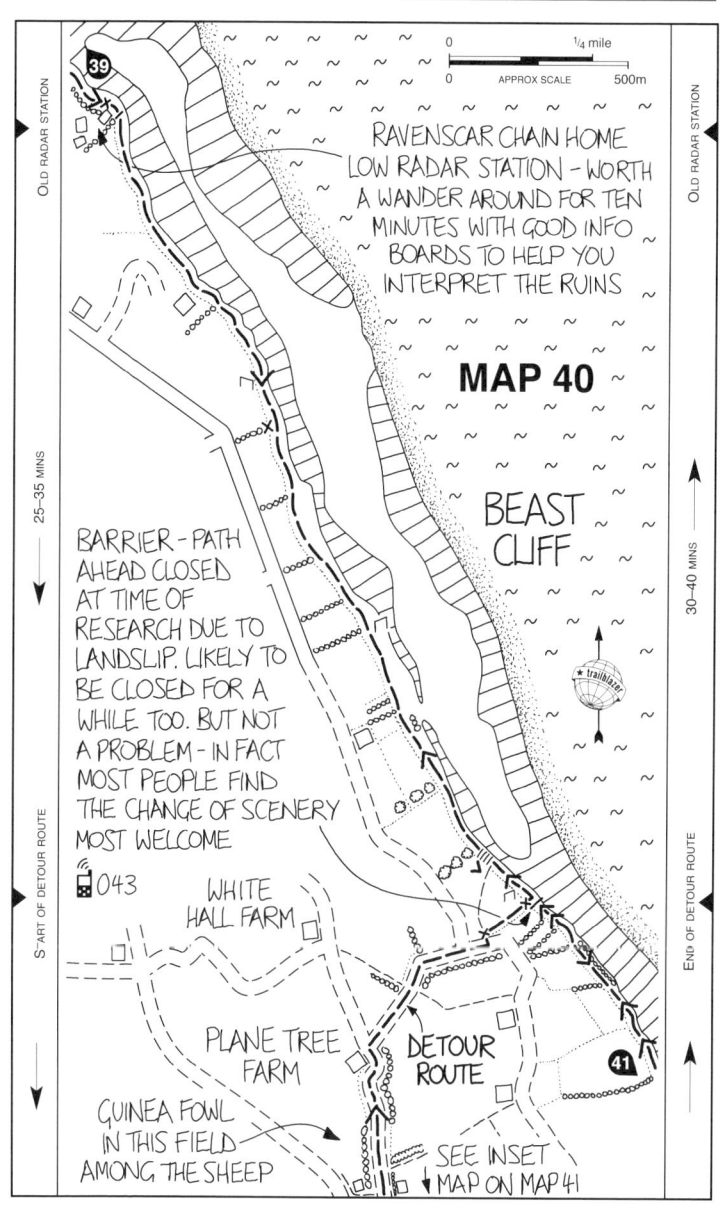

MAP 40

RAVENSCAR CHAIN HOME LOW RADAR STATION – WORTH A WANDER AROUND FOR TEN MINUTES WITH GOOD INFO BOARDS TO HELP YOU INTERPRET THE RUINS

BEAST CLIFF

BARRIER – PATH AHEAD CLOSED AT TIME OF RESEARCH DUE TO LANDSLIP. LIKELY TO BE CLOSED FOR A WHILE TOO. BUT NOT A PROBLEM – IN FACT MOST PEOPLE FIND THE CHANGE OF SCENERY MOST WELCOME

043

WHITE HALL FARM

PLANE TREE FARM

DETOUR ROUTE

GUINEA FOWL IN THIS FIELD AMONG THE SHEEP

SEE INSET MAP ON MAP 41

39

41

Old radar station

25–35 MINS

Start of detour route

Old radar station

30–40 MINS

End of detour route

ROUTE GUIDE AND MAPS

¼ mile
APPROX SCALE
500m

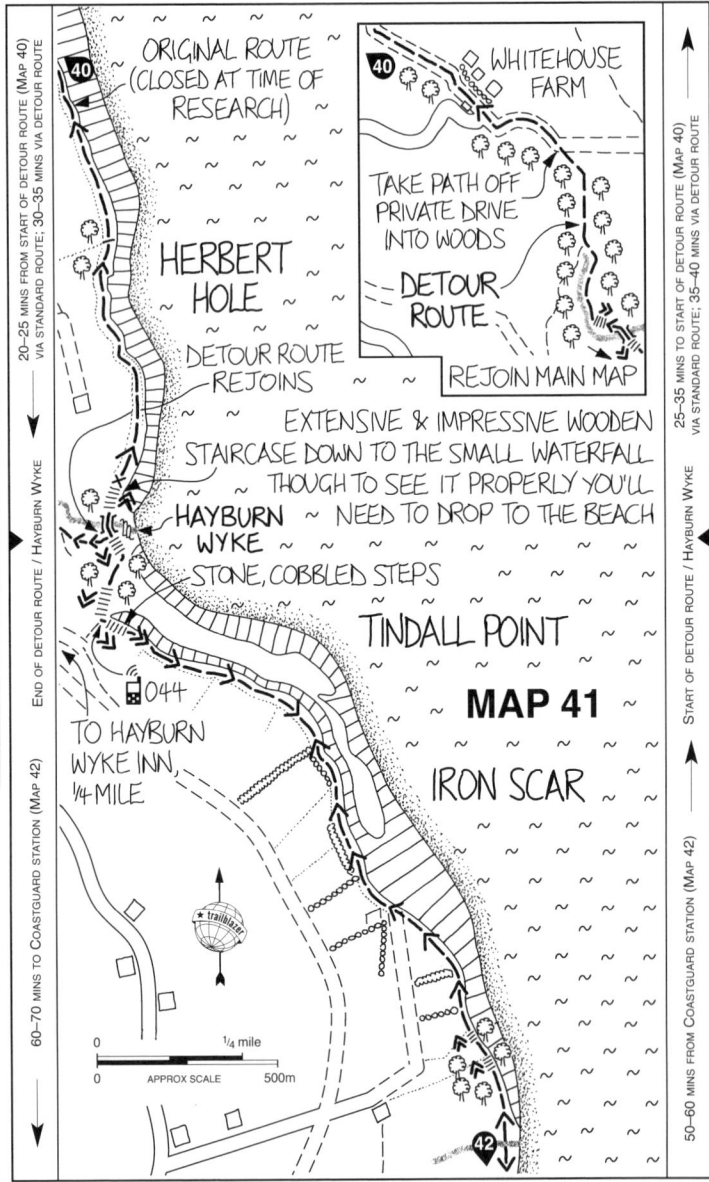

ORIGINAL ROUTE
(CLOSED AT TIME OF
RESEARCH)

40

WHITEHOUSE
FARM

40

TAKE PATH OFF
PRIVATE DRIVE
INTO WOODS

DETOUR
ROUTE

REJOIN MAIN MAP

HERBERT
HOLE

DETOUR ROUTE
REJOINS

EXTENSIVE & IMPRESSIVE WOODEN
STAIRCASE DOWN TO THE SMALL WATERFALL
THOUGH TO SEE IT PROPERLY YOU'LL
NEED TO DROP TO THE BEACH

HAYBURN
WYKE

STONE, COBBLED STEPS

TINDALL POINT

044

TO HAYBURN
WYKE INN,
¼ MILE

MAP 41

IRON SCAR

★ trailblazer

0   ¼ mile

0   APPROX SCALE   500m

42

20–25 MINS FROM START OF DETOUR ROUTE (MAP 40)
VIA STANDARD ROUTE; 30–35 MINS VIA DETOUR ROUTE

End of detour route / Hayburn Wyke

60–70 MINS TO COASTGUARD STATION (MAP 42)

ROUTE GUIDE AND MAPS

25–35 MINS TO START OF DETOUR ROUTE (MAP 40)
VIA STANDARD ROUTE; 35–40 MINS VIA DETOUR ROUTE

Start of detour route / Hayburn Wyke

50–60 MINS FROM COASTGUARD STATION (MAP 42)

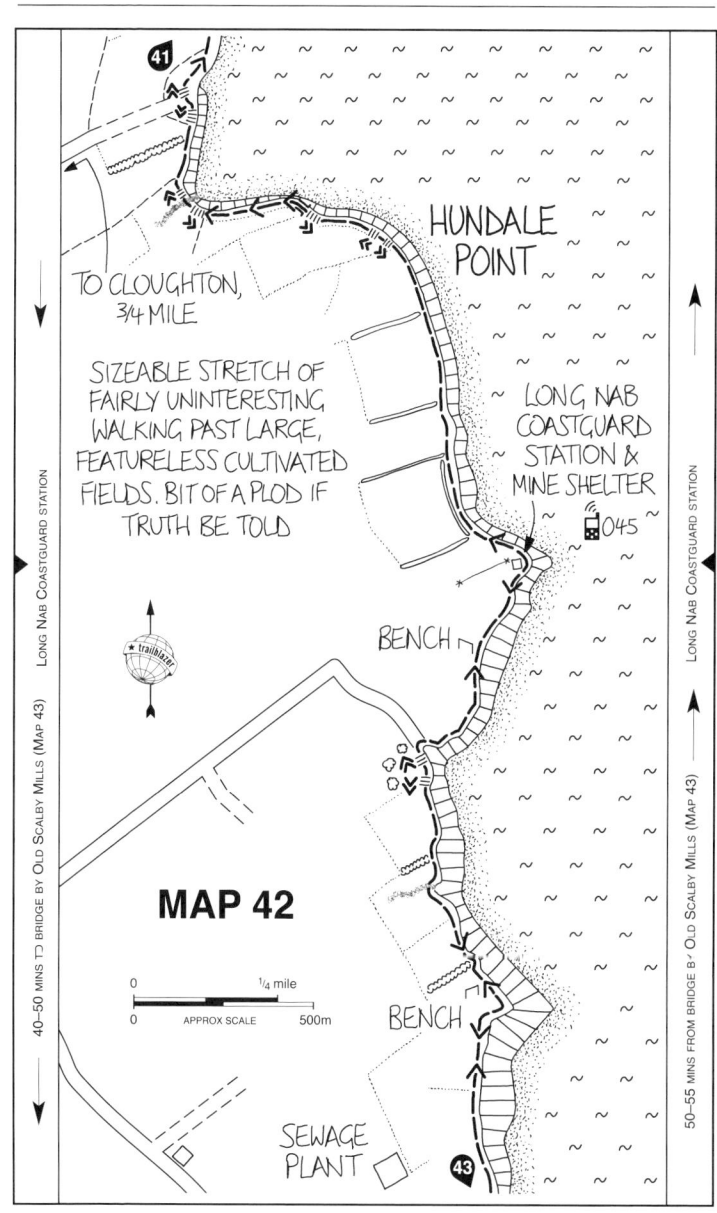

41

HUNDALE POINT

TO CLOUGHTON, 3/4 MILE

SIZEABLE STRETCH OF FAIRLY UNINTERESTING WALKING PAST LARGE, FEATURELESS CULTIVATED FIELDS. BIT OF A PLOD IF TRUTH BE TOLD

LONG NAB COASTGUARD STATION & MINE SHELTER

045

BENCH

★ trailblazer

MAP 42

0   1/4 mile

0   APPROX SCALE   500m

BENCH

SEWAGE PLANT

43

LONG NAB COASTGUARD STATION

40—50 MINS TO BRIDGE BY OLD SCALBY MILLS (MAP 43)

LONG NAB COASTGUARD STATION

50—55 MINS FROM BRIDGE BY OLD SCALBY MILLS (MAP 43)

ROUTE GUIDE AND MAPS

there – it's a great and secluded spot for a picnic. If you forgot to bring any grub but are feeling peckish, the excellent *Hayburn Wyke Inn* (☎ 01723-870202, 🖥 hayburnwykeinn.co.uk; WI-FI; Ⓛ; 🐴 bar only) lies around a quarter of a mile from the trail and it serves **food** (Tue-Sat noon-2.30pm & 6-9pm, Sun noon-7pm, Mon noon-2.30pm only); most mains cost £10 or less. They also have rooms (4D/2Tr, all en suite); **B&B** costs from £35pp (sgl occ from £38). Despite its isolated location – the only way of getting here by car is on a rough, 'corkscrew' track – this place is heaving in summer, particularly on a sunny Sunday. Note there is often live music on a Saturday night, and the rooms are directly above the bar.

Leaving the woods behind, the Cleveland Way returns to the cliff-edge for what, in all honesty, is a bit of a dull trudge, with little to see save the blank sea on your left and some vast, prairie-style cultivated fields on your right. Landmarks along the way include the vast, warehouse-style **sewage plant** (Map 42) on the right, topped with a rather incongruous weather vane, and **Long Nab Coastguard Station and Mine Shelter**. Originally built to give assistance to shipwrecks and protect seagoing vessels, as well as combat smuggling, in 1939 a mine shelter was added to protect those manning the station; later, during the Cold War, it was linked to the Nuclear Warning system, before finally being given to the local birdwatching society to study migration and monitor local bird populations. Keep on plodding, however, aim towards the castle that's been beckoning you onwards since leaving Ravenscar – and eventually you'll drop down to the funfairs and fleshpots of **Scarborough**.

SCARBOROUGH [map p169]

Scarborough is the largest settlement on the Cleveland Way by quite some margin – its population of over 50,000 dwarfs the next biggest, Whitby's, by a factor of four. That figure of 50,000 increases many times over in summer when tourists flock to the Yorkshire Riviera's main draw.

If we're being honest, the town isn't everyone's cup of Yorkshire tea, particularly if one happens to be visiting on a sunny bank holiday when the pavements are packed and the decibel level from the traffic and tourists comes as a bit of a shock to Cleveland Way hikers used to having the distant calling of a kittiwake as the backing track to their walk. It has to be said, too, that while there are some lovely examples of Victorian architecture, Scarborough is also rather run-down in parts (and I'm being kind here). Still, to be fair, the Cleveland Way does a good job in keeping its followers away from the less appetising areas (the 'isthmus' area between the Castle and the railway station, for example),

instead showcasing Scarborough's more salubrious sections (ie the seafront). It must also be owned that the town has more facilities, better transport links and a greater number of sights and attractions than any other part of the trail. So rather than be sniffy about Scarborough, maybe instead it's time to don your kiss-me-quick hat, grab your bucket and spade and take a day off from your walk – because there is something for everyone here.

What to see and do

The Cleveland Way takes you along Scarborough's two great **beaches**, North Bay and South Bay, each with plenty to tempt both tourist and trekker. The following attractions are listed in approximate order from north to south, ie the order in which you encounter them when walking along the Cleveland Way, with the town centre attractions – which are a little further from the trail – listed last.

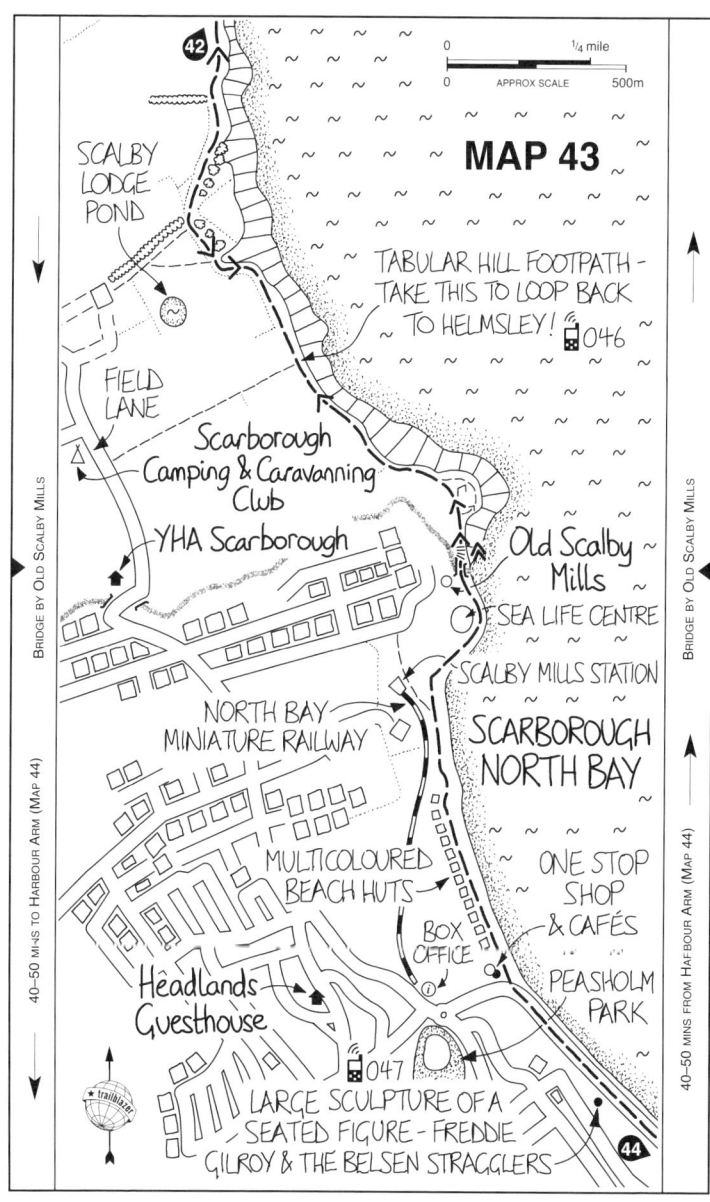

MAP 43

42

SCALBY
LODGE
POND

TABULAR HILL FOOTPATH -
TAKE THIS TO LOOP BACK
TO HELMSLEY! 046

FIELD
LANE

Scarborough
Camping & Caravanning
Club

YHA Scarborough

Old Scalby
Mills

SEA LIFE CENTRE

SCALBY MILLS STATION

NORTH BAY
MINIATURE RAILWAY

SCARBOROUGH
NORTH BAY

MULTICOLOURED
BEACH HUTS

ONE STOP
SHOP
& CAFÉS

BOX
OFFICE

PEASHOLM
PARK

Headlands
Guesthouse

trailblazer

047

LARGE SCULPTURE OF A
SEATED FIGURE - FREDDIE
GILROY & THE BELSEN STRAGGLERS

44

0   1/4 mile
0   APPROX SCALE   500m

BRIDGE BY OLD SCALBY MILLS

BRIDGE BY OLD SCALBY MILLS

40–50 MINS TO HARBOUR ARM (MAP 44)

40–50 MINS FROM HARBOUR ARM (MAP 44)

ROUTE GUIDE AND MAPS

North Bay This is the first beach you come to if walking the Cleveland Way and is really quite fabulous, particularly with the line of brightly coloured **beach huts** that fringe it. There are also attractions aplenty here too: almost as soon as you walk along the beach after crossing the bridge at Scalby Mills you come to the **Sea Life Centre** (Map 43; 🖳 visitsealife.com/scarborough; Mon-Fri 10am-4pm, to 5pm on Sat & Sun; £19 though can be up to 50% off if booked online) which, rather oddly, has a pirate-themed mini-golf course next door. Nearby is Scalby Mills Station, a terminus on the **miniature North Bay Railway** (🖳 nbr.org.uk; £3/4 single/return) that runs to Peasholm Park, 15 minutes away.

South Bay This is the busier of the two, with most of the cafés and restaurants lining its western side.

At the northern end is a small funfair called **Luna Park** (daily Easter to Sep, weekends only Oct-Easter), while next door is the **harbour**, still home to a small fishing industry and well worth a nose around. South Bay is also where you'll find the Grade II listed *Grand Hotel Scarborough* (see Where to stay), built in 1863 and at the time the largest hotel and brick building in Europe. The hotel was designed according to the theme of time, with four towers, 12 floors, 52 chimneys and, originally, 365 bedrooms, the numbers corresponding to the seasons, months, weeks and days in the year respectively. The hotel is also laid out in the shape of a 'V', in honour of the monarch who was

on the throne when it was built, Queen Victoria.

Next to the hotel is one of two **cliff lifts** – the oldest such lifts in the country. The first, **Central Tramway** (🖳 central tramway.co.uk; Feb-Oct daily 9.30am-4.45pm; £1 one way) was opened in 1881; the entrance to it is squashed between the Grand Hotel and the **Olympia Leisure complex** on Foreshore Rd and heads up to Marine Parade and the excellent Cat's Pyjamas Café (see p171). The second lift, **Spa Lift** (🖳 scarboroughspa.sivtickets .com; opening times vary but usually summer daily 9.30am-10.30pm, rest of year 10am-5pm; £1) opened even earlier, in 1873, and is also right by the Cleveland Way; it takes people up to the Esplanade from the Spa Complex.

Between the two, and set a couple of hundred metres up from the seafront, is **Rotunda Museum** (🖳 scarboroughmu seumstrust.com/rotunda-museum; Tue-Sun 10am-5pm); one of the world's first purpose-built museums, having been built in 1829 by William 'Strata' Smith (see p58). It's a fascinating place, the building as interesting as the exhibits, and some of the displays, such as the Gateway to the Dinosaur Coast Gallery, will be of particular interest to Cleveland Way walkers. Entry is just £3 and this includes entry to **Scarborough Art Gallery** (same opening times) too which lies a couple of hundred metres away to the west in an Italianate villa on the Crescent.

Town centre Separating the two bays is the headland, where kittiwakes and fulmars

---

❑ Sir Alan Ayckbourn and Stephen Joseph Theatre
The associations of one of the UK's most prolific and celebrated playwrights, **Sir Alan Ayckbourn**, with his hometown of Scarborough are well documented. The author of over 70 plays, Sir Alan was actually born in Hampstead, north London, and didn't move to Scarborough until he was 18, where he worked in the Library Theatre under the director Stephen Joseph, after whom the theatre is now named. (The theatre was originally established on the first floor of the local library – hence its original name – and was the first theatre-in-the-round in the UK.) Ayckbourn was the Artistic Director for almost forty years until 2009 and to this day his plays traditionally have their première at the theatre, which is situated opposite the railway station.

make their homes in the steep cliffs. Atop this headland – and the first thing you see of Scarborough when you're on the trail – is its **castle**, standing on the head of the promontory above the town. The edifice that you see today was built in the 12th century, though given that this is the only spot from where you can see both North and South Bay, and that it is surrounded on three sides by steep cliffs, the site provides such a strategic advantage that it's no surprise to find that there has been some sort of fort here since at least 500BC, when Bronze Age man settled and built a hill fort. Archeological digs at this location uncovered a 3000-year-old sword from this time, a replica of which is on display inside the castle. Subsequently the Romans built one of their signal stations here and the Anglo Saxons a church, though both have long since gone. The castle was built on the order of Henry II, to provide a statement of power and a royal stronghold in the north. As the monarch's grip on England became more sure, however, so the castle declined in importance though was never entirely abandoned. The castle is now in the same parlous state as Helmsley Castle; see p77), and for a similar reason too. In 1645, the largest cannon in the country was used by the Parliamentarians to blast away at the castle's defences, partially destroying the castle's keep, as they attempted to remove the Royalist-supporting Sir Hugh Chomley during the English Civil War – Scarborough at the time was the only port still in Royalist hands. Following the Parliamentarian's victory and the subsequent return to power of the monarchy, the castle became a prison – George Fox, founder of the Quakers, was held here by Charles II for his religious activities.

The castle is now run by English Heritage (🖳 english-heritage.org.uk; Mar-Oct 10am-5pm, Nov-Feb Sat, Sun & hols only 10am-4pm; entrance £6.50; free for EH members). The quickest way to the castle is to take the steep path up from North Bay or from the path heading up the hill near the harbour. Either way, it's a steep climb. Incidentally, the church below the castle, **St Mary's**, is the last resting place of

Anne Brontë, who died in Scarborough aged just 28 and who was the only one of the famous literary sisters not buried at their home in Haworth.

Services
Surprisingly for a major tourist resort, Scarborough has no manned tourist office. Instead, they have several '**tourist points**' dotted around town including at Scarborough Lifeboat House near the harbour, on the ground floor of Stephen Joseph Theatre, and at The Open Air Theatre Box Office opposite Peasholm Park.

The first two offer a freephone service linking you to the central bureau which is based in the town hall on St Nicholas St (though you can't visit them there). This line is manned daily in summer 9am-5pm, winter Monday to Saturday only; if not in Scarborough you can call this office (☎ 01723-383636) during those hours for information on Scarborough, Whitby and Filey. Other than the phones these tourist points are little more than a collection of leaflets on bus times and local businesses. The official website is 🖳 discoveryorkshire coast.com; 🖳 scarboroughvisitorguide.com and 🖳 visitscarborough.com may also be able to provide further help.

Most other services can be found near the main shopping district to the north of the station, including the **post office** (Mon & Wed-Fri 9am-5.30pm, Tue from 9.30am, Sat 9.30am-12.30pm) at 11-15 Aberdeen Walk, and a Boots the **Chemist** (Mon-Sat 8.30am-5.30pm, Sun 10.30am-4.30pm), round the corner on Westborough. There are several **ATMs** around here too. as well as the **outdoor shop** Mountain Warehouse (Mon-Sat 9am-5.30pm, Sun 10am-4pm) at 14 Westborough; competition is provided by Trespass (Mon-Sat 9am-5.30pm, Sun 10.30am-4.30pm) in Brunswick Shopping Centre.

For a **supermarket** there's a Tesco (Mon-Sat 6am-midnight, Sun 10am-4pm) south of the station on Westwood, though nearer to the path is One Stop (daily 7.30am-10pm), as you join the road on North Bay.

Transport

Scarborough has the best transport links of any place on the Cleveland Way. Unfortunately, few of these are near the trail itself, which means you need to head to the centre of town and the railway station – where the bus services stop too – to get transport to anywhere.

The only **buses** that go near the seafront (and thus the trail) are EYMS's 8/8A and the 109 that travels between North and South Bay; and while the 8/8A does indeed go to the railway station, it takes an awfully long time to get there (about half an hour from the Sea Life Centre for example).

The most useful bus service for Cleveland Way walkers that departs from Scarborough is Arriva's X93 to Middlesbrough. Scarborough also connects to: Ravenscar (EYMS's No 115), Filey (EYMS's No 12, 13 and X21, and SS's 555); Leeds (Transdev's No 843 and the seasonal X43); and Helmsley (EYMS's No 128) – the latter would be useful for those who left their car at the start of the trail. See box pp52-3 for details.

For destinations further afield there's National Express **coach** No 563 and No 327 (see p51).

Scarborough not only has the busiest **railway station** on the Cleveland Way but also has trains to places where you might actually want to go including TransPennine Express's service to Liverpool Lime St and Northern's to Hull (see box p49).

Where to stay

The nearest **campsite** to Scarborough is back along the path at *Scarborough Camping & Caravanning Club* (Map 43; ☎ 01723-366212, 🖳 campingandcaravanningclub.co.uk; WI-FI; 🐾; Mar/Apr to early Nov) on Field Lane, about two miles from the town centre but is best reached from the path (Map 43). It's one of the more family-friendly, facility-filled places (there's even a chip shop on site, as well as a well-stocked shop) that accepts walkers too; prices start at £8.35pp.

Not too far away from here is *YHA Scarborough* (Map 34; ☎ 01723-361176, ☎

0345-260 2896, 🖳 yha.org.uk/hostel/yha-scarborough or 🖳 scarboroughhostelcom.ipage.com; 46 beds in 4- & 6-bed rooms; one en suite; Mar-Oct), housed in a 17th-century former water mill on a quiet river-bank about 1½ miles from town in Burniston. It's certainly one of the simpler hostels on the path (there's no wi-fi, for example), though you'll still find a self-catering kitchen and breakfast and packed lunches are available) and the prices reflect this, with a dorm bed from just £13pp and private rooms start from £45 for up to four sharing. Note that check-in is after 5pm but then there is 24hr access. This hostel is independently managed but can only be booked through the YHA website.

Given how far outside of the town centre the YHA hostel is, we recommend that you maybe look to see if the **Boat Shed** (☎ 07889-180925, 🖳 boatshedhostel.co.uk) is up and running again, though it is unlikely their new accommodation will be available before summer 2020. Just a pebble's throw from the beach and path at 22A Quay St, the place has always had an excellent reputation and when it reopens the owner wants it to be, in her words, 'all-singing-and all-dancing' with private rooms in addition to the bunk barn; they may even allow dogs – most unusual for a hostel.

There are plenty of **B&Bs** in Scarborough. Several roads seem to be dominated by them, including Queen's Parade, overlooking North Beach. Here you'll find places such as *Howdale* (☎ 01723-372696, 🖳 howdalehotel.co.uk; 2T/11D, all en suite; ✷; WI-FI; Apr-end Sep), at No 121, with rooms for £35-50pp (sgl occ room rate); amiable *Leeway* (☎ 01723-374371, 🖳 leewayhotel.co.uk; 3S/3D/3D or T, all en suite; WI-FI; Jan-end Oct), at No 71, one of the few places with single rooms (£35-40) as well as doubles and twins (£30-35pp, sgl occ room rate), some of which have a sea view; and the pleasant *Kimberley Seafront* (☎ 01723-372734, 🖳 kimberleyseafronthotel.co.uk; 5D/1T/2Tr, all en suite; WI-FI; at No 131, with B&B from £35pp (sgl occ room rate).

Eastborough is another street where you'll find several choices. Popular *Palace*

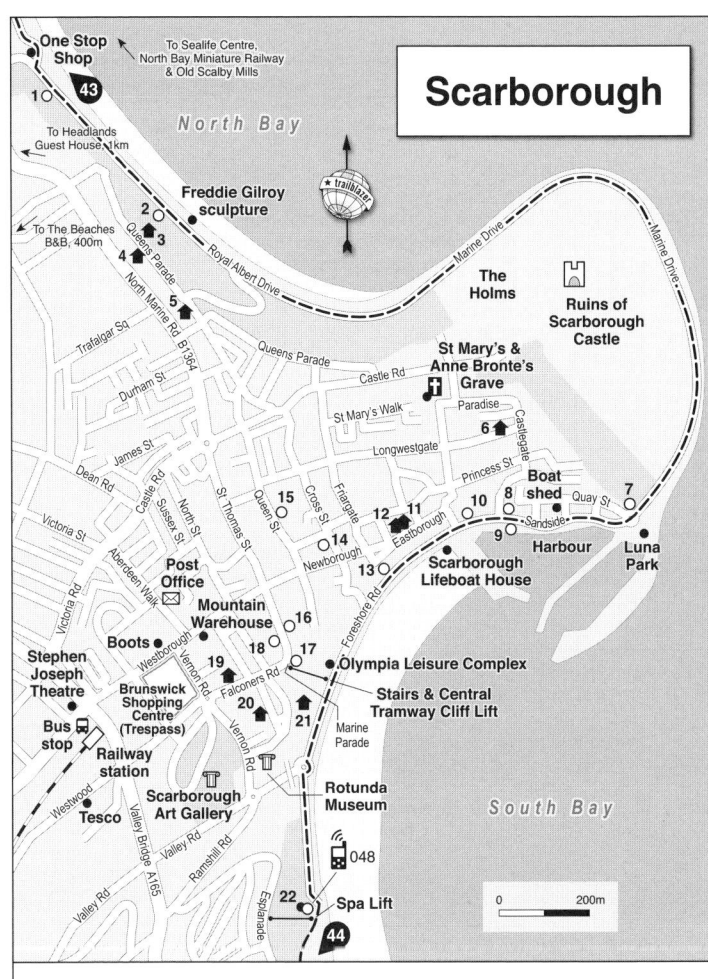

Scarborough

One Stop Shop
43
1

To Sealife Centre,
North Bay Miniature Railway
& Old Scalby Mills

North Bay

To Headlands
Guest House 1km

★ trailblazer

Freddie Gilroy
sculpture

2
Queens Parade
3
To The Beaches
B&B, 400m
4
North Marine Rd B1364
5

Royal Albert Drive

Marine Drive

Marine Drive

The
Holms

Ruins of
Scarborough
Castle

Trafalgar Sq

Queens Parade

Durham St

Castle Rd

St Mary's &
Anne Bronte's
Grave

James St.

St Mary's Walk

Paradise

Castlegate

Dean Rd

Longwestgate

6

Victoria St

Castle Rd

Sussex St

St Thomas St

Queen St

Cross St

Friargate

Princess St

Boat
shed

Quay St

7

Aberdeen Walk

North St

15

12 11

Eastborough

10 8

Sandside

9

Harbour

Luna
Park

14

Post
Office

13

Scarborough
Lifeboat House

Newborough

Mountain
Warehouse

16

Boots

18 17

Westborough

Vernon Rd

19

Olympia Leisure Complex

Stephen
Joseph
Theatre

Brunswick
Shopping
Centre
(Trespass)

Falconers Rd

Stairs & Central
Tramway Cliff Lift

Bus
stop

20

21

Marine
Parade

Railway
station

Vernon Rd

Westwood

Scarborough
Art Gallery

Rotunda
Museum

South Bay

Valley Bridge Rd

Tesco

Valley Rd

Ramshill Rd

048

Valley Rd A165

22

Esplanade

Spa Lift

44

0   200m

Where to stay
3 Howdale
4 Kimberley Seafront
5 Leeway
6 Tall Storeys B&B
11 Barrington Guest House
12 Palace Hill
19 Premier Inn
20 Travelodge

21 Grand Hotel
   Scarborough

Where to eat and drink
1 Watermark
2 Oasis
7 Ivy House
8 Anton's
9 Ask

10 Golden Grid
13 Bayview Coffee House
14 Eastern Paradise
15 Clark's
16 Scarborough Flyer
17 Cat's Pyjamas
18 Greensmith & Thackwray
22 Farrer's Bar & Brasserie

Hill (☎ 01723-374535, 🖳 palace-hill.co.uk; 1S/5D/3Tr, all en suite; WI-FI) is housed in an 18th-century property. B&B costs £27.50-35pp (sgl/sgl occ from £45). A few steps along, reasonable-value rooms can be found at No 3 and ***Barrington Guest House*** (☎ 01723-314864, 🖳 thebarringtonguesthouse.co.uk; 3D/2Qd, all en suite or private facilities; ▼; WI-FI; 🐕); rates are from £32.50pp (sgl occ room rate). Once again, these are the cheapest rates and can be gained only by booking direct.

Even closer to the castle, Grade II-listed ***Tall Storeys*** (☎ 01723-373696, 🖳 tallstoreyshotel.co.uk; 5D all en suite, 2D shared facilities; ▼; WI-FI best in the public rooms; 🐕) sits at 131 Longwestgate and is one of the more charming places in the town, with rooms boasting either four-poster beds or sea views – and sometimes both. Note, however, that some of the rooms are an odd shape and you may have to mind your head in a few. Rates are from £40pp (sgl occ room rate).

Other B&Bs that, while a little further out, are still worth recommending, include ***The Beaches*** (☎ 07812 195661, 🖳 thebeachesscarborough.co.uk; 3D/1Tr, one room sleeping up to five, all en suite; WI-FI; 🐕), at 167 Columbus Ravine, about 700m from the trail. It's in a pretty good location and it's a friendly place. To reach it, at the end of the beach huts of North Bay take a right past the supermarket to the roundabout, then head up Columbus Ravine from here. B&B costs from £27.50-35pp (sgl occ from £40).

Also on the northern side of town, ***Headlands Guest House*** (☎ 01723-373717, 🖳 theheadlandshotel.co.uk; 4D/ 2T/4D or T/3Tr, all en suite; ▼; WI-FI; Easter to end Oct), 16 Weydale Avenue, is a friendly and efficient place with rooms starting at £35.50pp, rising to £51pp in the larger rooms in summer (sgl occ £102, though it's negotiable in winter). Note that these are the rates if you contact them direct.

Scarborough is popular enough to have persuaded the national chain **hotels** to open branches of their operations here, including ***Travelodge*** (☎ 0871 984 6430, 🖳 travelodge.co.uk; 70D/70Tr, all en suite; ▼; WI-FI; 🐕), which is opposite The Grand on St Nicholas Cliff, and ***Premier Inn*** (☎ 0871-527 9292, 🖳 premierinn.com; 74D, all en suite; ▼; WI-FI) on Falconer Rd. Rates at both start online at about £30 per room if you book (and pay) far enough in advance but are likely to be double that.

Speaking of the ***Grand Hotel Scarborough*** (☎ 0871 222 0047, 🖳 britanniahotels.com/hotels/the-grand-hotel-scarborough; 413 rooms ranging from singles to rooms sleeping up to five people, all en suite; ▼; WI-FI; 🐕), while it can't quite muster up the standards and luxury of yesteryear (there are no leisure facilities, for example), that does at least mean that you can now book rooms for less than £20pp if you hunt around online (sgl occ from £34) – though note this will be for one of their internal 'windowless' rooms, which won't be to everyone's liking, and these prices don't include breakfast which is another £7.50pp. Single rooms cost from £40 and a room with window costs from £27.50pp (sgl occ room rate). Rates can either be: room only, B&B or dinner B&B. Still, there's no more historic a hotel than this one in the town and the location is unequalled.

Where to eat and drink

There are so many places to eat in Scarborough that reviewing them all would require us to double the size of this book. So in this section we have merely picked out a few places on the seafront (and thus on the trail too), with the reviews divided into separate sections for North and South Beach in order to help you locate them on the map. There is then a short, separate section highlighting some of the better places we found in and around the town centre.

North Bay The first building you come to as you set foot in Scarborough is also one of the best places for pub food in the town. Dog-friendly ***Old Scalby Mills*** (Map 43; ☎ 01723-500449, 🖳 oldscalbymills.co.uk; food served Sun-Thur noon-8pm, Fri & Sat to 9pm; 🐕) has a classic British pub menu with nothing over a tenner (the king prawns in garlic butter with salad & chips at £9.95

is the most expensive item), the service is friendly and efficient and the location overlooking the weir and the beach beyond is lovely.

After Scalby Mills there's surprisingly little around North Bay though there are a couple of OK places across the road from the beach including **Watermark** (Sun-Thur 6am-6pm, Fri & Sat 7am-6pm), which is a nice place to sit, read the papers and drink a coffee. Their breakfast sandwiches are particularly good (£4-5.15). They also host occasional live music in the evenings though otherwise they're shut by 6pm.

Even better value is provided by **Oasis** (daily 6am-9.30pm), a few hundred metres further along, where the Workman's Breakfast costs £8, though smaller breakfast fare such as egg (£1.80) or bacon (£2.20) sandwiches are cheaper.

South Bay Most of the action in Scarborough happens around South Beach and this is where the vast majority of eateries are too. Our favourite place for a coffee on the seafront road is **Bayview Coffee House** (daily 9am-5pm; ✼); there's nothing amazing about the place, the menu of paninis (£4.30), omelettes (£4-4.50), sandwiches (£3.75) and toasties (£4) is fairly standard but the coffee is good, the service is friendly and dogs are welcome.

If it's a full-on breakfast you're after we recommend heading far south to **Farrer's Bar and Brasserie** (☎ 01723-357860, 🖳 farrersbar.co.uk; food served summer Mon 9am-8pm, Tue-Sat 9am-7.30pm, Sun 9am-5.30pm, winter hours variable; WI-FI; ✼) in Scarborough Spa. The veranda is a great place for people-watching over a cuppa and the breakfast menu is fairly extensive, from egg muffins for £3 via salmon and scrambled egg (£5.70) all the way up to the Full English for £7.95.

Cheaper fare can be found back near the harbour at **Ivy House** (☎ 01723-361306, 🖳 ivyhousetearoom.com; food summer daily 9am-5pm, winter generally weekends only; WI-FI; ✼), which describes itself as a gastro tea room though it looks more like a pub than anything else. Even

the menu wouldn't look out of place in your average hostelry, with pub standards such as steak pie & chips for £8.95. Still, it's good value and, as a result, usually very busy. If you manage to find a table you can get a full English breakfast for just £4.95.

A little further along is the very popular fish restaurant **Golden Grid** (☎ 01723-360922, 🖳 goldengrid.co.uk; Sun-Thur 11am-9.30pm, Fri to 10pm, Sat to 10.30pm). The large menu is certainly one of the attractions, with every taste catered for from liquid lunches (they have an alcohol licence) to lobster. Their 'really good fish pie' certainly lives up to its name and is very good value at £11.50.

On the other side of the road is **Ask** (🖳 askitalian.co.uk; Sun-Thur 11am-11pm, Fri & Sat to 11pm), a branch of the nationwide Italian food chain. The pizzas (£8.25-12.95), of course, are reliably good but it is its position on the sea-side of the road that is the real draw.

Anton's Bar & Grill (☎ 01723-381445, 🖳 antonscafebar.com; food summer Tue-Sat 11am-9pm, Sun 11am-3pm, winter Tue-Fri 5-9pm, Sat 11am-9pm, Sun 11am-3pm) is most notable for being housed in the old Bethel Mission Chapel building. The menu is a curious hybrid of British staples supplemented with pizzas (from £8.50) and burgers; the Business Burger, a 100% Rump Steak Burger with cheddar cheese & smoked bacon, is fair value at £12.95.

In town There are several notable places in the centre of town. At the top of the Cliff lift on South Bay, **Cat's Pyjamas** (☎ 01723-375603, 🖳 thecatspyjamascafebars.co.uk; WI-FI; ✼; Sun-Thur 9am-5pm, Fri & Sat to 10pm) is a lovely place, a 1920s inspired eatery with jazz on the stereo and some great food, including a smashing fish butty made with cod goujons and tartare sauce (£7.50).

Nearby on St Nicholas St, for hot drinks there's **Greensmith & Thackwray** (Mon-Thur 9am-5pm, Fri & Sat to 9pm). Set in an old colonial outfitters, to be honest the place is suffused with pretension – they even give you an egg timer so you can brew your tea for the correct amount of time – but you have to give the young owners credit for trying to do something different.

Further down at 4-13 St Nicholas St is *Scarborough Flyer* (☎ 01723-366433, 💻 greatukpubs.co.uk/scarboroughflyer; WI-FI; food daily 10am-9pm), one of several Wetherspoon's venues in town, proffering their usual good-value, hearty menu (eg beef & double Gloucester pie with chips for £9.29).

At 5 St Helens Sq, *Eastern Paradise* (☎ 01723-375227, 💻 easternparadisescarborough.co.uk; Sun-Thur 5pm-midnight, Fri & Sat to 12.30am) is the best Indian restaurant in town, with mains for £5.95-10.95. The easiest way to get to it from the seafront is to climb up the expertly graffitied

Caravel Alley – the restaurant sits opposite Market Hall.

Finally, one of the smartest places to eat in town is *Clark's* (☎ 01723-447373, 💻 clarksrestaurant.co.uk; WI-FI; 🐾 but not on Fri or Sat; Mon & Wed-Fri 10am-2pm & 6.30-9pm, Sat 10am-2pm & 6-9.30pm), at 40 Queen St, which describes its food as 'British Tapas and Small Plate dishes' in a modern style. Using plenty of local ingredients, dishes are around the £4-5 mark each, or four for £16, and may include such delights as Serrano ham & black truffled quail's egg with white truffled mayonnaise, 'burnt' toast and mustard cress (£4.75); fancy, undoubtedly, but delicious nevertheless.

SCARBOROUGH TO FILEY   [MAPS 44-48]

To the relief of those whose trek has left them hurting from bonce to bunions, this final stage of the Cleveland Way is a nice, short **9½-mile/15.3km** jaunt (**2hrs 35mins to 3hrs 20mins**) that mercifully lacks the knee-knackering undulations of the previous stages.

Much of your time on this stage will be taken up with leaving Scarborough – and even when you think you have, it then returns in the form of **Osgodby** (Map 45), one of its suburbs, which the path visits for a few minutes. Thereafter the path drops down via sun-dappled woods to Cayton Bay.

CAYTON BAY   [Map 46, p175]
There are a couple of campsites here – *Flower of May* (☎ 01723-584311, 💻 flowerofmay.com; WI-FI; 🐾; Easter-Nov), where pitches start at £24 for up to two people, rising in £30 to high season, and *Crows Nest Caravan Park* (☎ 01723-582206, 💻 crowsnestcaravanpark.com; WI-FI; 🐾; Mar-Oct) which charges from £25 per pitch for up to four people.

But for most Cleveland Way walkers, if they have any interaction at all with Cayton Bay it will be with *Lucy's Beach Shack* (daily 9.30am-7pm; times, as

always, weather dependent), about 100m from the path down the hill towards the beach – it's the last place to get refreshments on the trail.

The impressive Victorian building to the north of Lucy's is an old Victorian **pumping station**.

EYMS's No 12 & 13, and SS's 555 **bus services** (see box pp52-3 for details) stop here as does National Express's 327 coach service (see p51).

Having regained the clifftops following Cayton Bay, the path skirts round the edge of the giant **Blue Dolphin Holiday Park** (Maps 46 & 47). Thereafter, with the steeples of Filey appearing ahead of you to your right, it's merely a case of rolling gently down the hill to the conspicuous promontory ahead on

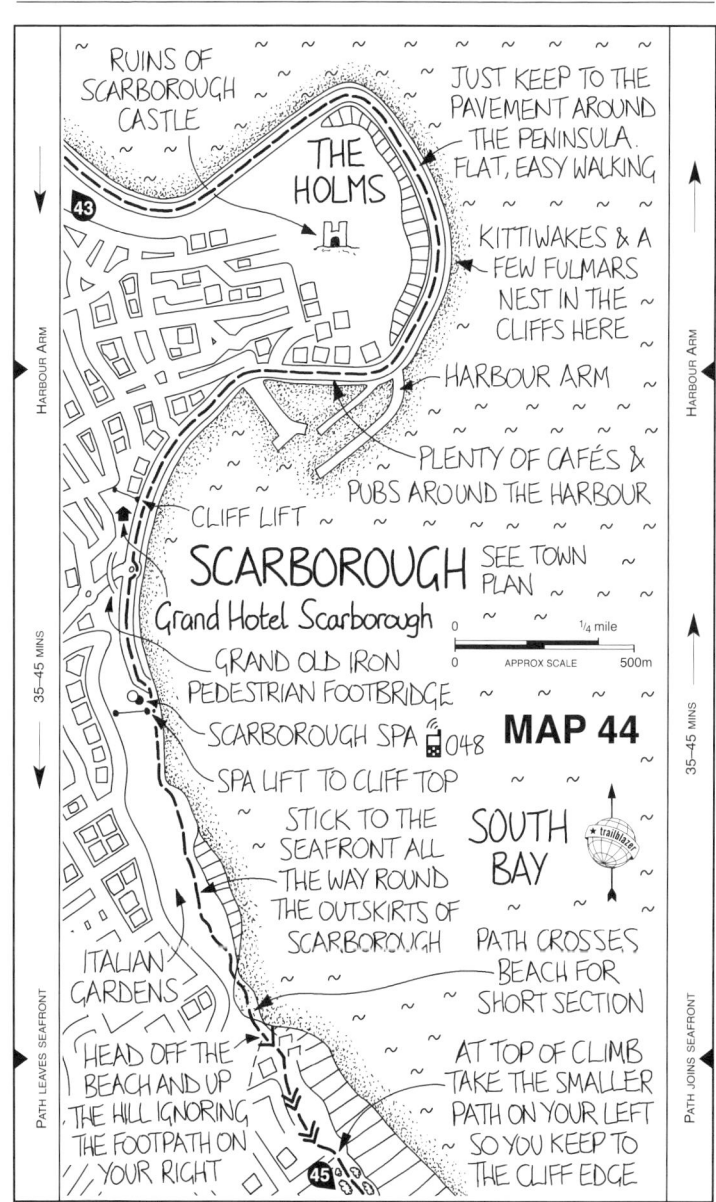

RUINS OF SCARBOROUGH CASTLE

THE HOLMS

JUST KEEP TO THE PAVEMENT AROUND THE PENINSULA. FLAT, EASY WALKING

43

KITTIWAKES & A FEW FULMARS NEST IN THE CLIFFS HERE

HARBOUR ARM

PLENTY OF CAFÉS & PUBS AROUND THE HARBOUR

CLIFF LIFT

SCARBOROUGH

SEE TOWN PLAN

Grand Hotel Scarborough

GRAND OLD IRON PEDESTRIAN FOOTBRIDGE

SCARBOROUGH SPA 048

SPA LIFT TO CLIFF TOP

0   ¼ mile
0   APPROX SCALE   500m

MAP 44

STICK TO THE SEAFRONT ALL THE WAY ROUND THE OUTSKIRTS OF SCARBOROUGH

SOUTH BAY

trailblazer

PATH CROSSES BEACH FOR SHORT SECTION

ITALIAN GARDENS

HEAD OFF THE BEACH AND UP THE HILL IGNORING THE FOOTPATH ON YOUR RIGHT

AT TOP OF CLIMB TAKE THE SMALLER PATH ON YOUR LEFT SO YOU KEEP TO THE CLIFF EDGE

45

HARBOUR ARM

HARBOUR ARM

35–45 MINS

35–45 MINS

PATH LEAVES SEAFRONT

PATH JOINS SEAFRONT

ROUTE GUIDE AND MAPS

your left. This is **Filey Brigg**, the landward end of which is known as **Carr Naze**; and it is here, near the site of an old **Roman Signal Station**, that you find a simple wooden signpost that marks the end of the Cleveland Way. Adjacent to the signpost is a commemorative, **carved stone seat** – the perfect place to sit, shoot a few selfies and celebrate your achievement.

So that's that: over 107 miles after leaving Helmsley your Cleveland Way odyssey is at an end. But that doesn't mean that your adventure is necessarily

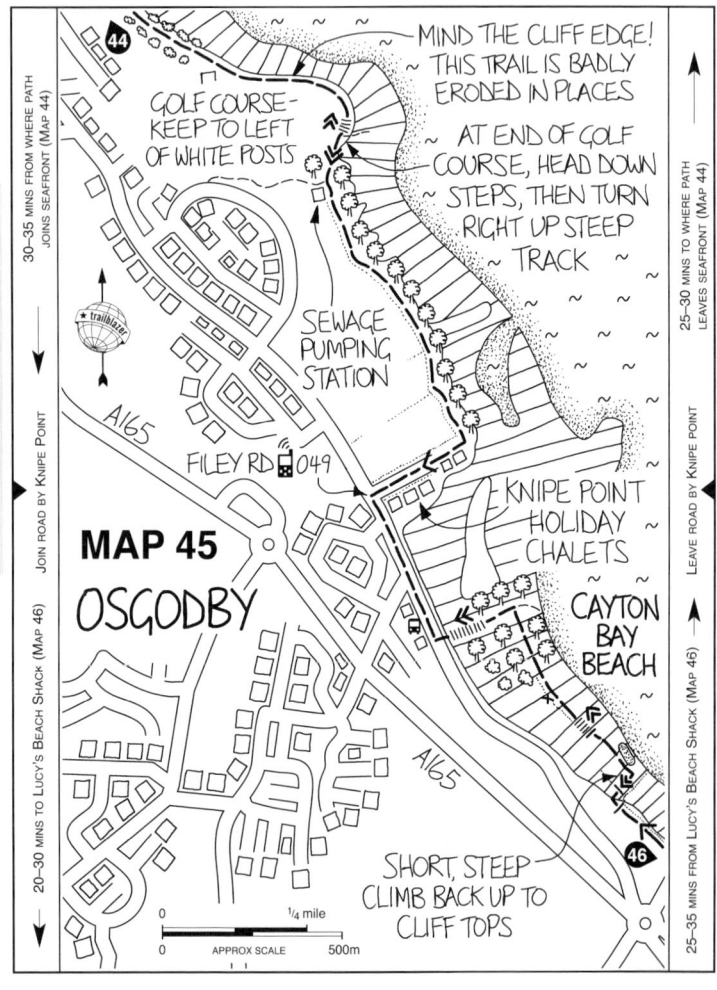

ROUTE GUIDE AND MAPS

30-35 MINS FROM WHERE PATH JOINS SEAFRONT (MAP 44)

JOIN ROAD BY KNIPE POINT

20-30 MINS TO LUCY'S BEACH SHACK (MAP 46)

25-30 MINS TO WHERE PATH LEAVES SEAFRONT (MAP 44)

LEAVE ROAD BY KNIPE POINT

25-35 MINS FROM LUCY'S BEACH SHACK (MAP 46)

44

MIND THE CLIFF EDGE!
THIS TRAIL IS BADLY ERODED IN PLACES

GOLF COURSE - KEEP TO LEFT OF WHITE POSTS

AT END OF GOLF COURSE, HEAD DOWN STEPS, THEN TURN RIGHT UP STEEP TRACK

trailblazer

SEWAGE PUMPING STATION

A165

FILEY RD 049

KNIPE POINT HOLIDAY CHALETS

MAP 45

OSGODBY

CAYTON BAY BEACH

A165

46

SHORT, STEEP CLIMB BACK UP TO CLIFF TOPS

0   ¼ mile

0   APPROX SCALE   500m

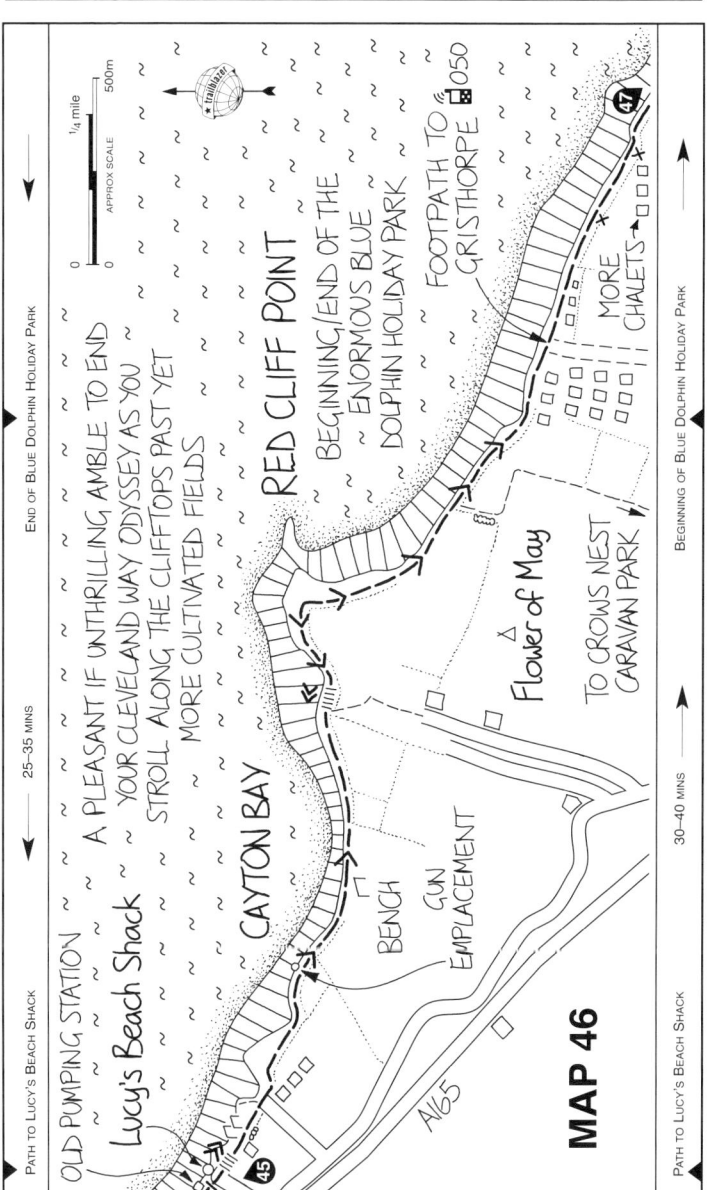

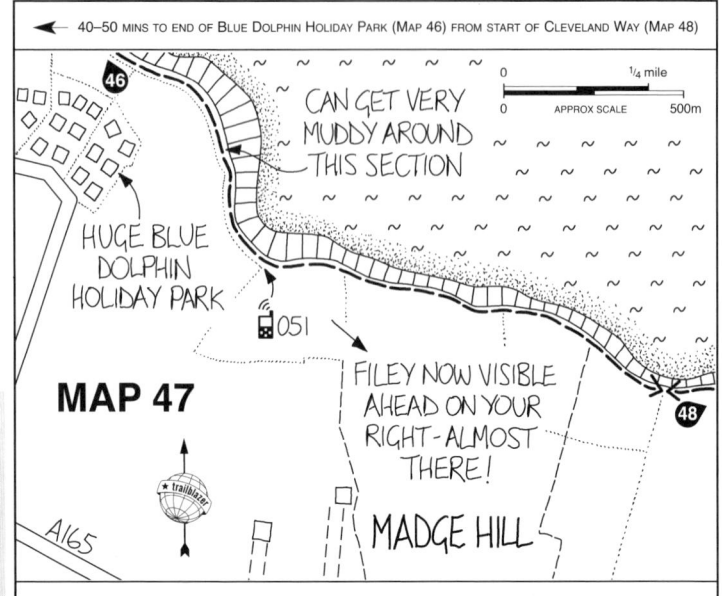

← 40–50 MINS TO END OF BLUE DOLPHIN HOLIDAY PARK (MAP 46) FROM START OF CLEVELAND WAY (MAP 48)

46

CAN GET VERY
MUDDY AROUND
THIS SECTION

0   ¼ mile
0   APPROX SCALE   500m

HUGE BLUE
DOLPHIN
HOLIDAY PARK

051

MAP 47

FILEY NOW VISIBLE
AHEAD ON YOUR
RIGHT - ALMOST
THERE!

48

★ trailblazer

A165

MADGE HILL

40–50 MINS FROM START OF BLUE DOLPHIN HOLIDAY PARK (MAP 46) TO END OF CLEVELAND WAY (MAP 48) ➤

ROUTE GUIDE AND MAPS

❑ Recording your achievement

We do think it's a bit of a shame that the end of the Cleveland Way is so 'low key'.
True, we weren't expect a marching band or bunting to greet our arrival; and it's also
true that pretty much every other long-distance trail suffers from the same lack of
'fireworks' at the journey's end. But it just seems to us to be a bit of a shame that
walkers have to make do with a photo of themselves by the signpost, or sitting on the
seat, to show that they've just finished a national trail and one of the great walks in
England.

You may also want to visit *Filey Country Park Café* (Map 48; see p180) a few
hundred metres from the end of the path, which keeps the 'official' register where
those who have completed the Cleveland Way or Wolds Way can sign their name and
jot down their thoughts. Though to be honest, it's clear that many walkers don't bother: after all, the same book has been in use since 2000 and still isn't full, and we were
the first people to sign it in 2018, having completed the trek in late April. Still, it's
another piece of evidence to prove your achievements, and afterwards you can continue to the railway station via St Oswald's Church (it's the easiest way there), walk
down the slope to the Wolds Way, visit the beach – or simply sit, tuck into one of the
café's sausage sandwiches and remind yourself that, as with any long-distance trail,
it's not the destination that's important – but the journey itself.

over, of course. Look closely at the seat and you'll see the names of a few of the places you've visited carved into the stone – but also the names of several places that you haven't, at least not yet: Wintringham, for example, and Thixendale, and Ganton. These, of course, are places on the **Wolds Way**, which continues for a further 79 miles to the south. So what are you waiting for? You've still got your boots on, you've never been fitter – and it seems a shame to quit now when there's another national trail right there, waiting for you…

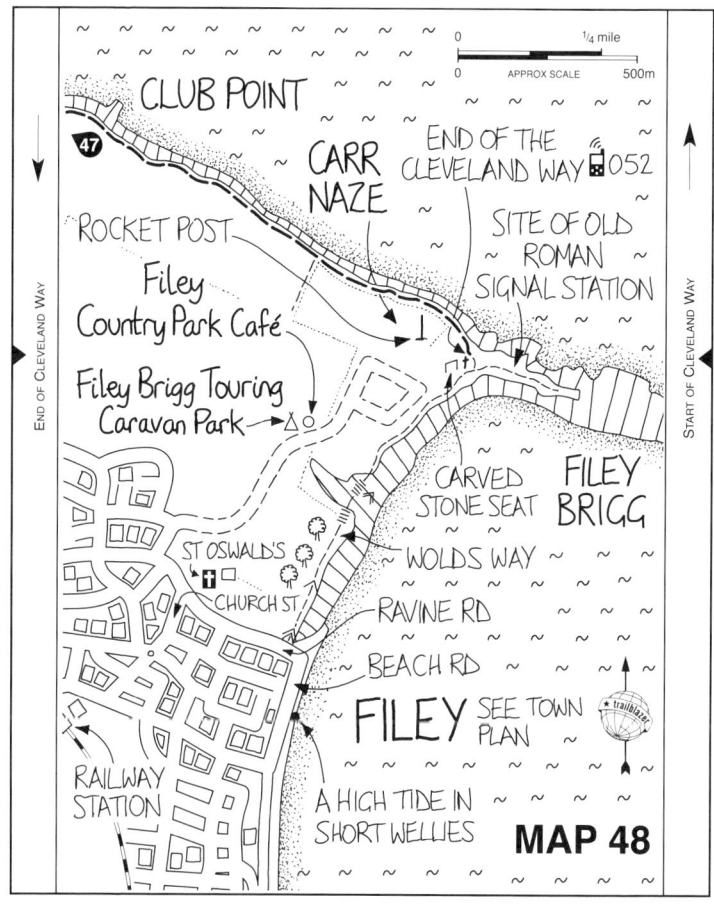

CLUB POINT

47

CARR NAZE

END OF THE CLEVELAND WAY 052

ROCKET POST

SITE OF OLD ROMAN SIGNAL STATION

Filey Country Park Café

Filey Brigg Touring Caravan Park

END OF CLEVELAND WAY

START OF CLEVELAND WAY

CARVED STONE SEAT

FILEY BRIGG

ST OSWALD'S

WOLDS WAY

CHURCH ST

RAVINE RD

BEACH RD

FILEY SEE TOWN PLAN

trailblazer

RAILWAY STATION

A HIGH TIDE IN SHORT WELLIES

MAP 48

ROUTE GUIDE AND MAPS

0   ¼ mile

0   APPROX SCALE   500m

FILEY

Filey has an unusual claim to fame in the world of walking. There are a few places in England and Wales where two national trails meet: Goring in Berkshire and its neighbour Streatley-on-Thames, for example, are visited by both the Ridgeway national trail and the Thames Path; and the tiny hamlet of Twice Brewed in Northumbria is crossed by both the Hadrian's Wall and Pennine Way national trails. But with the arrival of the England Coast Path, Filey is the first place where *three* paths meet.

We like the fact that Filey holds such a unique position, especially as the town is such an unassuming place. Less gaudy, less attention-seeking, less 'shouty' than its noisy neighbour to the north, Filey is pretty much the epitome of pleasant. One of Scarborough's residents said to me that visiting Filey was like stepping back to the 1950s, and while the town doesn't *look* like it's stuck in the middle of the 20th century, its atmosphere does seem to hark back to a more genteel and civilised time. Even Filey's seafront is tranquil and, surprisingly, largely residential, its 'pleasure beach' section tucked away at the north-eastern end of the seafront, out of sight of the main part of town up the hill.

With good cafés and B&Bs for those who are staying, and decent transport links for those who just want to get back home, we think it's a lovely place to end a national trail....or, of course, to begin one.

Services

The **tourist information point** (⌨ discoveryorkshirecoast.com) is in the Concert Hall on John St. It's mostly just leaflets but there is also a freephone linking you to a dedicated Tourism Bureau team based in Scarborough. This line is manned daily in summer 9am-5pm, winter Monday to Saturday only; if not in Scarborough you can call this office (☎ 01723-383636) during those hours for information on Scarborough, Whitby and Filey.

The **post office** (Mon-Fri 9am-5.30pm, Sat to 4pm) is next door.

Maybe reflecting the age of many of its residents, Filey can boast no fewer than three Boots the **chemists**; the one halfway down Murray St (Mon-Sat 9am-5.30pm, Sun 10am-4pm) is the largest and the only one open on Sunday.

West on Station Ave is a Tesco **supermarket** (Mon-Sat 7am-10pm, Sun 10am-4pm), while about 300m north of here at 2C Mitford St is the **trekking outfitters** Cammish Outdoors (☎ 01723-513319; school summer holidays daily 9am-5pm, rest of year Mon, Tue & Thur-Sat 9am-5pm). There is also a Spar (daily 7am-10pm) with an **ATM** at 3 Murray St.

Transport

Filey is a stop on Northern's **rail** services between Hull and Scarborough (see box p49).

National Express's No 327 and No 563 (see p51) also visit Filey bus station, which lies in front of Tesco.

Bus-wise, EYMS runs the 12, 13 & X21; there's also SS's 555 (the Filey Flyer). Transdev's seasonal X43 calls here en route between Leeds and Bridlington. See box pp52-3 for more details.

If coming by **car** see box p50 for information on parking here.

What to see and do

There's not a huge amount to do in Filey – but that's just fine. There is a **museum** (⌨ fileymuseum.org.uk; Easter-end Oct Sun-Fri 11am-5pm, Sat 2-5pm; £2.50) that's entirely run by volunteers and tucked away at 8-10 Queen St. Studying the history of the town over seven rooms, the museum includes exhibitions on the local lifeboat service and Victorian Filey. The highlight for us, however, was the room dedicated to local 19th-century photographer Walter Fisher and the pictures of the locals that he took while residing here, that give a great insight into how the town looked back then in the days before mass tourism.

If you happen to be strolling in **Crescent Gardens**, overlooking the beach, do seek out the **five stones** found on Carr

Naze in the middle of the 19th century following a landslip, and which were later determined to be pillar bases of Roman origin. You can still make out the 'hunting' scene of a dog chasing a stag on the middle of the stones.

Down on the seafront at Coble Landing there is another large sculpture, *A High Tide in Short Wellies* (see photo overleaf), by local artist Ray Lonsdale, who is also responsible for *Freddie Gilroy and the Belsen Stragglers* in Scarborough (see pp124-5).

Where to stay

For once, **campers** actually have the most convenient accommodation for the trail. *Filey Brigg Touring Caravan Park* (Map 48; ☎ 01723-513852, 🖳 fileybriggcaravan park.campmanager.com; 🐾; Mar-Dec) has pitches for around £11 per night for up to two people.

Filey is well-stocked with **B&Bs**. West Ave is a good place to start looking, with well-appointed *Binton Guest House* (☎ 01723-513753, 🖳 bintonguesthouse.co.uk; 2T/2D/1D or T, all en suite, 1Tr, private

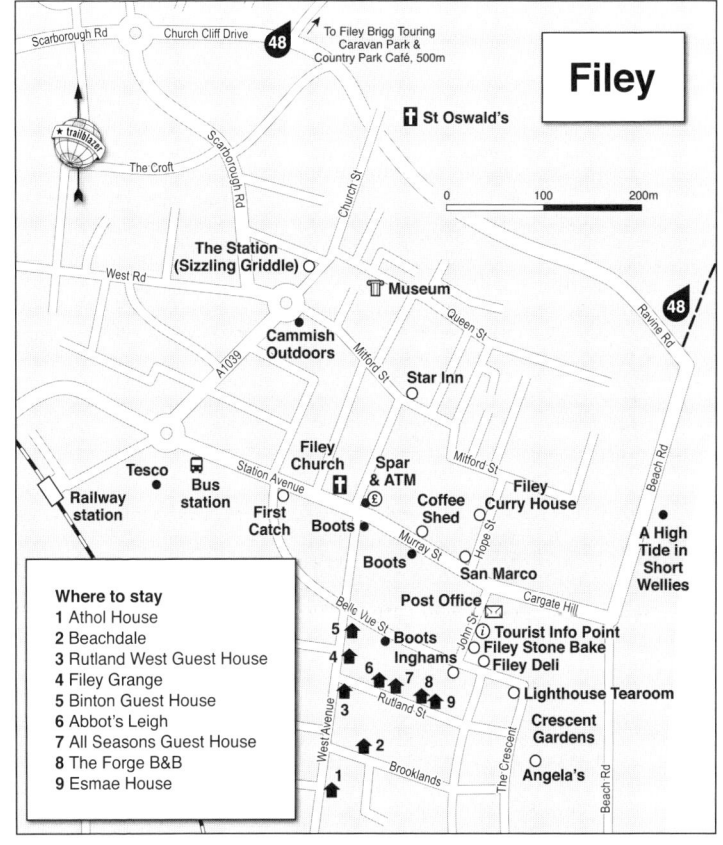

Where to stay

1 Athol House
2 Beachdale
3 Rutland West Guest House
4 Filey Grange
5 Binton Guest House
6 Abbot's Leigh
7 All Seasons Guest House
8 The Forge B&B
9 Esmae House

ROUTE GUIDE AND MAPS

facilities; WI-FI), at No 23, where rates are around the £39-42pp mark (sgl occ from £60, though full room rate required on bank hols and in summer).

Just along the Avenue at No 27 is *Filey Grange* (☎ 01723-513396, 🖳 fileygrange .co.uk; 3D/1Qd, all en suite; 🖤; WI-FI). All the rooms have a fridge and the twin and double rooms on the third floor have a connecting door and can sleep up to four people. Rates are £40-57.50pp (sgl occ rates on request); note that there's often a two-night minimum stay policy in high season but it is always worth calling to check. From Feb 2019 a continental-style breakfast will be served in the rooms; a cooked breakfast will no longer be available.

Further along still, at No 67, is *Athol House* (☎ 01723-515189, 🖳 athol-guest house.co.uk; 3D/1T/1Qd, all en suite; WI-FI), one of the cheaper options if you're travelling alone, with single occupancy from £45, two sharing from £35pp.

Rutland St, just around the corner is another happy hunting ground. At No 2A, where Rutland St meets West Ave, is the smart *Rutland West Guest House* (☎ 01723-514750, 🖳 rutlandwestfiley.co.uk; 1D/2D or T/1Qd, all en suite; 🖤; WI-FI; 🐕), one of the few places in town that allows dogs in its rooms, with rooms from £37pp (sgl occ from £60).

Moving down the road, at No 7 there's cheerful *Abbot's Leigh* (☎ 01723-513334, 🖳 abbotsleighguesthouse.co.uk; 3D/2D or T/1Tr, all en suite; 🖤; WI-FI), where rates start at £37.50pp (sgl occ from £50, though full room rate in summer). *All Seasons Guest House* (☎ 01723-515321, 🖳 allsea sonsfiley.co.uk; 4D/1D or T/1Tr, all en suite; WI-FI), at No 11, which charges £42.50-50pp (sgl occ from £65); *The Forge* (☎ 01723-514646, 🖳 theforgefiley .com; 4D/1T, all en suite; WI-FI) at No 23, one of our favourites with some very nicely furnished rooms (rates are from £39.50pp, sgl occ from £60); and, next door, at No 25, *Esmae House* (☎ 01723-515493, 🖳 esmae-house.co.uk; 4D/1D or T, all en suite; WI-FI; Feb-Nov), perhaps the smartest of the lot, with rates £37.50-45pp (sgl occ room rate).

Away from these two streets, at 2 Brooklands is *Beachdale Guesthouse* (☎ 01723-317560, 🖳 beachdalefiley.co.uk; 3D/2D or T, all en suite; 🖤; WI-FI; Ⓛ) charges £40-45pp (sgl occ from £70).

Where to eat and drink

If you're up early in the morning and need a hit of caffeine, *Filey Country Park Café* (daily 6.30am up to 6pm, closed Wed outside of school holidays) seems to be the first place to open; see box p176. The menu is fairly standard 'caff' style but good value, with a sausage bap for £3.

Of those that open at more civilised times, our favourite café is *Coffee Shed* (Mon-Sat 8.30am-4.30pm), on Murray St, whose menu seems unremarkable (breakfasts, with beans on toast £2.50, sandwiches, cakes and snacks) but which seems to be the most popular with locals – always a good sign.

Special mention must also be made of *Angela's* (Mon-Sat 10am-5pm, to 3pm outside of summer), largely because of its agreeable location hidden away below Crescent Gardens, where you can pick up a bacon sarnie with a hot drink for £4.50; the popular *Filey Deli* (daily 9.30am-3pm), with fairly priced sandwiches (£1.50-2.50); and the excellent *Lighthouse Tearoom* (Sat-Thur 10am-4pm; at the seaward end of Belle Vue Terrace) because it's very friendly and the items on their menu, particularly the freshly home-baked scones (cheese and fruit), are smashing.

Amazingly, finding a **pub** in Filey that serves food is actually quite difficult though there are a couple that are recommendable. The first is the popular *Star Inn* (☎ 01723-512031, 🖳 thestar filey.co.uk; food Tue-Sat 5-8.30pm, Sun noon-4pm; WI-FI) at 23 Mitford St. Open evenings only during the week, mains are £9.45-17.95 and there's a decent veggie selection (all veggie mains £9.45); they also do a decent value Sunday lunch (£6.95-8.95 depending on the size).

The second option is **The Station** on Church St which plays host to *Sizzling Griddle* (Mon-Wed 3-7.45pm, Fri noon-7.45pm, Sat 11am-7.45pm, Sun noon-

4pm); it offers pizzas from £4.95 and burgers that range from £8.95 up to £18.95 for the Towering Inferno, a monster of a burger that includes four beef patties and *twelve* rashers of bacon, all smothered with a mountain of cheese and chilli con carne! They also do an array of pub classics (lasagne, chilli etc) which are all reasonably priced at £8.95.

The only problem with both these pubs is that they are a few minutes' walk from the town centre, which may be too much for those who finished their trek and decided that, for the next few days at least, they want to do as little walking as possible. If that's you, and you're staying in the town centre, you may need to rely on the restaurants for your evening dining. The best of them include the Italian, *San Marco* (☎ 01723-515457, 💻 sanmarcofiley.co.uk; Tue-Sun 5-10pm), on Murray St, with pizzas and pasta for £7.30-9.40; and the simply named *Filey Curry House* (☎ 01723-514567, 💻 fileycurryhouse.com; daily 5-11pm) with dishes from £5.95.

Alternatively, the **fish & chips** can be found either at *Inghams* (Mon-Thur 11.45am-2pm, Fri & Sat 11.45am-2pm & 4.15-6.45pm, Sun noon-6.45pm), on Belle Vue St, or on the way to the railway station at the much smarter *First Catch* (daily 11.30am-9pm), 16 Belle Vue Crescent.

Finally, the top place for **fast food** is *Filey Stone Bake* (☎ 01723-518333, 💻 filey-stone-bake.business.site; Sun-Thur 4pm-midnight, Fri-Sat to 2am), centrally located on John St, with pizzas from £4.50, kebabs from £4 and free local delivery.

Above: *A High Tide in Short Wellies*, by Ray Lonsdale (see box pp124-5).

APPENDIX A: GPS WAYPOINTS

MAP	WAYPOINT	OS GRID REF	DESCRIPTION
1	001	N54° 14.780' W1° 03.698'	Market Cross, Helmsley
2	002	N54° 15.060' W1° 07.203'	Rievaulx Bridge
3	003	N54° 15.188' W1° 10.750'	Junction by scruffy barn before Cold Kirby
4	004	N54° 13.508' W1° 12.798'	White Horse
4	005	N54° 14.423' W1° 12.641'	Sutton Bank National Park Centre
5	006	N54° 15.817' W1° 13.508'	Junction with path to Boltby
6	007	N54° 17.529' W1° 13.701'	High Paradise Farm
7	008	N54° 19.225' W1° 14.861'	Location of Old Limekiln House
8	009	N54° 19.884' W1° 14.782'	Gate & cattle grid before distinctive bend in Hambleton Street
9	010	N54° 21.387' W1° 15.831'	Square Corner
10	011	N54° 22.119' W1° 17.975'	Osmotherley's central square
11	012	N54° 23.791' W1° 16.352'	Scarth Nick
12	013	N54° 24.279' W1° 13.418'	Second huge cairn
13	014	N54° 25.220' W1° 11.597'	Lord Stones
14	015	N54° 25.328' W1° 07.113'	Clay Bank Top
15	016	N54° 24.341' W1° 05.196'	Boundary marker known as the 'hand stone'
16	017	N54° 24.315' W1° 03.172'	Bloworth Crossing
17	018	N54° 27.250' W1° 03.633'	Take the right-hand (easterly) path through the green gate
17	019	N54° 27.269' W1° 03.598'	Path meets road
18	020	N54° 28.123' W1° 04.005'	Turn-off to Park Farm
19	021	N54° 28.598' W1° 03.854'	Glebe Cottage (tearoom), Kildale
20	022	N54° 28.979' W1° 05.444'	Captain Cook Monument
20	023	N54° 30.329' W1° 06.436'	Roseberry Topping
21	024	N54° 30.971' W1° 03.521'	Highcliff Nab (viewpoint)
22	025	N54° 31.959' W1° 00.309'	Slapewath
23	026	N54° 32.497' W1° 00.225'	Airy Hill Farm
24	027	N54° 34.343' W0° 58.775'	Footbridge under viaduct
25	028	N54° 35.144' W0° 58.132'	Where the Cleveland Way meets the sea!
26	029	N54° 34.421' W0° 54.090'	Skinningrove jetty
27	030	N54° 34.046' W0° 52.214'	Information board by farmhouse
28	031	N54° 33.959' W0° 50.443'	Turn-off to trig point on Boulby Cliff
29	032	N54° 33.451' W0° 47.392'	Left turn after Church St
30	033	N54° 31.973' W0° 45.006'	Top of slipway at Runswick Bay
31	034	N54° 31.658' W0° 44.492'	Turn-off from Runswick Beach up second gully
32	035	N54° 31.144' W0° 41.314'	Footpath to Lythe
33	036	N54° 29.563' W0° 38.689'	Sharp turn left off A174 onto path through golf course.
34	037	N54° 29.423' W0° 36.959'	Captain Cook statue and Whalebone Arch
35	038	N54° 28.683' W0° 34.143'	High Lights Lighthouse
36	039	N54° 27.649' W0° 32.955'	Where the Cleveland Way meets the Coast to Coast Path

37	040	N54° 25.824' W0° 31.952'	Turn-off Robin Hood's Bay's Albion St onto flagstone steps
38	041	N54° 25.090' W0° 31.550'	YHA Boggle Hole
39	042	N54° 24.041' W0° 29.465'	Start of Station Rd, Ravenscar
40	043	N54° 22.466' W0° 27.314'	Start of (possibly temporary) diversion by stile
41	044	N54° 21.435' W0° 26.928'	Junction with path to Hayburn Wyke Inn
42	045	N54° 19.885' W0° 25.120'	Long Nab Coastguard Station
43	046	N54° 18.473' W0° 24.981'	Tabular Hill footpath
43	047	N54° 17.391' W0° 24.132'	Freddie Gilroy and the Belsen Stragglers sculpture
44	048	N54° 16.568' W0° 23.830'	Scarborough Spa
45	049	N54° 15.120' W0° 22.612'	Filey Rd, Osgodby
46	050	N54° 14.125' W0° 19.763'	Footpath to Gristhorpe
47	051	N54° 13.666' W0° 18.789'	End of Blue Dolphin Holiday Park site
48	052	N54° 13.116' W0° 16.585'	End of the Cleveland Way

APPENDIX B: TAKING A DOG

TAKING DOGS ALONG THE WAY

Many are the rewards that await those prepared to make the extra effort required to bring their best friend along the trail. But you shouldn't underestimate the amount of work involved. Indeed, just about every decision you make will be influenced by the fact that you've got a dog: how you plan to travel to the start of the trail, where you're going to stay, how far you're going to walk each day, where you're going to rest and where you're going to eat in the evening etc.

But if you're sure your dog can cope with (and will enjoy) walking 10 miles or more a day for several days in a row, and you can cope with the responsibility of looking after him or her, then you need to start preparing accordingly.

Looking after your dog

To begin with, you need to make sure that your dog is fully **inoculated** against the usual doggy illnesses, and also up to date with regard to **worm pills** (eg Drontal) and **flea preventatives** such as Frontline – they are, after all, following in the paw-prints of many a dog before them, some of whom may well have left fleas or other parasites on the trail that now lie in wait for their next meal to arrive.

Pet insurance is also a very good idea; if you've already got insurance, do check that it will cover a trip such as this. On the subject of looking after your dog's health, perhaps the most important implement you can take with you is the **plastic tick remover**, available from vets for a couple of quid. These removers, while fiddly, help you to remove the tick safely (ie without leaving its head buried under the dog's skin). Being in unfamiliar territory also makes it more likely that you and your dog could become separated.

All dogs now have to be **microchipped** but make sure your dog also has a **tag with your contact details on it** (a mobile phone number would be best if you are carrying one with you).

When to keep your dog on a lead
● **On cliff tops** It's a sad fact that, every year, a few dogs lose their lives falling over the edge of the cliffs. It usually occurs when they are chasing rabbits (which know where the cliff-edge is and are able, unlike your poor pooch, to stop in time).

● **When crossing farmland**, particularly in the lambing season (March to May) when your dog can scare the sheep, causing them to lose their young. Farmers are allowed by law to shoot at and kill any dogs that they consider are worrying their sheep. During lambing, most farmers would prefer it if you didn't take your dog at all. The exception is if your dog is being attacked by cows. Some years ago there were three deaths in the UK caused by walkers being trampled as they tried to rescue their dogs from the attentions of cattle. The advice in this instance is to let go of the lead, head speedily to a position of safety (usually the other side of the field gate or stile) and call your dog to you.

● **On National Trust land**, where it is compulsory to keep your dog on a lead.

● **Around ground-nesting birds** It's important to keep your dog under control when crossing an area where certain species of birds nest on the ground. Most dogs love foraging around in the woods but make sure you have permission to do so; some woods are used as 'nurseries' for game birds and dogs are only allowed through them if they are on a lead.

What to pack
You've probably already got a good idea of what to bring to keep your dog alive and happy, but the following is a checklist:

● **Food/water bowl** Foldable cloth bowls are popular with walkers, being light and taking up little room in the rucksack. You can get also get a water-bottle-and-bowl combination, where the bottle folds into a 'trough' from which the dog can drink.

● **Lead and collar** An extendable one is probably preferable for this sort of trip. Make sure both lead and collar are in good condition – you don't want either to snap on the trail, or you may end up carrying your dog through sheep fields until a replacement can be found.

● **Medication** You'll know if you need to bring any lotions or potions.

● **Bedding** A simple blanket may suffice, or you can opt for something more elaborate if you aren't carrying your own luggage.

● **Tick remover** See p183.

● **Poo bags** Essential.

● **Hygiene wipes** For cleaning your dog after it's rolled in stuff.

● **A favourite toy** Helps prevent your dog from pining for the entire walk.

● **Food/water** Remember to bring treats as well as regular food to keep up the mutt's morale. That said, if your dog is anything like mine the chances are they'll spend most of the walk dining on rabbit droppings and sheep poo anyway.

● **Corkscrew stake** Available from camping or pet shops, this will help you to keep your dog secure in one place while you set up camp/doze.

● **Raingear** It can rain!

● **Old towels** For drying your dog.

When it comes to packing, I always leave an exterior pocket of my rucksack empty so I can put used poo bags in there (for deposit at the first bin reached). I always like to keep all the dog's kit together and separate from the other luggage (usually inside a plastic bag inside my rucksack). I have also seen several dogs sporting their own 'doggy rucksack', so they can carry their own food, water, poo etc – which certainly reduces the burden on their owner!

Cleaning up after your dog
It is extremely important that dog owners behave in a responsible way when walking the path. Dog excrement should be cleaned up. In towns, villages and fields where animals graze or which will be cut for silage, hay etc, you need to pick up and bag the excrement.

Staying (and eating) with your dog

In this guide we have used the symbol 🐾 to denote where a place welcomes dogs. However, this always needs to be arranged in advance and some places make no extra charge and for others the fee may be anything from £1 to a whopping £20.

Many B&B-style places have only one or two rooms suitable for people with dogs; hostels do not permit them unless they are an assistance (guide) dog; smaller campsites tend to accept them, but some of the larger holiday parks do not – however, in either case it is likely the dog will have to be on a lead. Before you turn up always double check whether the place you would like to stay accepts dogs and whether there is space for them.

When it comes to **eating**, some cafés accept dogs and most landlords allow dogs in at least a section of their pubs, though few restaurants do. Make sure you always ask first and ensure your dog is on a lead and secured to your table or a radiator so it doesn't run around.

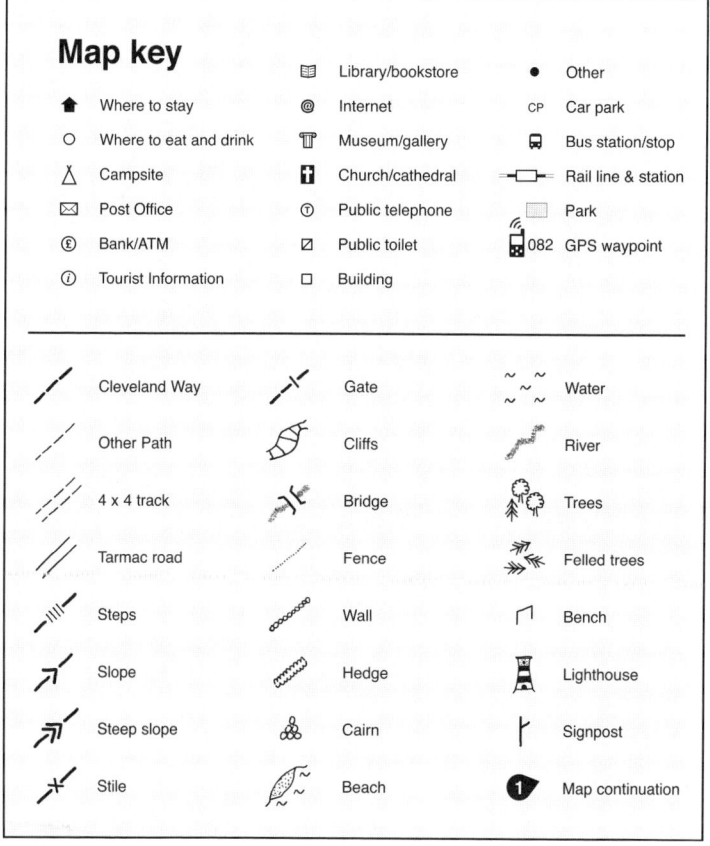

Map key

🛏 Where to stay	📖 Library/bookstore	● Other
○ Where to eat and drink	@ Internet	CP Car park
△ Campsite	🏛 Museum/gallery	🚌 Bus station/stop
✉ Post Office	✝ Church/cathedral	▪━▪ Rail line & station
(£) Bank/ATM	☎ Public telephone	▨ Park
(i) Tourist Information	☑ Public toilet	📱082 GPS waypoint
	□ Building	

Cleveland Way	Gate	Water
Other Path	Cliffs	River
4 x 4 track	Bridge	Trees
Tarmac road	Fence	Felled trees
Steps	Wall	Bench
Slope	Hedge	Lighthouse
Steep slope	Cairn	Signpost
Stile	Beach	❶ Map continuation

INDEX

Page references in **bold** type refer to maps

TRAILBLAZER TREKKING GUIDES

Europe
British Walking Guides – 18-title series
Scottish Highlands – The Hillwalking Guide
Tour du Mont Blanc
Walker's Haute Route: Mt Blanc – Matterhorn

South America
Inca Trail, Cusco & Machu Picchu
Peru's Cordilleras Blanca & Huayhuash

Africa
Kilimanjaro
Moroccan Atlas – The Trekking Guide
Asia
Nepal Trekking & The Great Himalaya Trail
Sinai – the trekking guide
Trekking in the Everest Region
Australasia
New Zealand – The Great Walks

Kilimanjaro – the trekking guide
Henry Stedman, 5th edn, £14.99
ISBN 978-1-905864-95-9, 368pp, 40 maps, 50 colour photos
At 5895m (19,340ft) Kilimanjaro is the world's tallest freestanding mountain and one of the most popular destinations for hikers visiting Africa. Route guides & maps – the 6 major routes. City guides – Nairobi, Dar-es-Salaam, Arusha, Moshi & Marangu.

Peru's Cordilleras Blanca & Huayhuash
The Hiking & Biking Guide
Neil & Harriet Pike, 1st edn, £15.99
ISBN 978-1-905864-63-8, 242pp, 50 maps, 40 colour photos
This region, in northern Peru, boasts some of the most spectacular scenery in the Andes, and most accessible high mountain trekking and biking in the world. This practical guide contains 60 detailed route maps and descriptions covering 20 hiking trails and more than 30 days of paved and dirt road cycling.

Sinai – the trekking guide *Ben Hoffler,* 1st edn, £14.99
ISBN 978-1-905864-41-6, 288pp, 74 maps, 30 colour photos
Trek with the Bedouin and their camels and discover one of the most exciting new trekking destinations. The best routes in the High Mountain Region (St. Katherine), Wadi Feiran and the Muzeina deserts. Once you finish on the trail there are the nearby coastal resorts of Sharm el Sheikh, Dahab and Nuweiba to enjoy.

Moroccan Atlas – the trekking guide
Alan Palmer, 2nd edn, £14.99
ISBN 978-1-905864-59-1, 420pp, 86 maps, 40 colour photos
The High Atlas in central Morocco is the most dramatic and beautiful section of the entire Atlas range. Towering peaks, deep gorges and huddled Berber villages enchant all who visit. With 73 detailed trekking maps, 13 town and village guides including Marrakech.

Trekking in the Everest Region
Jamie McGuinness 6th edn, £15.99
ISBN 978-1-905864-81-2, 320pp, 95 maps, 30 colour photos
Sixth edition of this popular guide to the world's most famous trekking region. Covers not only the classic treks but also the wild routes. Written by a Nepal-based trek and mountaineering leader. Includes: 27 detailed route maps and 52 village plans. Plus: Kathmandu city guide

TRAILBLAZER'S LONG-DISTANCE PATH (LDP) WALKING GUIDES

We've applied to destinations which are closer to home Trailblazer's proven formula for publishing definitive practical route guides for adventurous travellers. Britain's network of long-distance trails enables the walker to explore some of the finest landscapes in the country's best walking areas. These are guides that are user-friendly, practical, informative and environmentally sensitive.

'The same attention to detail that distinguishes its other guides has been brought to bear here'.
THE
SUNDAY TIMES

● **Unique mapping features** In many walking guidebooks the reader has to read a route description then try to relate it to the map. Our guides are much easier to use because walking directions, tricky junctions, places to stay and eat, points of interest and walking times are all written onto the maps themselves in the places to which they apply. With their uncluttered clarity, these are not general-purpose maps but fully edited maps drawn by walkers for walkers.

● **Largest-scale walking maps** At a scale of just under 1:20,000 (8cm or 3¹/₈ inches to one mile) the maps in these guides are bigger than even the most detailed British walking maps currently available in the shops.

● **Not just a trail guide – includes where to stay, where to eat and public transport** Our guidebooks cover the complete walking experience, not just the route. Accommodation options for all budgets are provided (pubs, hotels, B&Bs, campsites, bunkhouses, hostels) as well as places to eat. Detailed public transport information for all access points to each trail means that there are itineraries for all walkers, for hiking the entire route as well as for day or weekend walks.

● **Includes dowloadable GPS waypoints** – Marked on our maps and downloadable from the Trailblazer website.

Cleveland Way *Henry Stedman*, 1st edn, ISBN 978-1-905864-91-1, 208pp, 58 maps
Coast to Coast *Henry Stedman*, 8th edn, ISBN 978-1-905864-96-6, 268pp, 110 maps
Cornwall Coast Path (SW Coast Path Pt 2) *Stedman & Newton*, 5th edn, ISBN 978-1-905864-71-3, 352pp, 142 maps
Cotswold Way *Tricia & Bob Hayne,* 3rd edn, ISBN 978-1-905864-70-6, 204pp, 53 maps,
Dales Way *Henry Stedman,* 1st edn, ISBN 978-1-905864-78-2, 192pp, 50 maps
Dorset & South Devon (SW Coast Path Pt 3) *Stedman & Newton*, 2nd edn, ISBN 978-1-905864-94-2, 336pp, 88 maps
Exmoor & North Devon (SW Coast Path Pt I) *Stedman & Newton*, 2nd edn, ISBN 978-1-905864-86-7, 224pp, 68 maps
Great Glen Way *Jim Manthorpe,* 1st edn, ISBN 978-1-905864-80-5, 192pp, 55 maps
Hadrian's Wall Path *Henry Stedman*, 5th edn, ISBN 978-1-905864-85-0, 224pp, 60 maps
Norfolk Coast Path & Peddars Way *Alexander Stewart*, 1st edn, ISBN 978-1-905864-98-0, 224pp, 75 maps,
North Downs Way *Henry Stedman*, 2nd edn, ISBN 978-1-905864-90-4, 240pp, 98 maps
Offa's Dyke Path *Keith Carter*, 4th edn, ISBN 978-1-905864-65-2, 240pp, 98 maps
Pembrokeshire Coast Path *Jim Manthorpe*, 5th edn, ISBN 978-1-905864-84-3, 236pp, 96 maps
Pennine Way *Stuart Greig*, 4th edn, ISBN 978-1-905864-61-4, 272pp, 138 maps
The Ridgeway *Nick Hill*, 4th edn, ISBN 978-1-905864-79-9, 208pp, 53 maps
South Downs Way *Jim Manthorpe*, 6th edn, ISBN 978-1-905864-93-5, 204pp, 60 maps
Thames Path *Joel Newton*, 2nd edn, ISBN 978-1-905864-97-3, 256pp, 99 maps
West Highland Way *Charlie Loram*, 6th edn, ISBN 978-1-905864-76-8, 218pp, 60 maps

'The Trailblazer series stands head, shoulders, waist and ankles above the rest.
They are particularly strong on mapping ...'
THE SUNDAY TIMES

TRAILBLAZER TITLE LIST

For more information about Trailblazer and our
expanding range of guides, for guidebook updates or
for credit card mail order sales visit our website:

www.trailblazer-guides.com

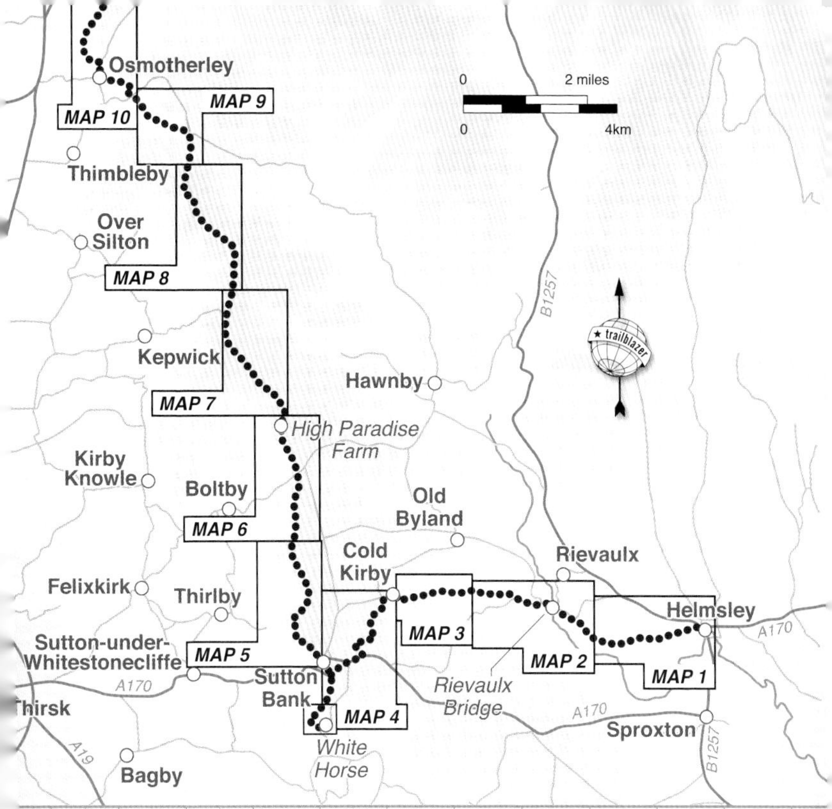

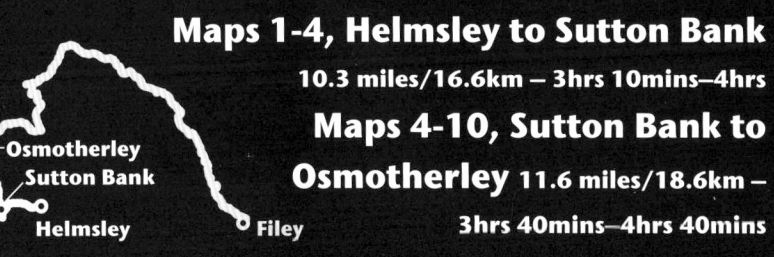

Map scale

0		2 miles
0		4km

Osmotherley

MAP 9

MAP 10

Thimbleby

Over
Silton

MAP 8

Kepwick

MAP 7

Hawnby

★ trailblazer

High Paradise
Farm

Kirby
Knowle

Boltby

MAP 6

Old
Byland

Rievaulx

Felixkirk

Thirlby

Cold
Kirby

Helmsley

A170

Sutton-under-
Whitestonecliffe

MAP 5

MAP 3

MAP 2

MAP 1

Thirsk

A170

Sutton
Bank

MAP 4

Rievaulx
Bridge

A170

Sproxton

A19

White
Horse

B1257

Bagby

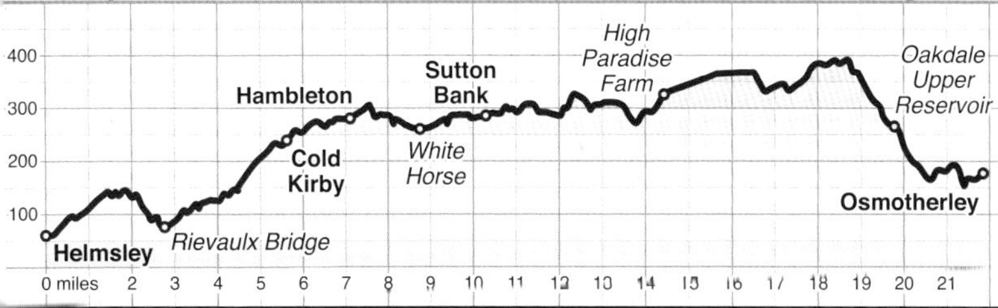

Elevation profile

	High Paradise Farm		Oakdale Upper Reservoir
400		Sutton Bank	
300	Hambleton		
200	Cold Kirby	White Horse	
100			Osmotherley
	Helmsley	Rievaulx Bridge	

0 miles 2   3   4   5   6   7   8   9   10   11   12   13   14   15   16   17   18   19   20   21

Maps 1-4, Helmsley to Sutton Bank
10.3 miles/16.6km – 3hrs 10mins–4hrs
Maps 4-10, Sutton Bank to
Osmotherley 11.6 miles/18.6km –
3hrs 40mins–4hrs 40mins

Osmotherley
Sutton Bank
Helmsley
Filey

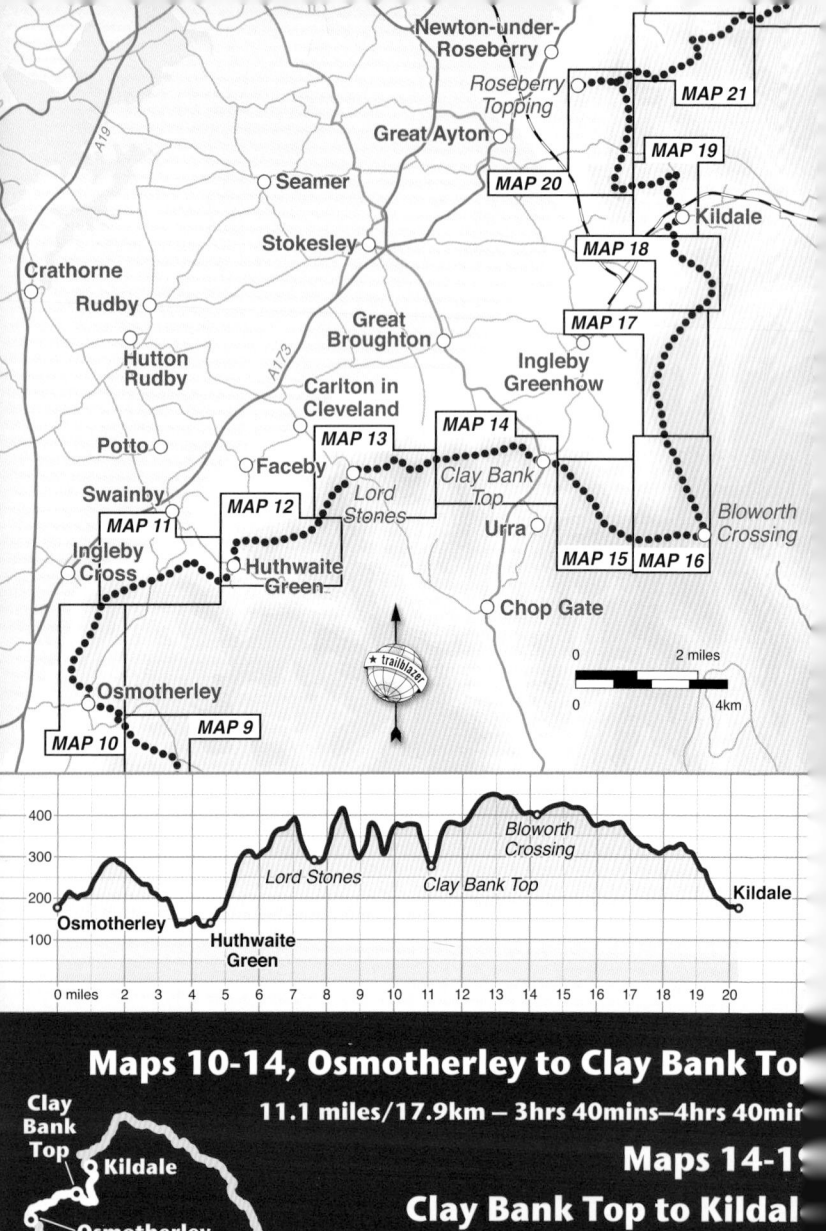

Maps 10-14, Osmotherley to Clay Bank Top

11.1 miles/17.9km – 3hrs 40mins–4hrs 40min

Maps 14-19

Clay Bank Top to Kildal

9.1 miles/14.6km –

2hrs 35 mins–3hrs 20 mir

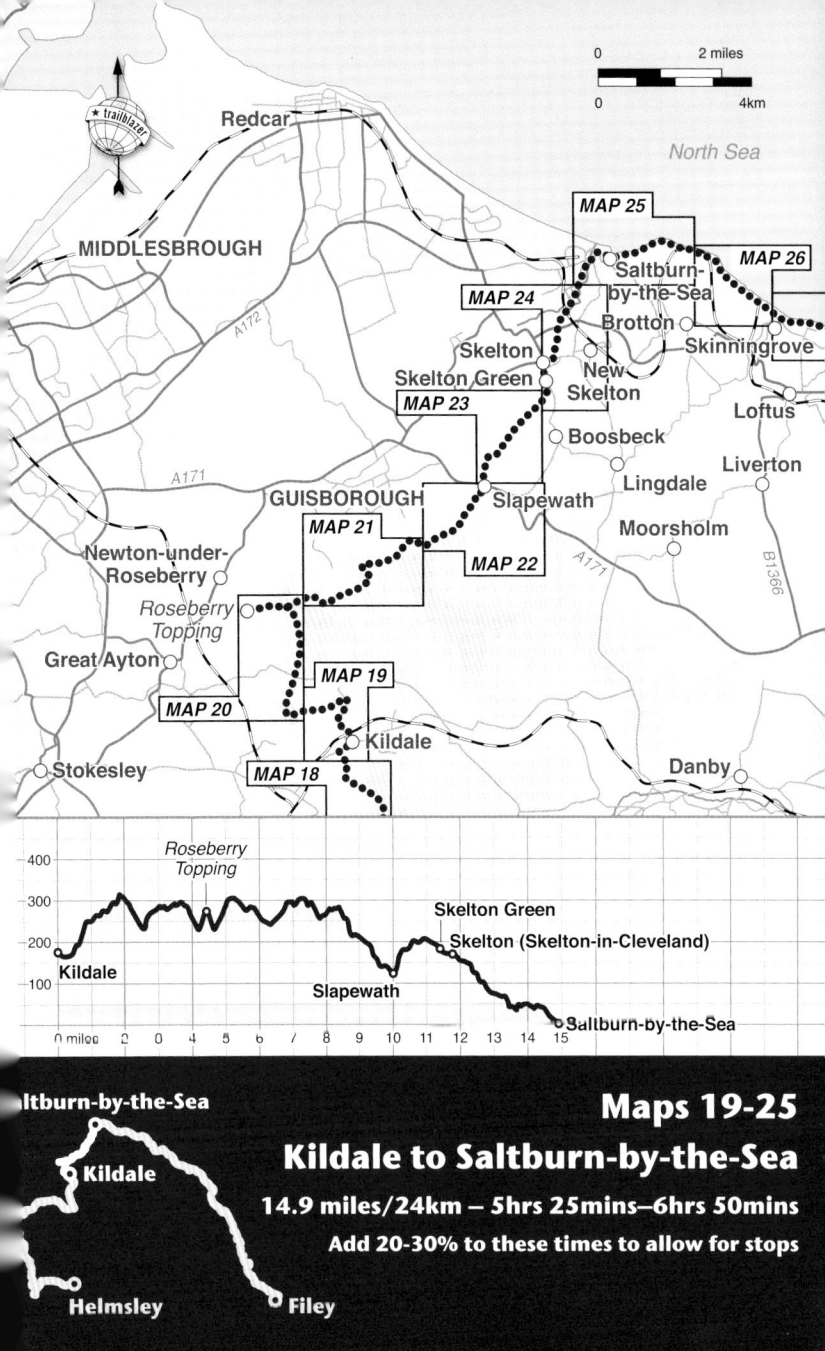

Maps 19-25

Kildale to Saltburn-by-the-Sea

14.9 miles/24km – 5hrs 25mins–6hrs 50mins

Add 20-30% to these times to allow for stops

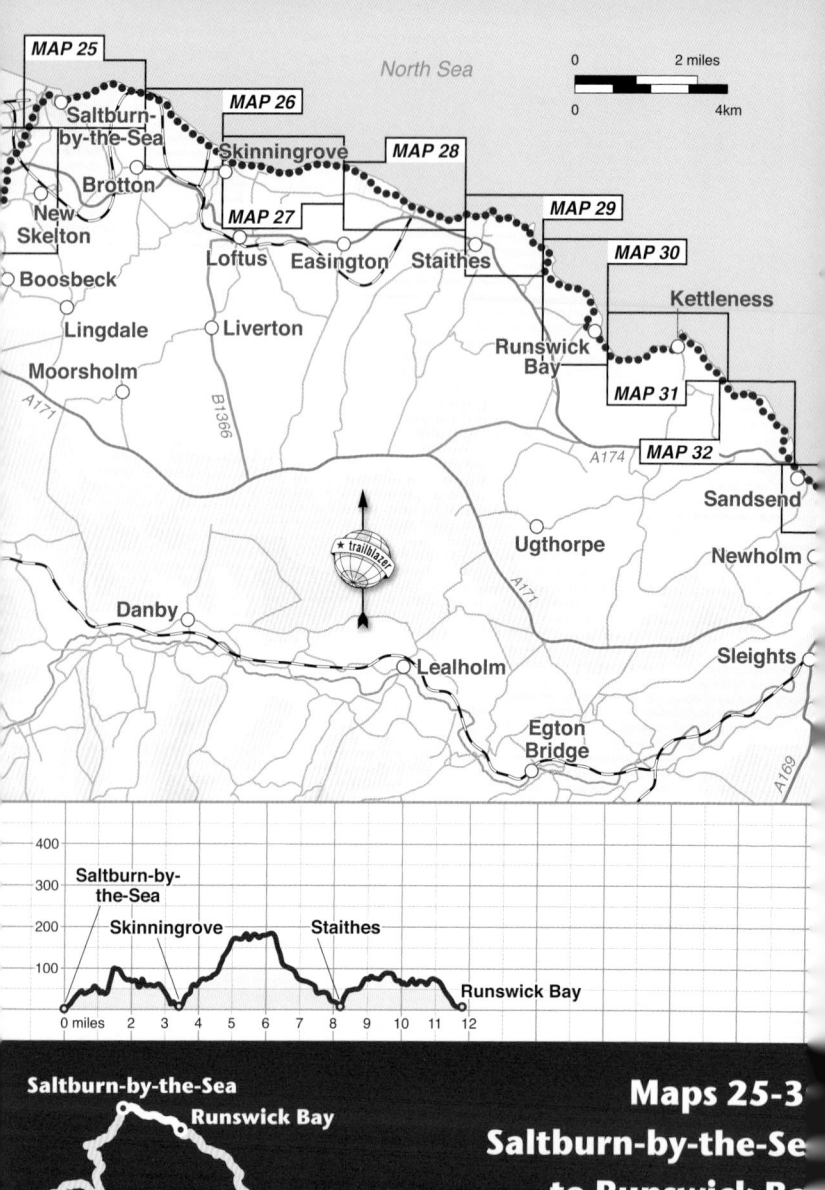

North Sea

0   2 miles
0   4km

MAP 25
MAP 26
MAP 28
MAP 29
MAP 27
MAP 30
MAP 31
MAP 32

Saltburn-by-the-Sea
Skinningrove
Brotton
New-Skelton
Loftus
Easington
Staithes
Kettleness
Runswick Bay
Sandsend
Boosbeck
Lingdale
Liverton
Moorsholm
Newholm
Ugthorpe
Danby
Sleights
Lealholm
Egton Bridge

Maps 25-3
Saltburn-by-the-Se
to Runswick Ba

11.8 miles/19km – 3hrs 55mins–4¾h
Add 20-30% to these times to allow for sto

Saltburn-by-the-Sea
Runswick Bay
Helmsley
Filey

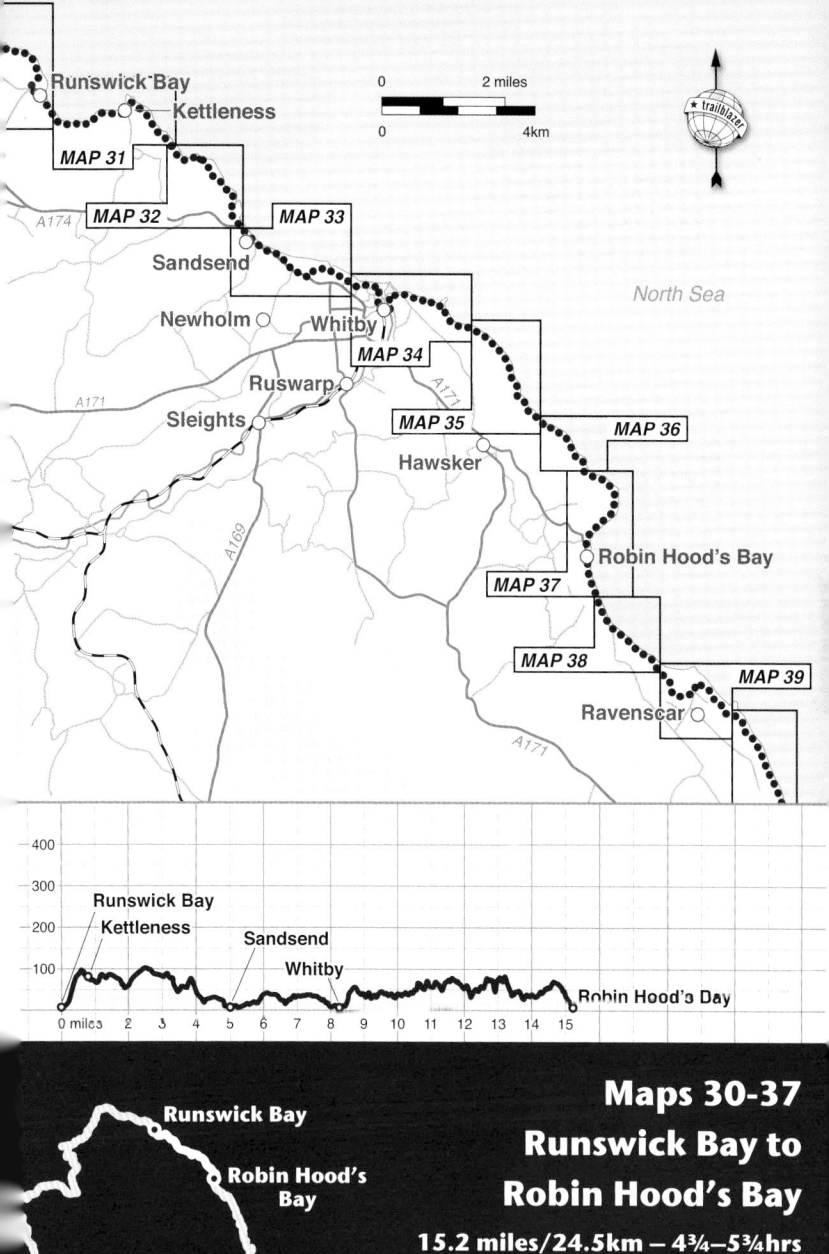

| 0 | 2 miles |
| 0 | 4km |

North Sea

Runswick Bay
Kettleness

MAP 31

A174

MAP 32

MAP 33

Sandsend

Newholm ○ Whitby

MAP 34

A171

Ruswarp

A171

Sleights

MAP 35

MAP 36

Hawsker

A169

Robin Hood's Bay

MAP 37

MAP 38

MAP 39

Ravenscar

A171

400
300
Runswick Bay
200
Kettleness   Sandsend
100   Whitby   Robin Hood's Bay

0 miles 2   3   4   5   6   7   8   9   10   11   12   13   14   15

Maps 30-37
Runswick Bay to
Robin Hood's Bay

15.2 miles/24.5km – 4¾–5¾hrs

Add 20-30% to these times to allow for stops

Runswick Bay

Robin Hood's
Bay

Helmsley   Filey

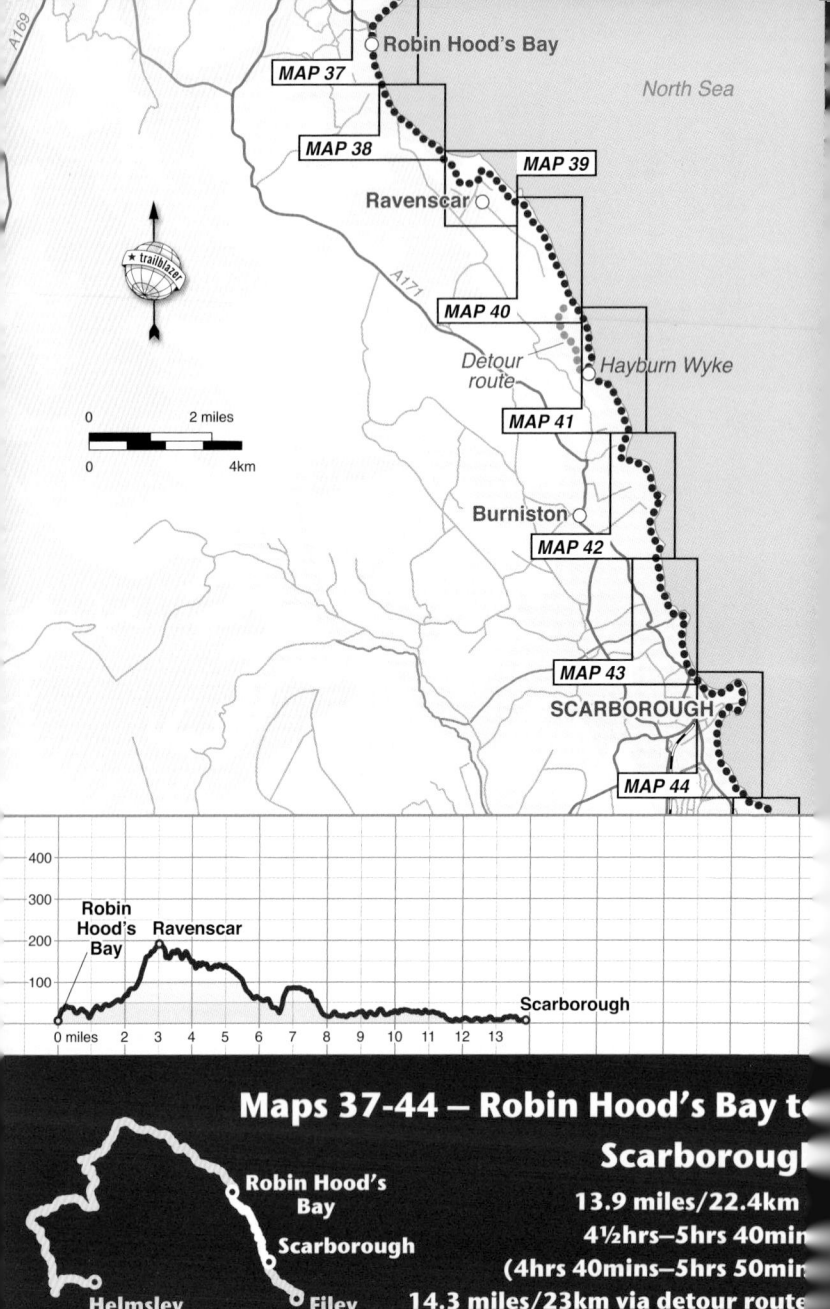

North Sea

Robin Hood's Bay

MAP 37

MAP 38

MAP 39

Ravenscar

A171

MAP 40

Detour route

Hayburn Wyke

MAP 41

Burniston

MAP 42

MAP 43

SCARBOROUGH

MAP 44

0   2 miles
0   4km

400
300
200
100

Robin Hood's Bay   Ravenscar

Scarborough

0 miles 2 3 4 5 6 7 8 9 10 11 12 13

Maps 37-44 – Robin Hood's Bay to Scarborough

Robin Hood's Bay

Scarborough

Helmsley   Filey

13.9 miles/22.4km
4½hrs–5hrs 40min
(4hrs 40mins–5hrs 50min
14.3 miles/23km via detour route

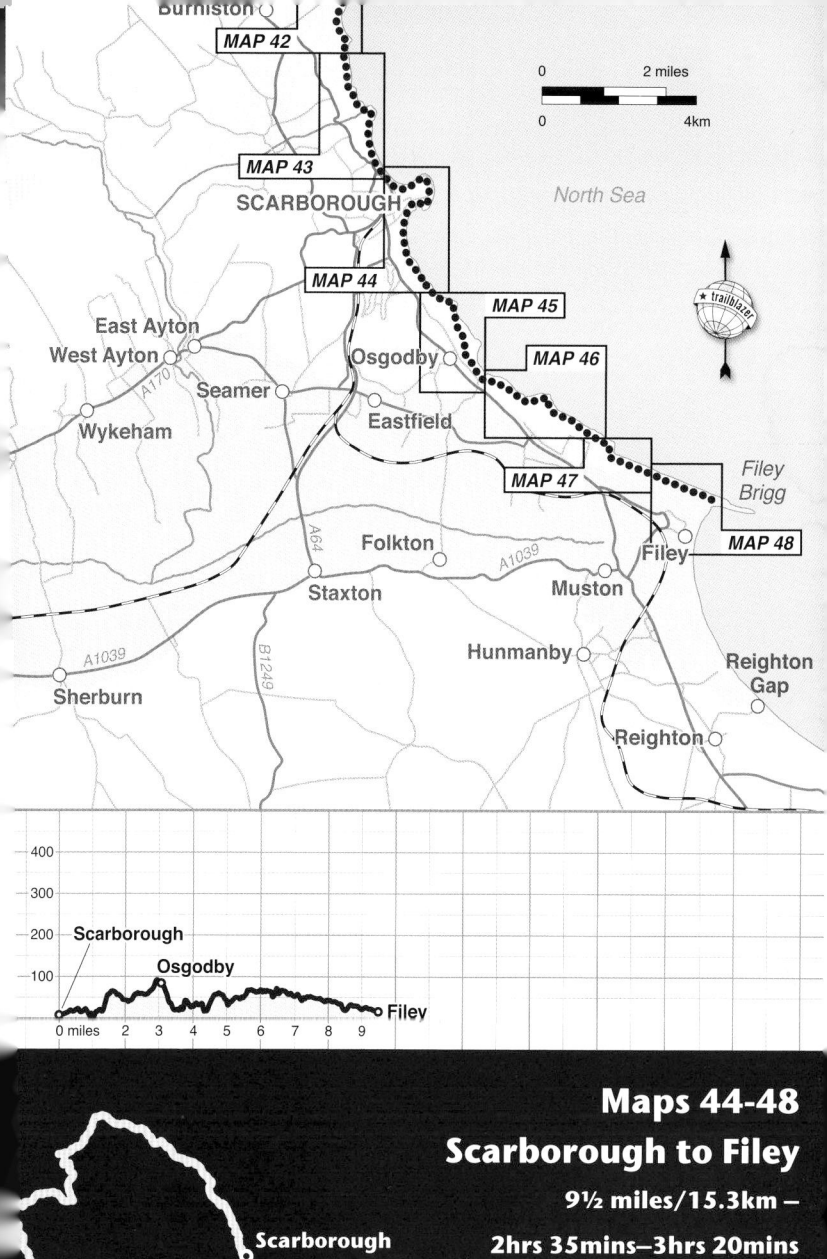

North Sea

Burniston

MAP 42

MAP 43

SCARBOROUGH

MAP 44

East Ayton
West Ayton

Seamer

Wykeham

Osgodby

Eastfield

MAP 45

MAP 46

MAP 47

Filey
Brigg

MAP 48

Folkton

Staxton

Muston

Filey

Hunmanby

Sherburn

Reighton
Gap

Reighton

Scarborough

Osgodby

Filey

0 miles 2 3 4 5 6 7 8 9

Maps 44-48
Scarborough to Filey

9½ miles/15.3km –
2hrs 35mins–3hrs 20mins
Add 20-30% to these times to allow for stops

Helmsley   Filey   Scarborough

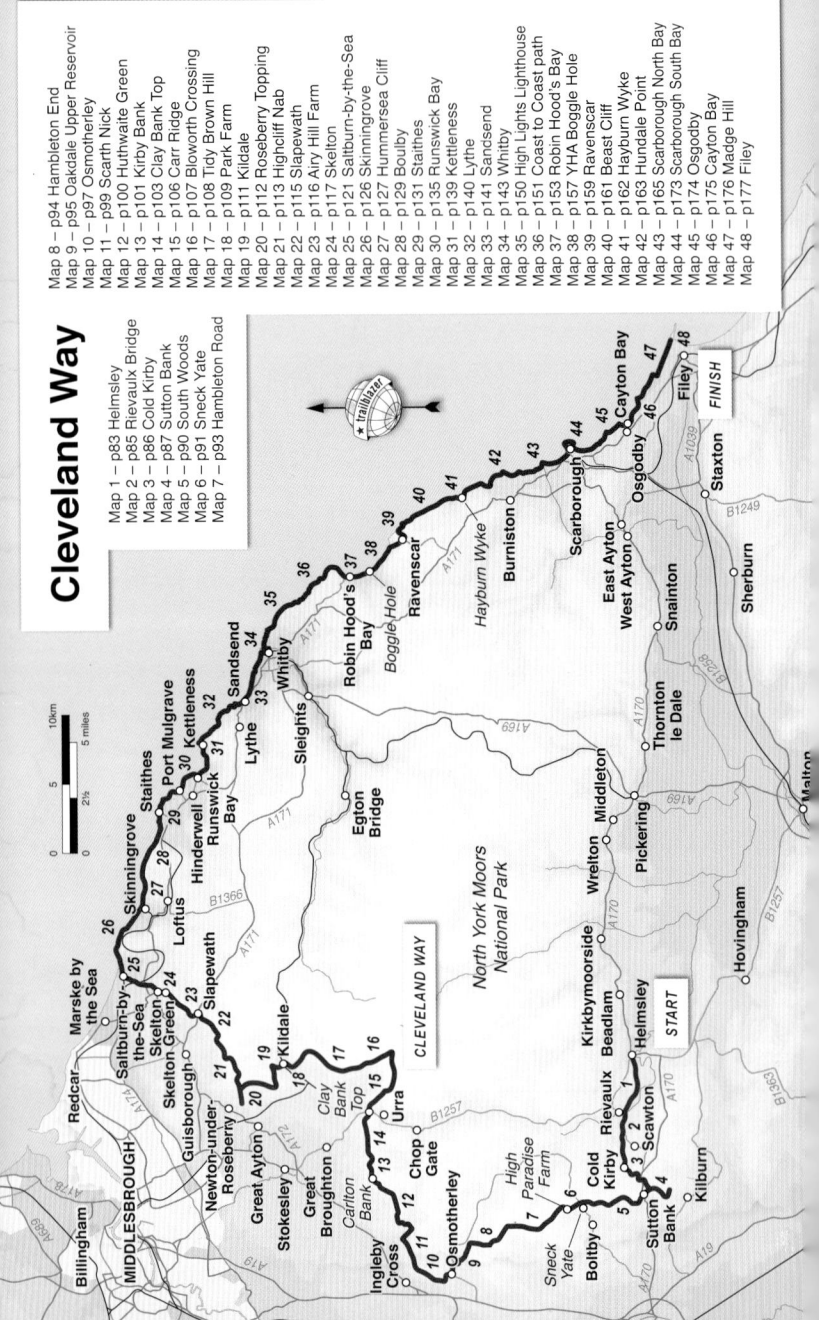

Cleveland Way